A TOPOGRAPHY
OF CATALOGUING

showing the most important
landmarks, communications
and perilous places

A TOPOGRAPHY OF CATALOGUING

showing the most important landmarks, communications and perilous places

Mary Piggott

THE LIBRARY ASSOCIATION

LONDON

© Mary Piggott 1988

Published by
Library Association Publishing Ltd
7 Ridgmount Street
London WC1E 7AE

First published 1988

British Library Cataloguing in Publication Data

Piggott, Mary
   A topography of cataloguing : showing the
   most important landmarks, communications
   and perilous places.
   1. Documents. Cataloguing
   I. Title
   025.3

ISBN 0-85365-758-0

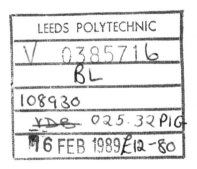
Typeset in 11/12 pt Baskerville by Library Association Publishing Ltd
Printed and bound in Great Britain by
Butler & Tanner Ltd, Frome and London

Contents

v

UNISIST, International Serials Data System, Centres of information about information, IFLA's concern with cataloguing, standards for bibliographic description (ISBD)s, UNIMARC, Universal Bibliographic Control – Standardizing work still to be done – References

thesaurus – Terminology as an artificial
language: a systematic nomenclature illustrated
by Botany – A note on the terminology of
librarianship – References

Codes of filing rules: basic filing order, characters
disregarded in filing, abbreviations, initialisms
and acronyms, same entry word or words;
sequence of entries by catalogue function, grouped
entries under a single personal name – Helping
the catalogue user, the divided catalogue –
Towards an international standard for bibliographic filing – References

Preface

This book endeavours to map the intellectual environment in which the cataloguer works, to show, using selected and specific examples, how language, social organization and the methods of intellectual communication determine the decisions that the cataloguer makes. The book is a record of explorations that I needed to undertake myself before I could expound, justify or criticize modern cataloguing practices. As such, it is not a straightforward textbook, although some of it is, indeed, didactic, and will, I hope, be used for reference.

It is a foolish thing, I am told, not only to make a long prologue, but also to make a long book. This volume, therefore, while setting out in general terms the problems and solutions that confront the cataloguer, does not consider specific materials and their treatment, neither does it refer, except in rare instances, to specific codes and rules. Such a necessary continuation forms the matter of a companion volume entitled *The cataloguer's way: from document receipt to document retrieval.*

The first four chapters of the book set the scene in which contemporary cataloguing takes place. They are followed by a general statement of the first requirement of cataloguing: how to describe a document unequivocally.

In order to understand the detailed rules of descriptive cataloguing it is necessary to look at the underlying problems of language. Although the chapters entitled Script and transcript I and II are superficial and perforce only illustrative, they indicate the variety of forms that language may take and also point to ways by which librarians can lessen the difficulties presented by that variety.

Equally dependent upon language and its precise and consistent use are subject catalogues. These have been described in some detail. Included are methods of determining the subject matter of documents, the structure of subject catalogues, the sources of terminology and its use, and the arrangement of catalogues and indexes.

I am greatly indebted to the following people: Mr K. G. B. Bakewell, who read the whole manuscript and offered most valuable suggestions for its improvement; Mr C. G. Allen and Professor J. D. Pearson, who read and made most helpful comments on Chapters 6 and 7; Ms Janet Shuter, who solved the problem of length by suggesting publication in two parts; the librarians in the University of London libraries and in the British Library Library Association Library; and not least to Miss Ann Rowen, MBE, who typed and retyped my manuscript with patience and accuracy.

I acknowledge also with thanks permission from the Forest Press Division, Lake Placid Foundation, owner of copyright, to use in the diagram in Chapter 11 excerpts from the Dewey Decimal Classification, edition 19, 1979.

1
Are catalogues necessary?

This chapter looks at the questions: What is a catalogue? Are catalogues necessary? If so, who should make catalogues?

What is a catalogue?

By definition a catalogue is a list. In a library the term catalogue is used to refer to the ordered lists of the various materials collected there: catalogue of works in the reference library, catalogue of periodicals, catalogue of sound recordings, catalogue of books in the lending library, catalogue of the whole library. Such a list is necessary because the librarian cannot store in his memory all the information about the books and other materials in his library which is likely to be wanted by his readers, nor can he be available personally to conduct the readers to all the books they need to see. The catalogue stands in as his permanent substitute to answer the simpler questions about what is in the library and where it is to be found. It is a medium of communication, necessarily formal, but not necessarily formidable.

The term catalogue denotes a wide variety of physical forms: card catalogue, sheaf catalogue, printed book, visible index, microfilm, microfiche, magnetic tape, online terminal. It denotes also a variety of intellectual approaches: catalogues may distinguish and arrange individual items according to the author's name, the subject content, the language of the text, suitability for particular readers or any other pertinent characteristics. Their functions may range from finding-lists, which merely identify the individual items and say where they are to be found on the library shelves, through more detailed descriptions which permit a preliminary choice to be made before approaching the shelves, to bibliographical or textual summaries which allow selection or rejection of material to be made at the catalogue itself. Even the barest of such lists may be a good catalogue if it does what is required of it. A catalogue that offers information which is never wanted is only confusing to the reader and wasteful of the cataloguer's time and therefore of the library's money. It cannot be emphasized too strongly, that cataloguing should always be done with a particular aim in view, and also that the catalogue's suitability for its purpose, and the reader's satisfaction in using it, must depend on the knowledge, understanding and skill of the cataloguer.

Why make catalogues?

With the impressive efficiency of Boston Spa in mind, where the then National Lending Library's collection – to which no readers had access – was arranged alphabetically by title within three chronological divisions, M. W. Grose and Maurice Line questioned whether, in keeping catalogues of their own stock, individual libraries were not in reality maintaining white elephants, and whether a simpler shelf arrangement and the use of published bibliographies might not make catalogues dispensable.[1]

An important function of a library is to display to students the literature of their subjects and to permit browsing among it. Libraries also may have the function of providing suitable furniture and lighting for the consultation of maps and other special materials. Granted the necessity for grouping their collections into separate sequences, librarians must provide guides to them. Besides the general guides, such as brochures, wall displays and diagrams which locate the different areas of a library, the librarian must provide a catalogue which describes and locates each publication of more than ephemeral interest. In addition to showing the reader whether and where a book or cassette or any other medium of information may be found, the catalogue description – or its absence – will be used by the acquisitions librarian or the reference librarian to save a journey to the shelves and to save repeated handling and comparison of books at the shelves.

Certain materials are difficult to handle and do not plainly reveal what they are, possibly needing apparatus to scan them, so that it is easier to use information discovered and plainly set out by the cataloguer than to resort to the document itself, and possibly run through several frames of a film, or consult both sleeve and label of a sound recording, before being able to say whether the document is required or not. ('Document' has been used above in its original sense of 'medium of instruction', from which is derived its current use as the general designation for all kinds of library materials.)

The suggested use of printed bibliographies to identify titles of probable usefulness, although essential to research, could be a hindrance to the casual use of the library. A library's own catalogue is itself a bibliography of material selected over the years for a particular community. In a university, for example, the community consists of the members of the several faculties for whose benefit special library collections have usually been built up carefully by academic and library staff working together.

A library's catalogue should be easier to use than a published bibliography. In conjunction with the displayed plans and shelf-guides it orients a reader within the library and leads to material which is immediately available. There are times when a book in the hand is worth two in a remote repository, even if the book must be a second or third choice because the first choice is already in use. Incidentally, the National Lending Library, incorporated in the British Library as its Lending Division (BLLD) and from 1986 known as the British Library Document Supply Centre (BLDSC), itself admits to publishing – not of course 'catalogues' but – 'lists of various categories of its holdings', including, for example, a microfiche record of recent monographs in English.[2]

Consider some different types of library and their cataloguing requirements.

In the lending department of a small public library, the collection is general and is displayed round the room on shelves to which readers have access. When they, and the library staff, consult the catalogue it is generally to discover where a particular book, or books by a particular author, are shelved, or where books on a certain subject are to be found. Since readers have only to stretch out their hands to have the book itself, there is no point in giving a detailed description of it in the catalogue.

In a large university or city library the book-stock may be housed in several different departments, possibly in separate buildings, some of them of limited access to the readers. It will be necessary for the reader to locate material of an appropriate level and in a suitable form for his study, before going off to find it or requesting that it should be brought to him. According to the form the expression of his need takes – a precise citation, a misremembered citation, a subject term – his need will be for a name or a subject catalogue with sufficient information about what is available to enable him to select, say, the latest edition of critical studies on a literary figure, or a film illustrating the geological structure of an area, or a tape-slide presentation of a laboratory technique, or a simple textbook on chemistry. He may well not have suspected the existence of the highly pertinent non-book materials revealed by the catalogue – an argument for treating such materials in the same way as books and incorporating them, with suitable differences in description, into the general catalogues.

In the library of an industrial concern, most of the material wanted will be periodical articles, research reports, house bulletins and memoranda, trade papers of various kinds, and illustrations. A specific answer to a specific question may be available among such documents but unless the librarian has anticipated the kind of question likely to be asked, it will require a tedious and time-consuming search to find the answer. The librarian will expect readers to ask for papers by individuals and by teams of research workers who are known to have studied a certain problem, and for information about different substances, sometimes under names of chemical compounds, sometimes under trade names, and about laboratory or manufacturing or marketing processes. He will therefore provide an author catalogue containing names not only of individuals but also of university departments, research associations and commercial firms, and also a very detailed subject catalogue. He may decide that the most relevant of the documents acquired by the library shall be scanned on receipt and that an abstract of each paper selected for cataloguing shall form part of the catalogue entry. Thus, in such a specialized industrial library, not only may the catalogue contain many entries for one item, but the entries themselves may contain

4

abstracts, as well as a note of any special diagrams in the text. A very good guide to abstracting, read as a paper to the first Informatics Conference, distinguishes the possible purposes of an abstract, identifies the elements necessary for each purpose, and suggests a style of presentation.[3] There is also an American national standard for writing abstracts.[4]

Union catalogues

A combined catalogue of the holdings of several libraries – a union catalogue – can lead to a wider range of literature than is available in any one library. Contributions to a union catalogue are made by a group of libraries that have some common characteristic, such as being located in a particular geographical area, having the same subject interest or serving the same class of reader, and that are willing to make their stock available for use by others outside their own registered readership in return for a reciprocal privilege for their own readers. Collaboration for lending goes hand-in-hand with collaboration in acquisition, facilitated equally by a union catalogue.

Union catalogues may incorporate records of all kinds of materials for which compatible entries are available, as *The national union catalog, pre-1956 imprints* incorporates entries for books, pamphlets, atlases, music and serials contributed by more than 1,000 North American libraries, and as the bibliographic databases maintained by some of the networks described in Chapter 2 incorporate records for audio-visual materials with those for the older forms of publication. Other union catalogues are restricted by format, language or subject of the material recorded, or by a combination of such restraints. For example, the University of London maintains a union catalogue of periodicals which is of great value, particularly when a sought journal is held uniquely by a single library; the *Union catalogue of Asian publications* records material held in 64 British libraries owning oriental collections; other specializations are served by union catalogues in medicine, legal materials, music, Latin-American newspapers, and so on.

Who should make catalogues?

The availability of published abstracts and of selective indexing services will affect the amount of detailed cataloguing which is necessary in any one library. An overview of abstracting and indexing services by Stella Keenan summarizes what the services are, how they are used, how they must be cost-effective, and also how useless they are if a bibliographic reference cannot be substantiated by production of the document itself.[5]

Therefore a decision must be made as to how much indexing needs to be done within an organization and to what extent publicly available services – printed or online – can be relied on or afforded. Most university libraries will subscribe to some published indexes, such as *Chemical abstracts*, and will supply either from their own resources or by obtaining from the British Library Document Supply Centre materials their readers have identified as being potentially useful. On the other hand some establishments will generate documents for internal use only, and these will need to be analysed and recorded within the library, possibly for retrieval by designated categories of users only. Comments from two librarians serving readers with specialist but different needs illustrate the response to local needs. One librarian found it unnecessary to do any in-house indexing of the laboratory reports in her collection because they were all adequately indexed by commercially available services.[6] The second librarian, running a government department's library, found that centralized analysis and indexing were inadequate for his local needs, where topics of interest were highly specialized and subject to rapid change.[7] To exploit a limited stock, detailed subject cataloguing, particularly for a clientele with known requirements, is an obvious means. A technical college librarian, writing in 1983, notes that her 'home-made' subject catalogue on cards is 'very well used', economically making a limited stock go further.[8]

Although it would thus seem that each catalogue should be made to suit a particular collection and a particular group of readers, in fact the same *kinds* of demand are made on catalogues in all libraries. The nature and use of the collections determine only the details: whether authors need to be

6

identified or only named, whether many editions of the same work need to be distinguished from one another, whether terms denoting subjects shall be chosen from a general or a special list, how much annotation is required. A certain amount of standardization is therefore possible, and this should be applied as widely as circumstances permit, so that readers accustomed to using one library's catalogue can turn easily to another's, cataloguers can transfer from one library to another knowing that basic practice will be the same, co-operation between libraries can be facilitated, particularly with the use of automated records, union catalogues can be compiled and used more easily and economically if a single form of description of the same publication is submitted by all contributing libraries and also by libraries seeking to borrow, and, above all, ambiguity in citation, with its consequent delays and disappointments, can be avoided. This is strikingly demonstrated by the experience of libraries linked by the Joint Academic Network (JANET) which find direct access to the catalogues of certain other member libraries less 'direct' than it might have been because of variations in cataloguing practice.

Because so much uniformity is possible and desirable in recording material the case is strong for having a central agency to do the recording once and for all. The case is strengthened by the degree of multiplication of the individual items which form the stock of different libraries. Many attempts have, in fact, been made to provide a centralized cataloguing service, as the following chapter notes in more detail. Here it suffices to say that successful services now operate, through the national libraries of many countries, and also through co-operative schemes through which the catalogues of individual libraries can be produced outside the libraries in so far as their collections are covered by the records produced by the agencies.

Then why learn to catalogue?

Why, it may well be asked, if every book is authoritatively catalogued somewhere, is it necessary for the individual librarian to study cataloguing?

It goes without saying that there must be some skilled cataloguers to do the authoritative cataloguing. There must also be cataloguers in individual libraries to manage and select from the material offered by the centralized agency and to catalogue those publications which have eluded the centralized agency or which have not appeared speedily enough in its distributed output, or those which are outside its scope, together with material which for one reason or another is not published but which forms part of the library's collection. In some libraries it will be more economical to make catalogues within the organization than to subscribe to centralized services. It is often considered more apt to the library's own purposes. In small libraries, in-house production of card catalogues, possibly with the aid of a word-processor, is likely to continue.[9]

There is also the consideration that a knowledge of what is involved in cataloguing – the background knowledge required, the skills and techniques of compiling and maintaining catalogues and continuous appraisal of their efficacity – is necessary in making decisions that affect the whole library: the deployment of staff, the best means of co-operation, the choice of what bibliographic aids shall be produced within the library and what bought from outside agencies, how a single record can most economically be used, and so on.

Almost all library work involves the *use* of catalogues and of correct bibliographical citation.

Effectiveness as a reference librarian depends upon skill in using catalogues, bibliographies and indexes, and on the ability to assess their quality and reliability. A bibliographer must know intimately the make-up of a book, how books and other library materials come into being, how they may be related among themselves, what variations in description to be aware of. Variations in nomenclature, both in proper names and in names of things, must be expected and their forms recognized when handling readers' enquiries, booksellers' lists and other bibliographical data coming from outside the library. The terminology of document description must be learnt for easy exchange of information with colleagues. The recurrent vocabulary of title pages and colophons should not call for the use of a dictionary. Ignorance in these matters can result in wasted time, or even failure in carrying out a piece of work. How better to overcome ignorance than by handling documents themselves, describing them, appraising their contents, and offering the knowledge gained as clearly and helpfully as possible to others? As William Warner Bishop puts it, 'If you are to administer libraries, you must know libraries, you must be able to work your machine, you must have practical knowledge of its parts. Nothing in the craft should be foreign to you, least of all the art of cataloguing'.[10] Of more immediate import, perhaps, is the fact that cataloguers are still required to fill posts in libraries. One third of the advertisements in a recent list of 42 vacant library posts specifically asked for ability in cataloguing, indexing or the compilation of bibliographies.

Notwithstanding what I have just written, the preceding paragraphs of this chapter will have made it abundantly clear that no library's cataloguing department – even though it consists of only a single cataloguer – can proceed without reference to cataloguing information which may be available elsewhere.

It is equally clear that all areas of library administration and operation are changing continually, not least cataloguing. An overview of recent developments in Britain, *British librarianship and information science*, is published five-yearly by the Library Association, with chapters devoted specifically to cataloguing, indexing and related topics. The North American cataloguing scene is surveyed annually in *Library resources and technical services*. Reports of work in progress and accounts of the current situation are indexed and abstracted in *Library and information science abstracts* which covers journals and conferences throughout the world.

References

1 Grose, M. W. and Line, M. B., 'On the construction and care of white elephants: some fundamental questions concerning the catalogue', *Library Association record*, 70 (1), January 1968, 2 – 5.
2 *BLLD publications and other publications distributed by the BLLD.*
3 Harris, B. and Hofmann, T. R., 'Regularized abstracting', *in Informatics I: proceedings of a conference held by the Aslib Co-ordinate Indexing Group on 11 – 13 April, 1973, at Durham University.* London: Aslib, 1974, 98 – 107.
4 *American national standard for writing abstracts*, ANSI Z39.14 (1971).

5 Keenan, Stella, 'Abstracting and indexing services', *in* Bourne, Ross (ed.), *Serials librarianship*. London: Library Association, 1980.
6 Newman, Wilda B., 'Managing a report collection for zero growth', *Special libraries*, 71(5/6), 1980, 276 – 82.
7 Hamilton, Geoffrey, 'Government department libraries', *in* Bourne, Ross (ed.), *Serials librarianship*. London: Library Association, 1980.
8 Hone, Grace, Letter, *Library Association record*, 85(6), 1983, 229.
9 Whitsed, N., 'Reflections on word processing: the experience of a small medical library', *Aslib proceedings*, 34(9), 1982, 415 – 19.
10 Bishop, William Warner, 'Cataloguing as an asset', *in* the author's *The backs of books and other essays in librarianship*. Freeport, N.Y.: Books for Libraries Press, 1968.

2

Co-operation, centralization and computerization

The idea of universal bibliography

When Charles Coffin Jewett was librarian of the Smithsonian Institution in Washington in the 1850s, he envisaged the library of that institution as the bibliographical centre for the United States. As a preliminary step towards realizing this ideal he began to compile a union catalogue of all the books in the public libraries of America. Jewett also hoped that the Smithsonian could undertake the centralized printing, from stereo blocks, of each of those libraries' own catalogues. Each library would notify the Smithsonian of its extant stock by depositing a copy of its printed catalogue, and would subsequently send in notification of its additions and deletions, so that from time to time the catalogues could be reprinted as an up-to-date record of local holdings. The considerable multiplication of individual titles in libraries would make it possible to use a single stereotyped entry again and again. In the middle of the nineteenth century the printed volume was the only appropriate form for a library catalogue.

Jewett described his project as looking towards the accomplishment of that cherished dream of scholars, a universal catalogue. 'If the system', he said – meaning his projected collaborative compilation of a union catalogue – 'If the system should be successful in this country, it may eventually be so in every country of Europe. When all shall have adopted and carried out the plan, each for itself, the aggregate of general catalogues, thus formed, – few in number – will embrace the whole body of literature extant, and from them it will be no impossible task to digest and publish a universal bibliography'.[1]

Jewett was prevented from carrying out his project. For one

reason, the composition of his stereo blocks was faulty, so that printing by that means proved impossible. (Mechanical problems are, however, always overcome if the need, and the rewards, are great enough, and printing from stereo plates was soon afterwards perfected.) A greater and more lasting drawback was the impossibility of reconciling the peculiar catalogue entries received from contributing libraries. When were they, and when were they not, describing the same books? Displaying an almost naive optimism, Jewett published a set of cataloguing rules designed for general adoption and thence the standardization of descriptive cataloguing. But other troubles of a more personal nature led Jewett to leave the Smithsonian after only five years' service, and his plans for that institution were forever abandoned.

The idea of a universal bibliography was sufficiently persistent for others to attempt its fulfilment. At the first international conference on bibliography, held in Brussels in 1895, it was again put forward, by two Belgian lawyers, Paul Otlet and Henri La Fontaine. This time the catalogue was to be sponsored by an international body, the Institut international de bibliographie, founded at that conference to promote the organization of a comprehensive subject index to the accumulating records of intellectual achievement. The catalogue, or *répertoire universel*, was to be arranged according to a scheme of subject classification, the Universal decimal classification (UDC), and so overcome the problem of reconciling entries in different languages. A vast number of records were amassed, but the universal bibliography collapsed under the weight of increasing publication which its limited resources proved inadequate to record. The Institut, however, under its later names (see p.42) and acronym FID, continues to be concerned with problems of bibliography, its best-known activity being promotion of the various editions of the UDC.[2]

Even the Royal Society's limited objective of making and publishing an international catalogue of scientific literature, begun at the same period, had to be abandoned in 1919 because production of the literature out-stripped its cataloguing.[3]

'Scholars' dreams' have today been replaced by a general realization that scientific and technological information is a national asset, and that knowledge once published – anywhere – should be made use of, that access to it should be convenient and prompt, so that time and labour are not wasted in rediscovering for the requirements of a particular task facts that are already known. Co-operation and division of labour, standardization and the substitution of the new electronic machinery for the insufficiency of hands to copy, rearrange and select published information are seen to be essential.

The application of automatic data processing in the more restricted spheres of certain national and special-subject bibliographies has enabled them, if not to keep pace with current production, at least not to lose sight of it. Of the many online bibliographic databases which are now accessible both nationally and internationally,[4-6] I have space to mention only a few examples. Probably the most famous specialist system is MEDLARS. The acronym denotes the Medical Literature Analysis and Retrieval System, referring directly to its genesis as the means of keeping the published *Index medicus* up to date. The basic work of collecting, cataloguing and indexing publications in medicine and related sciences is done in the US National Library of Medicine, whence machine-readable records of bibliographic and subject information are dispatched to centres from which further distribution is made on demand. Once online, the information can be used to generate both printed and tape output in a variety of categories. In the United Kingdom the Institution of Electrical Engineers maintains a database of information in Physics, Electrotechnology, Computers and Control (INSPEC) which is similarly accessible.

Centralized and co-operative cataloguing

Co-operation in compiling bibliographic records and sharing their use had long been practised before the advent of automatic data processing, which merely – albeit vastly – facilitated and extended the practice.

Centralized cataloguing agencies, or rather 'processing centres' were first set up in the United States although few of them predated the 1939 war. 'Processing' means preparing all the documentation that a book, or any other medium, needs for its life in a library. It entails cataloguing and classifying the item, providing the issuing card or other device, and the required number of catalogue and stock-list entries and labels. The centres were established to serve particular regional or subject groups of libraries.[7,8] Most of the American processing centres base their services on data made available by the Library of Congress, for it was that library, and not the Smithsonian, which assumed the position of bibliographical leadership in the United States.

Library of Congress

The Library of Congress (LC) began printing entries for its own dictionary catalogue on cards at the turn of the century, starting with books received by copyright in June 1898; after January 1901 cards were printed for all accessions.[9] The Library sent out a circular dated 28 October 1901, offering printed cards for sale at a generous price and showing a sample card. To be able to buy authoritative catalogue entries is so clearly an advantage that the great majority of American libraries adopted the style of Library of Congress cataloguing, basing both author and subject entries on those used in the national library. By 31 October 1902, 212 libraries were subscribing to the card service.[10] By 1967, there were approximately 20,000 subscribers and a total sale for the year of 74,503,000 cards.[11]

The development of a computerized cataloguing system within the Library of Congress has not altered the centralized cataloguing service in principle. The dissemination of cataloguing information on magnetic tape has reduced the number of LC printed cards distributed, but has not changed the dependence of subscribing libraries on the Library of Congress's Cataloging Division for the preparation of original cataloguing, although this may now come to them at second hand through another agency.

The increasing harmony of cataloguing practice which ensued from widespread dependence on LC cataloguing made it possible for a number of research libraries to contribute records of their specialized materials for printing and incorporation into a common catalogue with the records produced in the LC.[12-15] Improvements in the technique of photographic reproduction of printed matter, and later, photo-composition of new copy, made possible the publication in book form of an author catalogue of books represented by Library of Congress printed cards from 1898, which developed into the current and cumulative *National union catalog*[16,17] (The last general catalogue of Library of Congress holdings to be available in the form of a printed book had been issued in 1864.) These catalogues have played an important part in the bibliographical processes and services of all major libraries throughout the world. A list of the general and special catalogues produced by the Library of Congress, entitled *Catalogs and publications*, is issued by the Cataloging Distribution Service of the Processing Department.

Shared cataloguing

In the late 1960s the Library of Congress acquired additional burdens of collecting and describing published materials. In addition to United States imprints and the wide range of foreign imprints habitually collected, Congressional legislation imposed upon the Library of Congress the obligation to obtain and catalogue a vastly increased number of publications from many countries, grossly overstraining the Library's resources of skilled cataloguers. The legislation was the Higher Education Act of 1965, an act of great importance for US libraries. Among other provisions for the improvement of library services, the Act set in motion a national programme for the acquisition and cataloguing (NPAC) of virtually all currently published foreign monographs commercially available which were likely to be of use to American scholarship. Title II.C of the Act enjoined the national library to acquire such books and to make cataloguing information about them generally and speedily available.[18] Help in providing cataloguing data had long been accepted from other American libraries. Help was now sought from libraries and national bibliographies outside the United States in a programme of 'shared cataloguing'. It was natural, in the aftermath of the International Conference on Cataloguing Principles, which had revealed widespread unanimity on the aims and procedures of descriptive cataloguing, to think less in terms of national self-sufficiency and more in terms of sharing the load of original cataloguing with other countries whose national bibliographies and national libraries were perforce already cataloguing their national imprints.

The Shared Cataloging Division of the Library of Congress, established on 1 July 1966, set up offices in conjunction with national bibliographies in nine different countries, and by 1970 was utilizing bibliographical information prepared in 22 countries. The Division's language sections adapt the entries to the familiar Library of Congress style and the catalogue records are added to the MARC tapes (MARC is described on p.20). Author headings are sometimes changed to be in conformity with LC practice, but the body of the entry has been found to be as accurate and informative as LC's own cataloguing, and is therefore incorporated into the LC entry, with minor adjustments for machine manipulation.[19]

Herman Liebaers, then Director of the Bibliothèque Royale in Brussels and President of the International Federation of Library Associations (IFLA), concludes a descriptive and evaluative study of the Shared Cataloguing and NPAC programmes with the words: 'The Library of Congress Shared Cataloguing Programme proves there already exists adequate compatibility to ensure effective, worldwide co-operation. At present, however, the United States are alone in demonstrating this, at the cost of a considerable financial effort. Yet it is not possible to continue to rely on the willingness and resources of a single country to provide a supranational bibliographical service. European countries should now take the Library of Congress Shared Cataloguing Programme as an example in improving their national bibliographical services, and in reconsidering and modifying their current techniques in order to be in a position to make a valid contribution to a common pool'.[20] That was followed by a decade of constructive co-operation co-ordinated by IFLA, and the increasing accessibility across frontiers of nationally generated databases.

The British National Bibliography
In Great Britain, although the British Museum's *General cata-logue* served as a model for some other national and academic libraries, and all the printed catalogues of the British Museum library, both general and special, have been bibliographical tools of inestimable worth, the impetus towards uniformity

given by a centralized cataloguing agency did not come until publication of the *British national bibliography* (*BNB*) began in 1950.

The *British national bibliography* appears weekly. It lists a very large proportion of current British monographic publishing output in the classified order of the Dewey decimal classification scheme. The first appearance of a new serial is also recorded in *BNB*. Each entry in the *BNB* has a unique serial number by which it may be identified (the *BNB* number). The final issue of each month also contains a combined author and title index and a subject index, both of which refer to the class mark at which the full entry will be found in that month's issues. There are annual cumulations. There have been five cumulated subject sequences, covering the years 1951 – 4, 1955 – 9, 1960 – 4, 1965 – 7, and 1968 – 70, and five cumulated indexes, covering the same periods. From 1971 triennial indexes of authors and titles only have appeared. A cumulated author/title catalogue on microfiche covering the 35 years of British publishing recorded by the *BNB* was published in 1986. (The change to production of *BNB* files by computer is noted on p.22.)

The British National Bibliography Ltd, was founded as an independent, non-commercial undertaking whose Council comprised representatives of the British Museum, the National Central Library, and other bodies devoted to the dissemination and use of published matter. After the creation of the British Library on 1 July 1973, the *BNB* was taken over (in 1974), together with the British Museum's Copyright Receipt Office, to form the British Library's Bibliographic Services Division (BLBSD). In addition to the *BNB* the Division publishes the *British catalogue of music,* the *British catalogue of audio-visual materials*, various aids to cataloguing, and *Books in English*, the last being a combined list of *BNB* and LC records in an author/title sequence issued on microfiche in progressive cumulations every two months. The Bibliographic Services' Serials Office took over from the National Central Library in 1974 responsibility for compiling *BUCOP: new periodical titles*, which was superseded in 1981 by the quarterly *Serials in the British Library.*

From the beginning, the staff of the BNB has assumed

responsibility as a national cataloguing agency. Each publication recorded in *BNB* is described in accordance with standard cataloguing practice, which has followed the joint Anglo-American code: the 1908 edition (with amendments) until the end of 1967, the 1967 edition thereafter, until, by agreement with other national libraries, *AACR2 – Anglo-American cataloguing rules, 2nd edition* – was adopted by the British Library from 1 January 1981.[21-23] The classification and indexing, though not infallible, are highly reliable. The weekly lists and cumulations are therefore used not only as primary sources of information for book selection and ordering and for bibliographic reference, but also as sources for cataloguing data, the bibliographic descriptions being accepted as they stand or selectively, according to the needs of a particular library. A printed card service became available on subscription to individual libraries in 1956[24] and weekly tapes and COM catalogues from the date of computerization.

As a supplementary service to cataloguing, the British Library publishes a monthly *Name authority list* on microfiche, which lists all names established by the Bibliographic Services Division since the adoption of *AACR2*. The correct form of each name, according to *AACR2*, is given, together with associated references. Sources are noted, and also the work on which the authoritative name was first used, the field of activity of the author, the author's real name if a pseudonym has been used, and name headings with MARC codings.

Cataloguing-in-Publication

An imaginative idea that a book might be published with its catalogue entry printed inside its own covers led to an experiment in the Library of Congress in 1959. A number of publishers were asked to deposit with the library proof copies of forthcoming books, together with relevant information about them, in order that the library might catalogue the books before publication and send the catalogue entries to the publishers with the returned proofs in time for the books to be published with the cataloguing data printed inside them – either in the form of a facsimile reproduction of the Library of Congress card or in a form more compatible with each book's own design and typography. The experiment led to the conclusion within the library 'that a permanent, full-scale Cataloging-in-Source programme could not be justified from the viewpoint of financing, technical consideration or utility'.[25] However, faith persisted in the idea of what Ranganathan had called 'prenatal cataloguing'[26] and Verner Clapp 'the greatest invention since the title page',[27] and after a new trial period running from July 1971 to June 1973, in which the printed cataloguing data were reduced to those least liable to change before date of publication, Cataloguing-in-Publication (CIP), as it was renamed, seemed to be well on the way to fulfilling its aim of providing cataloguing data for most of the titles published annually by the American book trade.[28]

The CIP record is also available for distribution by the LC in advance of the full catalogue record established after handling the published volume. Noted as a CIP record, it is distributed in the same sequence as full records, and amended after receipt of the published volume.

The British Library also implements a CIP programme. From January 1977 the *BNB*, both in its printed form and as magnetic tape, has contained entries for forthcoming publications whose proofs and 'front matter' have been deposited with the CIP office (amalgamated in 1978 with the Copyright Receipt Office to form the Acquisitions Department). The *BNB* entry (indicated as being pre-publication cataloguing and appearing roughly two months before publication) is as complete as can be ascertained from the material in hand. Originally restricted in content, CIP entries have been upgraded to conform with *AACR2* level 2 (*AACR2* rule 1.0D2) to meet the wishes of contributors (publishers) and users,[29-31] but enforced economies in the British Library may modify this decision. The entries are compared with the books when the books come to hand, but, in order not to slow down the cataloguing of new books, a revised entry is published only if significant changes are found which could hinder finding it in the catalogue or on the shelves. About 90% of CIP entries are expected to be found authoritative. A facsimile of the Cataloguing-in-Publication sheet, together with some examples of CIP records, is shown in *Bibliographic Services newsletter* No. 35, February 1985. In those libraries where cataloguing-in-publication as found on the reverse of the title leaf forms the basis of local cataloguing of current imprints a critical reading of the entry is called for.

The automation of cataloguing

The computer, designed, as its name implies, as an aid to accounting, was recognized as being capable of development as a machine for manipulating bibliographic information and of transmitting it in a variety of forms for a variety of uses. It was seen as the source of supply of fresh material for the card catalogue, and also as the means of supplanting it. The computer's facility for manipulating data and putting them out in a number of pre-determined forms has led to the use of data prepared for cataloguing as the source of many other records: shelf registers, loan issue records, notification of new accessions, select subject lists, and so on. Aslib has published a series of bibliographies on library automation, of which the last issue seen is *An annotated bibliography of automation in libraries, 1975 – 1978*, compiled by Ainslie Dewe, 1980. Ongoing work is recorded in the journals, particularly in *Information technology and libraries*,[32] *Program*,[33] and *VINE*,[34] and in the annual survey issued by the American Society for Information Science.[35]

MARC

The Library of Congress's decision to transfer its current cataloguing data to machine-readable tape and to make the tape available for distribution set in motion a revolution in cataloguing that is reaching round the world. After an initial period of experiment, the Machine-Readable Cataloguing Service, called acronymically MARC, was judged to be viable and advantageous, and the tape distribution service began on a regular subscription basis in March 1969.

The MARC tape has all the flexibility of the card catalogue but its role is not limited to producing a series of catalogue entries. MARC has been developed as a 'communications format', a medium for the interchange of bibliographic information from which all users may extract such data, and only such data, as suit their purpose, and sort them how they wish. It stores far more information relating to each unit described than would in practice be wanted in an entry prepared for insertion in any one catalogue. Its capacity is redundant in that fields are available for each of several different kinds and parts of entries that will be needed for the description of different documents but not all for the same document. The MARC record lists, according to the characteristics of the document in hand: authors and other individuals and corporate bodies whose names are pertinent to the identification of the document; titles; LC and DC class marks (and the UDC class mark also where that is given in the document); an indication of the country of origin; the document's formal origin, as government publication, conference proceedings; its physical description; LC verbal subject headings, and, on tapes produced by the British Library, BNB PRECIS index entries; and possibly other data, by any of which, alone or in conjunction, a listing might be required or a single record called up; together with the record's unique code number which is sufficient to identify and retrieve it.

The MARC tape is thus seen to have many potential uses. Printed out or displayed on a screen – a visual display unit (VDU) – it can be consulted, as a printed bibliography is consulted, for verification of, or addition to, information already known about an item; for the discovery of entirely new material; for the grouping of records having some required characteristic in common. The weekly MARC tape may be perused for stock selection. If the interest of a library is limited to a single subject – let us say Crystallography – a listing from the tape can be made showing only such entries as have been given a classification mark relating to crystallography or which contain relevant terms in subject headings and titles. In addition, catalogue entries, accessions lists and restricted subject lists for departments or individuals can be produced selectively, the selection determining not only which entries, but also which elements of the full entry shall be reproduced. The full entry on the MARC tape, as I have said, contains redundancies precisely because it is offered for so many different uses. A library which keeps a classified catalogue arranged by the Dewey decimal classification chooses the DC number and rejects the LC classification notation. If the classification used is LC, then the DC number is rejected. If a dictionary catalogue is kept, then LC subject headings may be required. Similarly, for some uses collation or notes may not be required. They can be suppressed. On the other hand, an individual library can add to the tape elements considered essential in its own circumstances, such as location symbol, accession number, special collection code. The MARC record as the source of bibliographic information and its transformation into products to satisfy local needs may be tapped in various ways. An individual library with adequate computing facilities may subscribe to the full current MARC output on weekly magnetic tape and also to retrospective tapes, or it may buy reels of selected records in MARC format, and subject the tapes to manipulation in its own computer. Alternatively a library's own computer terminal may be used for online access to a central processing agency from whose store of MARC records individual entries may be called up for display on a screen and may then be edited to suit the library's needs. Where a library has no automatic data processing facilities it may still tap the MARC source through various agencies, as explained below.

UK MARC

The staff of the *BNB* played its part in broadening and developing MARC as an international communications medium. The British MARC project was initiated in 1967 and by 1973 the *BNB* was supplying tapes of its weekly output, selectively or in full, to about a score of libraries, most of which were still using them experimentally.[36] Close collaboration between *BNB* and Brighton Public Libraries – the BRIMARC project – had proved conclusively that an automated centralized cataloguing service through the national bibliography was feasible. By the beginning of 1975 a fully operational Local Catalogue Service (LOCAS) was available, primarily for libraries which had no computer of their own but wished to use an automated cataloguing system. Such libraries made their own selection from the MARC files and received catalogue entries in the medium of their choice. In addition, they sent for processing by the Bibliographic Services Division records for extra-MARC material (known briefly as EMMA) which they themselves created using the *UK MARC manual*. With more widespread installation of local online, stand-alone systems, the need for the LOCAS batch service is declining. The original cataloguing will, of course, continue to be needed by the British Library, but the cost of supplying the LOCAS service to individual users inevitably rises as it is shared among fewer subscribers, and they may well find it cheaper to subscribe to systems which can control acquisitions, loans, periodicals subscriptions, etc., as well as provide catalogues. The LOCAS service is to be reviewed in 1988.

The history and development of MARC in the Library of Congress have been recorded by the Chief of the MARC Development Office, Henriette Avram.[37] The development of UK MARC and its divergencies from LC MARC (now called US MARC) have been described by Anthony Long.[38] Current changes are noted in the *Bibliographic services newsletter*.

BLAISE

In April 1977 a new system became operational – the British Library Automated Information Service (BLAISE) – for both batch processing and online services, and for retrieval from databases generated elsewhere, such as MEDLARS (Medical Literature Analysis and Retrieval System) and CHEMLINE (Dictionary of Chemical Substances), as well as from its own centrally held records. The latter include the UK MARC, US MARC, AV MARC, *Index of conference proceedings*, and the *Eighteenth-century short-title catalogue (ESTC)*.

Networks and co-operative automation groups

In addition to the national agencies, networks of co-operating libraries have been established to serve regional groups.

OCLC

The largest centralized agency, which was one of the first to use an electronic database for such a purpose and is now the nodal point of a whole series of networks, is OCLC. OCLC was incorporated as a non-profit-making organization in 1967 as the Ohio College Library Center, to serve an association of colleges, universities and other educational institutions within the State of Ohio. Its services were extended to any kind of library, in any part of the country, to other regional centres, and finally to countries outside North America. Libraries have

23

online access, through regional centres, to bibliographic databases, that is, to stores of bibliographic information held on computer files. They may choose to receive additions to, or updated versions of, their own catalogues in a variety of forms. Entries for works not catalogued by the Library of Congress may be contributed by the participating libraries.[39]

Probably as a result of its early start on automated processing, in 1965, when few of the potential benefits of the developing technology had been fully grasped, and of its rapid growth, OCLC could be described by one speaker late in 1977, as being 'in certain respects both conceptually and technologically obsolete...essentially what it has been in the minds of its member libraries since its inception: a utility designed primarily to produce alphabetized catalogue cards customized to local idiosyncratic cataloguing practices'.[40]

By 1977, however, changes were already evident. Services were then being provided to more than 2,100 academic, public, special and federal libraries in 50 states of the US and in several countries outside America, and the local connotation of the name was minimized by the official change to OCLC Inc. (From 1981 the acronym's official expansion is Online Computer Library Center.) Services include access to the online union catalogue for all bibliographic reference needs, subsystems for cataloguing, inter-library loan, serials control, and acquisitions and circulation control.

From 1981 British libraries have had access, through OCLC (Europe) to OCLC's bibliographic database of more than 6,000,000 records to which another million a year are being added. This figure includes multiple records for single documents, varying in quality and fullness, because standardization at input stage has not been required. When consulted to find a record, the database appears to be unnecessarily large, requiring more search time, and hence cost, to identify certainly a single wanted record than would have been the case if a single, standard record had represented a single document.[41] In 1980 between three and four million records were changed to conform with the *AACR2*. Designs are in hand for reconstructing the database, to be implemented in 1987.[42]

The most up-to-date information on OCLC comes from OCLC itself. Leaflets explain each individual service and methods of participation, and an advisory service is ready to answer any questions.

CONSER

An outstanding contribution to bibliography made by OCLC was its participation in the CONSER (Conversion of Serials) Project. By the early 1970s a number of independent projects were under way in the United States and Canada to create machine-readable serials databases. In order to co-ordinate and standardize the work being done, the Ad Hoc Discussion Group on Serials Data Bases was formed in 1973 and with the help of the Council on Library Resources was instrumental in launching the CONSER Project. A contract was placed with OCLC at the end of 1974 to provide facilities for creating and maintaining a serials database, to which material was to be contributed by a number of libraries with major serials collections. Access to the file would be open to any library through OCLC. The basic input was the existing online Minnesota Union List of Serials, followed by the MARC serials records of the Library of Congress and the National Library of Canada (NLC) and later by the Pittsburgh Regional Library Center records. Other designated libraries initially contributed records for current titles, each being responsible for a portion of the alphabet, except for the National Library of Medicine and the National Agriculture Library which contributed according to their subject specializations. Later the participating libraries converted the remainder of their holdings.

In addition to contributing MARC serials records, LC and NLC are responsible for 'authenticating' records, that is, certifying the correctness and completeness of the bibliographic information accepted.

OCLC sends weekly tapes to LC for distribution through the MARC services. In addition, there are available a CONSER/ KWOC index and a microfiche file of authenticated records.

Besides the North American organizations which send members to the CONSER Advisory Group, the British Library, the National Library of Australia and the International Federation of Library Associations and Institutions are also represented.

25

UTLAS

The University of Toronto Library Automation System (UTLAS – now UTLAS International Inc) also developed from a local academic into a worldwide system. From supplying its own large campus it expanded to serve other libraries and by the mid-1980s it held MARC records from Canada, United States, France, Great Britain and Japan, together with updated authority files of LC name and subject headings. It provides a variety of automated systems for both large and small libraries.

Co-operatives in the United Kingdom

In Great Britain, where county libraries have been responsible for the service to many small towns, and where municipal schools and colleges were later in acquiring independent collections, cataloguing was generally centralized within the single library system. Regional systems existed solely as vehicles for interlibrary loans, maintaining union catalogues to which local libraries contributed, but from which no cataloguing material was distributed. The advent of automatic data processing machines – and the creative imagination to use them to enhance the value and use of library records – have led to a number of co-operative groupings, in addition to the direct link between individual libraries and the *BNB* and, later, BLAISE.

Southampton University Library was a pioneer with its Wessex Medical Library catalogues, several copies of which were required to serve the hospital region for which the University's Medical Library was responsible.[43] Newcastle University Library was another pioneer. Both university libraries have pursued a long programme of research into cataloguing, reported in *Program* and *VINE*.

BLCMP

BLCMP Library Services Ltd was begun experimentally in 1969 by the University of Birmingham, the University of Aston in Birmingham, and the Birmingham City Libraries as the Birmingham Libraries Co-operative Mechanisation Project. It has been fully operational from 1973, and serves a variety of libraries.[44,45] It makes use of *BNB* and LC MARC tapes and of locally generated records to produce a union

26

catalogue/database from which catalogues can be generated for each of the subscribing libraries in the form and frequency individually chosen. Author, title, name and classified cataogues are produced as requested, most popularly as microfiche, but also as film, bookform printout, cards, and online public access catalogues.

BLCMP pioneered centralized cataloguing of audio-visual materials and serials, not originally available through the BL. Still run from the University of Birmingham, BLCMP offers, in addition to its cataloguing and bibliographical enquiry services, automated systems for acquisitions, serials control and circulation control to libraries and regional centres throughout the country.

SWALCAP

The South West Academic Libraries Co-operative Automation Programme (SWALCAP), with its centre located in Bristol University, has provided an online service since 1976. From 1986 a private limited company with shareholders from among its 23 members, it provides circulation, acquisitions and cataloguing systems, and plans extensions.[46]

SCOLCAP

When the National Library of Scotland decided to automate its own catalogue production, the opportunity was seized to examine the possibilities of a national network in Scotland. By 1986, via the Scottish Libraries Cataloguing Automation Project (SCOLCAP), the holdings of six member libraries were being incorporated into a union catalogue – SCOLCAT – on COMfiche, with monthly cumulations. Updated COM catalogues of each library's holdings are supplied through the BLAISE/LOCAS service.

LASER

The London and South Eastern Library Region (LASER) has maintained a union catalogue of the stock of co-operating libraries since 1928. The catalogue was initiated solely to facilitate interlibrary loans, and it was to speed up interlending that automation was first used. As the whole LASER catalogue was converted to machine-readable form (after necessary editing and with access to the *BNB* files) so other services became possible.

A notable contribution to practical cataloguing was made after the local government reorganization of 1974 had altered the boundaries of many administrative areas and consequently of many library authorities. Kent County Library, for example, acquired, along with 15 new libraries, 15 catalogues so disparate in form that a straightforward amalgamation of them was impossible. The libraries had, however, over the years been notifying the union catalogue of successive accessions and withdrawals. Now that the need had arisen, the LASER automated catalogue could be sorted to provide a set of individual catalogues, compatible with each other and capable of being merged into a single catalogue. The combined LASER and *BNB* files were also used to provide partial catalogues for new local authorities in other parts of the country which needed to organize a sudden afflux of different book collections and to make new catalogues. Printouts supplied by LASER were used for stocktaking and for updating Decimal classification numbers, and, of course, as the base from which current catalogues could be derived. Once in automated form, a local catalogue could subsequently be kept up to date using the authority's own computer or through the agency of any of the centralized services.

LASER itself developed into such a service. It provides both a current and a retrospective cataloguing service to its members and remains a valuable medium for interlibrary loans. It has made available a microfiche copy of its complete database. The development of automation in LASER has been described by its Director, Jean Plaister.[47]

The British regional networks, together with co-operative groupings in support of specialist subject information collection and dissemination, are described in Jack Burkett's *Library and information networks in the United Kingdom* (London: Aslib, 1979), and in Alan Seal's *Automated cataloguing in the United Kingdom: a guide to services* (Bath: Bath University Library, 1980. (BLR&D Report 5545)).

Each of the regional networks issues its own manual and distributes its own newsletter to inform members of procedures and developments. BLAISE also issues at irregular intervals loose-leaf information sheets called *Cataloguing practice notes for UK MARC records.*

Assessment and development

Membership of a co-operative does not, of course, render carefree and effortless those library activities which have been automated, and some disappointment has been expressed at the degree of adjustment to new requirements which must be made by member libraries. The chief complaints voiced by members are of lack of standardization between systems, and even within systems; lack of currency in the central databases; insufficient coverage of publications, chiefly because EMMA records are not universally available; and the increasing cost of up-dating catalogues as they increase in size. Tony Lovecy draws attention to some of the particular problems, such as those created by, and for, libraries which do not need a full bibliographic record in all cases or whose cataloguing rules differ from the practice currently required by MARC, and also those which, while following identical rules in a common code, construe to different interpretations. Nevertheless, Lovecy ends his criticisms with a reminder that sharing implies some surrender of independence and giving as well as taking.[48]

Most of the co-operatives have, in fact, written into their constitutions a requirement for some degree of standardization for input and output. Stephen Massil has assessed the use of, and requirements for, standards in shared bibliographic systems as they appeared to him in 1982.[49] Here I will not go into the subject but refer the reader to the next two chapters, which consider standardization and bibliographic standards in some detail.

Constant change is a feature of all developing technologies and few are developing so rapidly as automated data processing. Existing provision gives rise to a demand for extended coverage and services, new advances are made, funding increases or decreases, and users become more aware of what is feasible and hence more able to influence development.

A body called the Co-operative Automation Group (CAG), consisting of representatives of the British Library and of the co-operatives – BLCMP, LASER, SCOLCAP and SWAL-CAP – and also of the Library Association, Aslib, Standing

29

Conference of National and University Libraries (SCONUL) and the Council of Polytechnic Librarians (COPOL), has been formed with the object of improving co-operation between networks and increasing standardization and coverage of records. CAG's recommendations for cataloguing input standards for all library materials have been listed in terms of the UK MARC format.[50]

Not all libraries using automated control systems operate through the networks. Some software packages offered by commercial firms have shown insufficient awareness of the complexities of bibliographic records, but some others, worked out in close collaboration with individual libraries, have proved to be highly successful, as in Cheshire and Derbyshire county libraries,[51] and recently many more software packages have become commercially available.

Computer output and catalogue reorganization

The end of an era was marked by the decision of the Library of Congress to stop filing new entries into its massive card catalogues on 1 January 1981 and to rely primarily on automated data to provide access to the collections. From that date forward the library possessed two catalogues – the 'frozen' manual card catalogue and a new multipartite one that included all records in the MARC data base. The older material did not long remain accessible only through the card catalogue. The retrospective conversion (RECON) of the catalogue to MARC format was begun selectively almost immediately. Renamed REMARC, the conversion was completed by the Carrollton Press who also publish a subject index to the MARC data base.[51a]

Services for retrospective conversion available in the United Kingdom, including REMARC, are reviewed in *VINE* 58, March 1985. That issue contains also an account of converting Edinburgh University Library's catalogue. REMARC applied in an American university library has also been described.[52]

The adoption of a new code of cataloguing rules or a new catalogue format is not an easy experience for a library's staff and readers to live through. This is particularly so when a change to computerized forms of cataloguing entails learning new techniques and organizing new work schedules, and when co-operation entails abandoning long-held practices and assumptions. The change requires careful planning and the understanding and goodwill of everyone concerned.

A decision on a new format must take into account the number of catalogue locations desirable within the organization and the feasibility of obtaining the catalogue in its final form through a national agency or one of the regional co-operatives, or of using an in-house computer to produce a COM or online output. In the latter case, the software packages that are available must be evaluated, and the different operations that can be co-ordinated; as must also the cost, reliability and performance of hardware installations available and their suitability for the preferred software; the cost and upkeep of installations; the staffing requirements; and what can be learned from the experience of others, both providers and users. The fate of the 'closed' catalogue must also be considered: to remain 'the old catalogue' or to be integrated with the new.

Demonstrations of the available software and hardware are frequent, and the professional literature is abundant. Juliet Leevis notes that 'the trend towards fully integrated in-house systems, covering all functions and including a facility to extract records from an external database if required, is now firmly established', and she has provided a buyer's guide which lists suppliers, and sets out in a standard sequence what each can do and at what cost.[53] Management aspects of online public access catalogues have been described in a manual by J. R. Matthews[54] and also in a report by Emily Fayen,[55] while various aspects of online public access to library files were discussed at two conferences held at the Centre for Catalogue Research, Bath, in 1983 and 1986,[56,57] and also in an Aslib compilation.[58] Decisions that must be taken in changing from a card to a COM catalogue have been set out by Philip Schwarz,[59] and individual experiences are currently recorded, as in the *MARC Users' Group newsletter*.

The drawbacks of not converting a 'frozen' catalogue have been summed up by Dwyer who finds that readers do not always bother, or realize the need, to look in more than one file.[60] A particular difficulty lies in checking the complete holdings of an author's works and in comparing editions.

31

Dwyer concludes that the conversion of an existing file into the same form and sequence as the current catalogue is the only satisfactory procedure. The relevant literature for the most part confirms his findings. Not all libraries need to keep their stock in perpetuity. Daniel Boorstin, Librarian of Congress, has reminded us that we cannot without committing the sin of arrogance predict what will be the matter of future research and that we must therefore accept and preserve somewhere whatever records society produces,[61] but indiscriminate acquisition and hoarding are not required of every library, as Wilfred Ashworth has pointed out,[62] and a library maintained sparely for current use brings the added benefit that its catalogues are easier and cheaper to maintain, and, if necessary, to renew, and also easier to consult.

References

1 Jewett, Charles Coffin, *On the construction of catalogues of libraries, and of a general catalogue; and their publication by means of separate, stereotyped titles. With rules and examples*. Washington: Smithsonian Institution, 1852, 7.

2 Hill, Michael, 'The International Federation for Documentation and Aslib', *Aslib information*, 10(11/12), November/December 1982, 301 – 4.

3 *International catalogue of scientific literature*. 1st to 14th annual issues. London: Royal Society, 1902 – 19.

4 Hall, James L., *Online bibliographic data bases: a directory and source book*. 4th ed. London: Aslib, 1986.

5 Hall, J. L., *Online information retrieval, 1976 – 1979: an international bibliography*. London: Aslib, 1980.

6 Stephens, J., *Inventory of abstracting and indexing services produced in the UK*. London: British Library, 1986. (Includes index of database processors, with the UK online databases they offer.)

7 Leonard, Lawrence E., *Co-operative and centralized cataloguing and processing: a bibliography, 1850 – 1967*. University of Illinois, Graduate School of Library Science, 1968. (Occasional papers, no. 93)

8 *Library trends*, 16(1), 1967, 1-175.

9 Library of Congress, *Annual report of the Librarian of Congress, 1902*, 101.

10 See reference 9 above, 106.

11 Library of Congress, *Annual report, 1967*, 53.

12 Ganning, Mary K. Daniels, 'Library of Congress cataloging distribution services, 1901 – 1976', *Library resources and technical services*, 27(4), Fall 1977, 317 – 25. (Describes current methods of ordering and production of catalogue records both for LC's own use and for distribution.)

13 Dawson, John M., 'The Library of Congress: its role in co-operative and centralized cataloging', *Library trends*, 16(1), 1967, 85 – 96.

14 Welsh, William J., 'The Processing Department of the Library of Congress in 1968', *Library resources and technical services*, 13(2), 1969, 175 – 97.

15 Dix, William S., 'Centralized cataloging and university libraries – Title II, Part C, of the Higher Education Act of 1965', *Library resources and technical services*, 13(2), 1969, 97 – 111.

16 Library of Congress, *A catalog of books represented by Library of Congress printed cards issued to July 31, 1942*. Ann Arbor, Mich: Edwards Bros., for the Association of Research Libraries, 1946. 167 vols.

17 *National union catalog*. 1953 – . Nine monthly and three quarterly issues and an annual volume. Five-yearly cumulations.

18 Stevens, Norman D. [and others], 'The National Program for Acquisitions and Cataloging: a progress report on developments under the Title IIc of the Higher Education Act of 1965', *Library resources and technical services*, 12(1), 1968, 7 – 29.

19 Library of Congress, *Annual report 1967*. Washington: LC, 1968, 36.

20 Liebaers, Herman, 'Shared cataloguing', *Unesco bulletin for libraries*, 24(2 & 3), 1970, 62 – 72 and 126 – 38. (Includes bibliography.)

21 *Cataloguing rules: author and title entries*; compiled by committees of the Library Association and of the American Library Association. English ed. London: LA, 1908 (facsimile reprint 1930).

22 *Anglo-American cataloguing rules*; prepared by The American Library Association, The Library of Congress, The Library Association and The Canadian Library Association. British text. London: LA, 1967.

23 *Anglo-American cataloguing rules*, 2nd ed.; prepared by The American Library Association, The British Library, The Canadian Committee on Cataloguing, The Library Association, The Library of Congress; ed. by Michael Gorman and

Paul W. Winkler. London: LA, 1978. (Supplemented by revisions, 1982, 1984, 1986.)

24 Johnson, T. J., 'The *BNB* card service: a brief history', *British Library Bibliographical Services Division newsletter*, 27 November 1982, 9 – 10.

25 Library of Congress. Processing Department, *The cataloging-in-source experiment: a report to the Librarian of Congress by the Director of the Processing Department.* Washington: Library of Congress, 1960. (Reviewed *Library resources and technical services*, 4(4), 1960, 269 – 84.)

26 Ranganathan, S. R., 'Prenatal classification and cataloguing on its way', *Annals of library science*, 6(4), December 1959, 113 – 25.

27 Clapp, V. W., 'The greatest invention since the title page? Autobibliography from incipit to cataloging-in-publication', *Wilson Library bulletin*, 46(4), December 1971, 348 – 59. (26 references)

28 Clapp, V. W., 'Cataloguing-in-publication: a new programme of pre-publication cataloguing in the United States of America, with comments on some similar programmes', *Unesco bulletin for libraries*, 27(1), 1973, 2 – 11. (24 references)

29 'Cataloguing-in-publication: what is happening? Proceedings of a one-day seminar held at the Library Association, 21 October 1981', *Catalogue & index*, 63/64, Winter 1981/Spring 1982.

30 'International cataloguing in publication meeting, Ottawa, August 1982', *British Library Bibliographic Services Division newsletter*, 27, November 1982, 6 – 9.

31 'The expansion of the UK Cataloguing-in-Publication programme: your questions answered', *Library Association record*, 86(12), December 1984 (insert).

32 *Information technology and libraries*, Vol. 1 – , 1982 – . Chicago: Library and Information Technology Association 1982 – . (Continues *Journal of library automation*.) Quarterly.

33 *Program: automated library and information systems*, 1966 – . From vol. 2 pub. London: Aslib, 1969 – . Quarterly.

34 *VINE: a Very Informal Newsletter of library automation*, compiled by the Information Office for Library Automation. Southampton: Southampton University Library. (About four times a year.)

35 *Annual review of information science and technology*. White Plains, N.Y.: Knowledge Industry Publications, 1966 – .

36 British National Bibliography. Research and Development Section, *BNB/MARC project: report September 1970 – March 1973*. London: BNB, 1974. (BNB/MARC documentation service, publ. no. 7)

37 Avram, Henriette, *MARC: its history and implications*. Washington: Library of Congress, 1975. (Includes bibliography.)

38 Long, Anthony, 'UK MARC and US MARC: a brief history and comparison', *Journal of documentation*, 40(1), March 1984, 1 – 12.

39 Long, Philip L., 'OCLC: from concept to functioning network', *in* Lancaster, Wilfrid (ed.), *Proceedings of the 10th Clinic on Library Applications of Data Processing, 1973, University of Illinois*. London, Bingley, 1974, 165 – 70.

40 Axford, H. William, 'The great rush to automated catalogs: will it be management or muddling through?' *in* Gore, Daniel (ed.), *Requiem for the card catalog: management issues in automated cataloging*. London: Aldwych P; Westport, Conn., Greenwood, 1979, 174.

41 Wanninger, P. D., 'Is the OCLC database too large? A study of the effect of duplicate records in the OCLC system', *Library resources and technical services*, 26(4), October/December 1982, 353 – 61. (13 references)

42 Buckle, David, 'AACR2 implementation five years on', *Catalogue & index*, 80, Spring 1986, 1 and 3 – 5.

43 Southampton University Library, *Library automation project. Final report*; compiled by R. G. Woods, 1975.

44 Buckle, David, 'The Birmingham Libraries' Co-operative Mechanisation Project, 1960 – 1975', *LIBER bulletin*, 5/6, 1974, 74 – 95 (2 tables, 16 references). Also in *Catalogue & index*, 34, Summer/Autumn 1974, 11 and 14. (The references cover the project from the date of the initial survey to the time of writing.)

45 Capewell, Pat, 'The customer and the network: a customer's view of BLCMP', *Catalogue & index*, 45, Summer 1977, 5 – 7.

46 'Breaking the silence: news of SWALCAP's local integrated library system', *VINE*, 61, December 1985, 3 – 11.

47 Plaister, Jean, *Computing in LASER: regional library co-operation*. London: Library Association, 1982.

48 Lovecy, Tony, 'What's in cooperatives for me?', *Catalogue & index*, 61, Summer 1981, 1 – 6.

49 Massil, Stephen W., 'Standards for sharing in bibliographic systems', *Catalogue & index*, 65, Summer 1982, 1 – 6. (7 references)

50 'Proposals for a recommended input standard', *VINE*, 57, December 1984, 36 – 47.

51 Gratton, Peter, 'What price independence?', *Catalogue & index*, 62, Autumn 1981, 1 – 4.

51a *Cumulative subject index to the MARC data base, 1968-1978 and Library of Congress Classification number index to the MARC data base,*

1968-1978. Quarterly supplements. Arlington: Carrollton Press, in progress.

52   Douglas, Nancy E., 'REMARC retrospective conversion: what, why & how?', *Technical services quarterly*, 2(3/4), Spring/Summer 1985, 11 – 16.

53   Leevis, Juliet, *Library systems: a buyer's guide*. Aldershot: Gower, 1987.

54   Matthews, Joseph R., *Public access to online catalogs: a planning guide for managers*, Weston, Conn: Online Inc, 1982. (Includes bibliography on pp.321 – 30.)

55   Fayen, Emily Gallup, 'The online public access catalog in 1984: evaluating needs and choices', *Library technology reports*, 20(1), January/February 1984, 5 – 59. (Includes bibliography.)

56   Seal, Alan (ed.), *Introducing the online catalogue: papers based on seminars held in 1983*, Bath: Centre for Catalogue Research, 1984. (Includes bibliography on pp.75 – 85.)

57   Kinsella, Janet (ed.), *Online public access to library files*. Oxford: Elsevier, 1986.

58   *Going online 1987*; compiled by G. Turpie. London: Aslib, 1986.

59   Schwarz, Philip, 'Management decisions and the COM catalog', *Microform review*, 11(3), Summer 1982, 156 – 71.

60   Dwyer, James R., 'The effect of closed catalogs on public access', *Library resources and technical services*, 25(2), April/June 1981, 186 – 95. (35 references)

61   In an interview with Sir Huw Wheldon during a programme on the Library of Congress shown on BBC television, 21 January 1979.

62   Ashworth, Wilfred, 'Future perfect', *Aslib proceedings*, 31(4), 1979, 158 – 69.

3

Standardization

The preceding chapter pointed to the need for standardization. The following chapters will speak of individual standards. Here I want to consider the questions: What is a standard? How is it determined? Why is it so important?

Used loosely the term *standard* refers to a consensus of opinion as to what is an acceptable level of goodness in any activity or product. We speak of 'a high standard' of work, behaviour, musicianship; of goods for sale not being 'up to standard'. The term is also used to imply compatibility between things we wish to use together. 'These are not standard fittings' we say, as we try to push a square peg into a round hole. Each of the things may, in fact, conform to a standard; it is the standards which are not compatible with each other. Certain American electrical appliances, for example, cannot be activated by a British electrical circuit, though each conforms to a norm in its own country.

Used technically, the word *standard* refers to an officially promulgated set of statements or technical requirements put out by a body of recognized standing, which has the respect of the trade, profession or other group for whose benefit the standard is prepared. The statements may comprise definitions, as a glossary of technical terms or a set of specifications for named materials or processes; they may constitute a code of practice, or, less stringently where complete uniformity is undesirable or inappropriate, a set of recommendations.

A standard is seen to be necessary for practical reasons. Everyday commerce requires that buyer and seller should quantify in the same measures – Magna Carta prescribed standard measures for wine, ale and cloth. If a published standard specifies the composition, dimensions and qualities of a product used in the manufacture of some other product, then the standard product can be continuously incorporated into the manufacturing process, each new batch of the standard product fitting into the place or performing the function assigned to it.

A standard is not an ideal. It is a desideratum within the possible. It embodies merely the highest measure of agreement which it has been possible to achieve among members of the committee which drafted it. The committee members represent different sectional interests, and they generally circulate their draft proposals to other interested parties, including individual experts, for comment before a definitive standard is published. The sectional interests may keep the level of a standard well below the ideal because organizations represented are unwilling to commit themselves to massive expenditure on changing existing production-machinery or using different raw materials or increasing manpower.

Standardization of nomenclature is necessary to ensure that there shall be no ambiguity as to the identity of a commodity and consequently as to its properties. To such an end, to take a practical example, the Forest Products Research Laboratory maintains a 'library' of samples of different woods, while the British Standards Institution keeps up to date a *Nomenclature of commercial timbers* (BS 881 and 589).

The British Standards Institution has also published a *Glossary of documentation terms* (BS 5408) which lists and defines terms used in cataloguing, classification, dissemination of information, the technical processes of printing and making books, data processing, reprographics, document storage and preservation, photography, and cartography. The glossary, of which a revised edition is expected in the late 1980s, naturally draws on and updates lists already available to the librarian, such as the *ALA glossary of library terms* published by the American Library Association in 1943 (updated as *ALA glossary of library and information science*, 1983), Anthony Thompson's *Vocabularium bibliothecarii* published by Unesco in 1953, in three languages, with other languages added in later editions, and Wersig's five-language *Terminology of documentation*.[1]

It is not always easy to define a concept in librarianship: it has no measurable colour, specific gravity, graining pattern.

38

Even the term 'cataloguing' is elastic. It is conveniently used to cover 'what the cataloguer, or the cataloguing department, does' and those activities will vary according to the size and organization of the library. Attempts to compare the costs of cataloguing in different libraries have always encountered this obstacle. Valid statistics depend upon rigid definitions.

Standardization leads designedly to savings in cost, time and effort because standard commodities are obtained more quickly and cheaply than custom-built goods, their quality should not vary, they fit into a standardized system, their familiarity makes them easier to use. Librarians are ever pressed by the need to economize, hence variations from the norm must be justified by appreciable, not simply marginal or supposed, advantages. There is enough in librarianship that is unique – the singularity of each work of literature and of each reader, the personal response of each librarian to his working environment – for standardization to be acceptable in those areas where it decreases repetitive labour – including intellectual but duplicated labour – and increases speed, clarity and understanding.

Standardizing organizations
National standardizing organizations were created to co-ordinate and harmonize the work being done by trade and professional associations. The British Standards Institution (BSI) developed from the British Engineering Standards Association, which had originally (in 1901) been set up as a joint Engineering Standards Committee of the three engineering institutions – Civil, Mechanical, and Electrical Engineers, the Iron and Steel Institute, and the Institution of Naval Architects. From engineering its interests spread to cover most British industries and trades.[2] They also now include technical activities of concern to librarians. The sectional list of British Standards on Documentation (SI 35) is subtitled 'standards for the editor, publisher, librarian and information scientist'. It comprises sections on Editing, Paper and printed matter, Information interchange, Micrographics, and the English editions of the Universal decimal classification (which BSI publishes in sections as they are completed or revised).

BSI has published *A standard for standards* which sets out the principles of standardization, the organization of BSI and its committees and the methods of drafting and presenting standards.[3]

Work in the same field of interest is initiated and co-ordinated in the United States by the National Information Standards Organization (Z39), a reincorporation in 1984 of the American National Standards Institute Committee Z39.[4] All other developed and developing countries have their own standards organizations.

There is also an International Organization for Standardization (ISO – founded as International Standardizing Association (ISA) in 1928). The ISO endeavours to bring national standards into line with each other, through the promulgation of international standards, whenever a need for international compatibility has been shown. Another of its functions is the dissemination of information about existing standards. The need frequently arises, for example, for an exporter to comply with certain standards in force in the country to which he hopes to export, or for an importer to ensure that the goods he imports will be compatible with products with which their use is intended. There is also the need to prevent ambiguity in the designation of products. Not least when a new national standard in any field is proposed, it is useful to know of similar standards already extant. To improve the flow of standards information ISO established, in 1974, a system to co-ordinate exchanges of information, working through national centres – ISONET. A manual and a thesaurus were drafted as an aid to the national centres in contributing to this network, and were presented at the ISONET symposium, organized by Unesco in 1977.[5] The manual provides for a description of each standard sufficient for its identification and characterization, while the thesaurus provides subject descriptors. Both are under revision at the time of writing. BSI's work on the revision has resulted in the publication of its own *Root thesaurus*, described in more detail on pp.164-6. ISO's Information Office publishes a series of bibliographies in support of ISONET. These include *International standards for documentation and terminology*, 1976 (3rd ed. Geneva 1981).

Both British and foreign standards are available through the BSI Sales Department.

For each individual country the only officially valid standard is the national standard for that country. Thus an ISO standard is the standard for an individual country only if that country's standardizing body promulgates it as a national standard. Even then it cannot necessarily be imposed. The importance of a national standardizing organization is attested by the financial support it receives from voluntary subscriptions and from governmental allocations, and by the widespread use of its publications and also of its testing services, which lead, in the case of compliance with a British Standard, to the right to use the Kitemark symbol of approval. Nevertheless, a national standard has merely the status of an authoritative recommendation backed by the knowledge and experience – and, to some extent, by the self-interest – of the organizations and individuals whose deliberations and decisions were embodied in its formulation. There are a few exceptions where standards are incorporated into the law of a country; for example, conformity with the relevant British Standard is required for certain building specifications and for certain safety regulations.

In addition to the official national standardizing bodies and the international body (ISO), there exist, as has already been noted, trade and professional bodies with a lively interest in the promotion of standardization. For librarianship there are primarily the national libraries and national bibliographies which provide services to, and collaborate with, the country's libraries, and also the general and specialized library associations which exist to improve the work done by libraries and to promote the education and welfare of librarians. It was the initiative of the British and American library associations which resulted in the creation of a joint Anglo-American cataloguing code, first published in 1908.[6] In its various revisions it has remained the standard descriptive cataloguing code for English-speaking countries.[7,8] There are also the international bodies whose aim is to improve library services throughout the world by co-operative action: the International Federation of Library Associations (IFLA) and the International Federation for Documentation (FID). (At its forty-

41

second meeting in 1976 the Council of IFLA changed its name to International Federation of Library Associations and Institutions, and on the ninetieth anniversary of its founding – 2 September 1885 – FID became the International Federation for Information and Documentation. In both cases the acronyms remain the same.) Unesco, in furthering educational, scientific and cultural exchanges, is inevitably concerned with the communication of bibliographic information at a level and to a degree of conformity which make its widespread use possible. Together with IFLA, and supported by funds from the (American) Council on Library Resources, Unesco sponsored the International Conference on Cataloguing Principles in 1961. Together with the International Council of Scientific Unions, it sponsored an inquiry into the feasibility of a world science information system – UNISIST – and subsequently a programme for implementing recommendations made in the report of the inquiry (see pp.51-2).

Certain other international bodies, not concerned primarily with documentation but recognizing its vital importance, such as the OECD and the EEC, have their special committees on information policy and procedures and maintain links with national bibliographical centres. The International Atomic Energy Agency (IAEA) and the International Nuclear Information System (INIS) produce jointly standards for descriptive cataloguing, authority lists for journal titles and names of corporate bodies, and a manual of indexing to be used in conjunction with the INIS thesaurus.

Because so many organizations are interested in promulgating normative codes there is a danger that in preparing a set of rules to be followed here and now, instead of in some Utopian future, certain needs will be overlooked or inconsistencies between closely related standards will arise. The international standard bibliographic descriptions (ISBDs) promulgated by IFLA are a case in point. (The ISBDs are described in more detail in the following chapter: here they are mentioned merely to illustrate the problem of conflict.) Concern over the rapid proliferation of ISBDs was expressed by four of the large national libraries in the English-speaking world which used the Anglo-American code and found themselves expected to conform to the new 'standards' without consultation and without confidence that their needs had been properly considered when the documents had been drawn up.[9] In replying to that criticism, the Director of IFLA's International UBC Office recalled the genesis of ISBDs in the IMCE meeting in Copenhagen (see pp.54-5) and enumerated the difficulties any international body had in making contact with all the people whose interests were affected by its actions, and who might wish to offer comment before it was too late.[10] For there is a time limit. At the meeting at which concern over the ISBDs had been expressed, one of the four national libraries had already announced that 'while LC hopes to use character sets conforming to or compatible with international standards, it will not feel bound to delay implementing its expansion of MARC coverage until such standards are available, as some of them are likely to be very long in coming'. Just so!

At a second meeting in 1978 the four national libraries mentioned above formally assumed the name ABACUS (Association of Bibliographic Agencies of Britain, Australia, Canada and the United States) and agreed on further co-ordination of policies, noting discrepancies that arose from the optional use of certain alternative rules in *AACR2* and the required use of two standards for serials cataloguing – ISBD(S) and ISDS – the lack of a filing standard for machine-readable records, and differing authority files.[11]

Revision of standards

From time to time the revision of a standard is called for, in order to incorporate information on new materials and practices and to deprecate the continued use of certain others, to respond to a changed environment and to make use of new technologies. The present policy of the British Standards Institution, for example, is to review existing standards published more than five years previously. In the light of suggestions received from interested organizations and individuals on such a standard, BSI may then

- withdraw it, as being no longer appropriate as a standard;
- confirm it, if it is still valid;

- update it, using an amendment slip, if only minor changes are necessary;
- revise it, if major changes are necessary.

IFLA proposes that a similar time-lapse should precede consideration of the revision of ISBDs. A warning is perhaps in order that any such standard cited with a date should be checked for a possible revision.

Until recently, standards in librarianship were considered to be valid for much longer than five years and even when acknowledged to be out of date were very slow in their updating. Today the urgency of making information available is accepted at all levels. Automatic data processing and alternatives to traditional methods of printing have so far penetrated our techniques and programmes of work that keeping up with their rapid development is seen to be a necessity. Nevertheless, inertia being generally a more comfortable human state than making the effort to redo work already done, and learn afresh in areas which had appeared to be areas of stable knowledge, and possibly submit established practices to searching analysis and replacement by entirely new systems, a revised standard will inevitably encounter some resistance.

Sixty years elapsed beteween the appearance of the first and second jointly agreed Anglo-American codes of cataloguing rules; eleven years between the appearance of the latter and its second edition; three sets of revisions to that edition were published within seven years.

Since the object of cataloguing is the communication of accurate bibliographical information, and a relevant definition of information is 'a message that means the same to the sender as to the recipient', it is inevitable that much of this book and its companion volume[12] will be about the use of the code and of other standards, and the compensatory measures that must be taken when standardization is lacking.

References

1   *Terminology of documentation. . . A selection of 1,200 basic terms in English, French, German, Russian and Spanish*; compiled by Gernot Wersig and Ulrich Neveling. Paris: Unesco, 1976. (Reviewed

by E. J. Coates in *Journal of documentation*, 32(4), 1976, 327 – 9).
2   Woodward, C. Douglas, *BSI: the story of standards*. London: BSI, 1972.
3   *A standard for standards. Part 1: General principles of standardization. Part 2: BSI and its committee procedures. Part 3: Drafting and presenting British standards*. London: BSI, 1981. (BS O: 1981)
4   Blum, Fred, 'Standards update: ANSI Committee Z39', *Library resources and technical services*, 18(1), Winter 1974, 25 – 9. (Reprinted in *The indexer*, 9(3), April 1975, 113 – 15, where it is followed (pp.116 – 18) by Michael Bardwell's 'Documentation standards at BSI'.)
5   Sutter, E., 'International dissemination of standards information – tools needed to operate the work: the ISO thesaurus and the ISONET manual', *The indexer*, 11(3), 1979, 157 – 9.
6   *Cataloguing rules: author and title entries*; compiled by committees of the Library Association and of the American Library Association. English ed. London: LA, 1908 (facsimile reprint 1930).
7   *Anglo-American cataloguing rules*; prepared by the American Library Association, The Library of Congress, The Library Association and The Canadian Library Association. North American text. Chicago: ALA, 1967. British text. London: LA, 1967.
8   *Anglo-American cataloguing rules,* 2nd ed.; prepared by The American Library Association, The British Library, The Canadian Committee on Cataloguing, The Library Association, The Library of Congress; ed. by Michael Gorman and Paul W. Winkler. London: LA, 1978. (Supplemented by revisions, 1982, 1984, 1986.)
9   'Summary minutes of the meeting on co-operative cataloging of the British Library, National Library of Australia, National Library of Canada and Library of Congress, Washington, D.C., Nov. 8 – 9, 1976', *LC information bulletin*, 36(14), 8 April, 1977, 251 – 2.
10 Anderson, Dorothy, 'A rejoinder: IFLA's role in standardizing bibliographic practices – the ISBD program', *LC information bulletin*, 36(34), August 1977, 600 – 4.
11 *BLBSD newsletter*, 11, November 1978, 5 – 10.
12 Piggott, Mary, *The cataloguer's way: from document receipt to document retrieval*. To be published by Library Association Publishing Ltd.

4

International standards for handling bibliographic information

There can be no doubt that if all the nationally produced bibliographies and bibliographic services are to be useable together to form a worldwide bibliographic reservoir, there must be compatibility in the way individual bibliographic units are described in the tributary sources. There must also be compatibility in the way the bibliographic information is transmitted. That is, there must be standardization not only in cataloguing but also in the communications format. A lack of correspondence must be remedied either by a specially written machine programme, or by intellectual application, both costly.

Much standardizing work is in progress. The *UNISIST guide to standards for information handling* gives an overview of some hundreds of existing standards, rules, guidelines and other documents of a normative character relevant to the generation, processing, dissemination and use of information.[1] But the mere existence of standards does not enforce their recognition, particularly as certain agencies have developed sophisticated rules to serve the needs of their own systems. The use of multiple 'standards' for the same purpose is a negation of standardization. Attempts which are being made to harmonize divergent practices are noted later in this chapter.

International standard numbers

ISBN

One way of minimizing the effects of discrepancies in bibliographic description is to use a code number which uniquely designates a particular record. Such numbers are familiar in LC card numbers and *BNB* numbers. Having little or no semantic content they cannot be used for systematic listing by which, for example, authors or subjects might be identified, but they can represent, both as shorthand and as a double check, a known entity. Such a code, internationally used, is the International Standard Book Number (ISBN) which uniquely identifies a published monograph. The ISBN is a ten-figure number made up of groups of digits which signify respectively country (or group of countries) of origin, publisher, the individual work in a particular issue, and a check digit by means of which the whole number can be validated. An individualizing book number was first used by a few publishers who were transferring their stock records to machine control. The then editor of the *BNB*, A. J. Wells, had the idea that a single, nationally valid code which could be applied to the output of all British publishers would provide a symbol which could be used both by people and by machines to specify and to recognize an individual bibliographic entity in library as well as bookselling operations. Wells was able to persuade many of the British publishing firms to accept his idea, and a numerical code was worked out by a committee of the Publishers' Association, with Professor Gordon Foster, of the London School of Economics, as consultant. The allocation of the standard numbers is made by a central agency, the SBN Agency Ltd, which keeps a master record of all numbers used. The advantage of extending the code to cover books produced in any country of the world was immediately recognized, and had, indeed, been foreseen by Professor Foster, whose mathematics allowed an extra group of numbers to precede the original nine-figure standard book number to indicate country of origin. Thus a preliminary nought indicates Great Britain, the United States, Canada and Australia; the figure two indicates France; and so on. The adapted code became an official international standard in 1969, and the literal prefix introducing the numeric group was changed from sbn to ISBN.[2,3]

Being of recent origin, however, ISBNs are found only in recent publications. If they are to be used as control numbers in catalogues which list also earlier publications, it is necessary to create a 'pseudo' or retrospective ISBN for each of the publications issued prior to the introduction of ISBNs. The retrospective conversion of existing catalogues which took place independently in many libraries has led to the creation of various control numbers for the same publication, thus making different libraries' lists incompatible. In addition, it must be remembered that the ISBN is applied to only one particular issue of a work, so that a linking system is also needed to recall all the entries in a single catalogue of all the versions of a work.

Research at the University of Bradford has resulted in a proposal for a Universal Standard Book Code that would provide a unique identifier and control code for bibliographic (and other) records, more reliable than the ISBN, and permit files to be satisfactorily merged and duplicates to be eliminated.[4]

ISSN and CODEN

A similar set of numbers, worked out originally by the American National Standards Institute, with later co-operation by the International Organization for Standardization, is available for serial publications.[5]

The international standard serial number (ISSN) consists of eight digits, the last of which is a check number. The figures are printed in two sets of four separated by a dash, as 0019-4131. The ISSN uniquely identifies a serial publication so long as it bears the particular title to which the number has been assigned. Any change in title necessitates a change in ISSN. The numbers are assigned by national centres working as part of the International Serials Data System, which is described on p.52.

Both ISBNs and ISSNs are useful shorthand for human communication (preferably with verbal expansion). They form ready-made control numbers for the entry of computer records, as in the LASER catalogue, and they are economical of computer time and of printout space. They have, however, no mnemonic value – apart from the code figures for certain publishers in the ISBN which usage may make familiar – and if they are wrongly transcribed they are useless. Neither man nor machine can make a correction without reference to a fuller record. This is why some serials librarians prefer CODEN, the alphabetical code developed by the American Society for Testing and Materials (ASTM).[6,7] CODEN uniquely identifies a journal by using a seven-character code, the first four characters of which are letters taken from the journal's title. The fifth character is a hyphen, the sixth another letter helping to individualize the journal, and the seventh a check character. The brevity and meaningfulness of CODEN make it particularly advantageous in printed indexes and abstracts – it is used by e.g. *Chemical abstracts* – and in checking the arrival of periodicals in libraries. It can even be used in reader service, since readers have no difficulty in translating CODEN into titles of the periodicals they use. Expanded with numerals, CODEN can identify a particular issue of a journal, as in AMLO-AD 5(3)165-256(1973), which represents *Annals of mathematical logic*, published in Amsterdam, volume 5, number 3, pages 165 to 256, dated 1973. For titles in a non-roman script unaccompanied by a roman transcription, the CODEN symbol is not necessarily obvious. The ISSN may be read independently of the wording of the title.

Just as there is a need for a correspondence listing or conversion programme between *BNB* entry numbers and ISBNs (and sometimes also between different sets of pseudo-ISBNs), there is a similar need for making automatic conversion possible between CODEN and ISSNs, as is done in the index volume to *International serials catalogue* (Paris: ICSU/AB, 1978). CODEN has been widely used since 1966, but ISSNs were adopted by the ISDS in 1973 and endorsed by the ISO, ANSI and the BSI. Unfortunately at present CODEN and ISSN are rival standards. A small survey undertaken by the Common Practices and Standards Committee of the (US) National Federation of Abstracting and Indexing (later Information) Services revealed almost equal use of ISSN and CODEN, some member services using both.[8]

Standardizing agents and systems
I have already mentioned the interest shown by governments and inter-governmental organizations in gathering and making use of available information. This interest covers the exploration of what constitutes information and how it is disseminated and used, as well as new ways of manipulating and retrieving it. The (British) Department of Education's Office for Scientific and Technical Information (OSTI) gave

support to the computerizing activities of the *BNB*. OSTI was absorbed on 1 April 1974 into the British Library's Research and Development Department, whose scope extends to research on information in the humanities. A resolution of the EEC Council adopted on 27 September 1985 requested the Commission to take action to help libraries in Europe, particularly by increasing co-operation, and instancing inter-linking of computerized catalogues.

Unesco's interest is shown in the work of its Ad Hoc Committee on Education and Training Policy and Programmes (whose fifth session, held in 1982, was attended by members of FID and IFLA),[9] and in publicity for educational facilities in information work,[10] as well as in its sponsorship of international meetings, such as the Conference on Cataloging Principles of 1961, and the International Congress on National Bibliographies of 1977. FID also publishes news of current training programmes.[11].

UNISIST

UNISIST is the international programme set up to co-ordinate the dispersed effort being put into the production of national bibliographies, the running of specialized information centres, and the committee work on standardization. Scientists had been growing more and more concerned that published information was running to waste and research being impeded or duplicated. Those who might profit from the published work of others did not always know of its existence because its indexing tended to be uneven and scattered throughout a number of different media and terminologies. As the Royal Society had done earlier, the International Council of Scientific Unions (ICSU) took steps to examine the situation and, if possible, improve it. Jointly with Unesco it appointed a committee in 1967 to consider the feasibility of establishing a world scientific information system, and to make recommend-ations as to the structure and functions of such a system. The Unesco/ICSU Central Committee presented its report in 1970.[12] The Committee was unanimously of the opinion that 'a world science information system, considered as a flexible network evolving from an extension of voluntary co-operation of existing and future services, is feasible. Further, from the point of view of the scientific and technological communities, such a flexible network of information services is both desirable and necessary'.

The near-acronym UNISIST is intended to convey the idea of the involvement of the United Nations and also of a united and international approach to the problems of presenting, disseminating and using scientific and technical information. (The scope of UNISIST was soon widened to take in technology and the social and economic sciences. To attract government support it needed to be seen as working towards industrial, social and economic as well as scientific development.) An official sub-title 'preferably to be used always in connection with UNISIST' was later adopted to reflect its settled status: Inter-governmental Programme for Co-operation in the Field of Scientific and Technical Information. The new sub-title was given in the *Newsletter* which reports the work of UNISIST, and from 1979 incorporates Unesco's *Bibliography, documentation, terminology*.[13]

The role of UNISIST was thus seen as a catalyst which would stimulate and fuse work observed to be already in progress in numerous places and organizations. It was hoped to get governments working with UNISIST, and indeed an intergovernmental conference was held in 1971 to launch the UNISIST action programme.[14] Although a small permanent secretariat has been formed for UNISIST with a steering committee established by the general conference of Unesco at its 17th session in 1972, there is no financial reserve from which to hand out funds in support of projects. The necessity of having scientific information and the cost of obtaining it are expected to be sufficient incentives to compel co-operation in providing and communicating it, now that a body has been established to keep track of ongoing work, to co-ordinate such work, and to suggest and encourage undertakings which appear to be most practical and most advantageous at any one time.

It may be asked why it was considered necessary to create yet another body to do what so many international bodies were known to be doing already. The answer is that without sufficient resources and the active participation of governments such bodies tend to move very slowly, and their achievements remain disparate and unco-ordinated and make little impact, especially in countries whose own lack of resources and unpreparedness make them unable to benefit from the work done. Herbert Coblans explained the catalytic function of UNISIST in a discussion which formed part of the 45th Aslib conference in Darmstadt in 1971.[15]

International Serials Data System

Serial publications being among the most important sources of information used by scientists, it is not surprising that UNISIST's first practical concern should be to see whether improvements could be made in recording the existence of serials and making their existence known through biblio-graphic records available in an unequivocal form. A system of universal bibliographic control of serials appeared to be possible by means of a network of national centres linked to a central co-ordinating agency, and a plan for the implement-ation of such a system was recommended to Unesco. Unesco accepted this plan for an International Serials Data System (ISDS) and was able to negotiate with the French government the establishment of a centre, within the Bibliothèque Nationale, which should act as the world centre of information about serial publications – information which would flow from and between the national serials data centres which were to be set up. The International Centre for the Registration of Serials was set up in 1971.[16,17] It aims to hold on the ISDS machine-readable file a record of all serials published since 1971 and all changes of title. Microfiche and magnetic tape copies of the database are available. The ISDS manual lays down pro-cedures to be followed by the national centres. Although individual centres are at liberty to design and maintain their own processing systems, the guidelines lay down that all computer-readable records emanating from ISDS centres must be available in a common interchange format, using a common set of data elements, a common data-element tagging scheme, and a common character set.[18] The United States centre was already in being, having been set up to co-ordinate the United States National Serials Data Program.[19,20] Britain and Australia were also quick to establish national centres, control of the British centre being one of the functions of the British Library.

Centres of information about information

In order that information about current research might be disseminated and duplication of effort avoided, the UNISIST programme included setting up two clearing-houses – at Case Western Reserve University in Ohio and at the Instytut Informacji Naukowej, Technicznez i Ekonomicnej (IINTE) in Warsaw – for information on classification schedules, word lists and thesauri, and an International Information Centre for Terminology (INFOTERM) at the Austrian Standards Institute in Vienna (see p.154). IINTE subsequently assumed full responsibility for the clearing-house function, receiving help from Toronto University Library, which forwards information from North and South America and from Australia.

IFLA's concern with cataloguing

The international bodies most active in the promotion of co-operation in cataloguing have been – besides Unesco – IFLA and FID. Certain national bodies, while promoting their own development, have also assumed obligations towards a wider service.

The revitalization in 1951 of IFLA's Committee on Cataloguing as the Working Group on the Co-ordination of Cataloguing Principles – its name was changed in 1970 to Committee (and later to Section) on Cataloguing – under the chairmanship of Hugh Chaplin, marks the beginning of a steady progress in international co-operation under the aegis of IFLA – a body which now has a record of more than 50 years' international librarianship.[21]

The first task assigned to the committee was to examine the degree of divergence between the two main theories of the descriptive cataloguing of anonyma and works of corporate authorship – the two areas where least agreement in practice was evident. The committee's findings that the differences in practice were diminishing and that there was a growing desire to reach uniformity in cataloguing practice, together with the belief of the Council on Library Resources that such uniformity should be encouraged by the provision of generous funds, led to the organization of the International Conference on Cataloguing Principles in Paris in 1961.

The Paris conference had a great influence on subsequent cataloguing codes and practice. Reference to its provisions will be made where relevant in later chapters. Here I note only the continued availability of its *Report* and *Statement of principles.*[22, 23]

The final session of the Paris conference passed a number of resolutions designed to promote the standardization of the form of headings in particular areas of publication. Work proceeding in accordance with those resolutions has resulted in the publication of a series of guides and authority lists, some of which have appeared in revised editions.[24-29]

Standards for bibliographic description (ISBD)

Not many years after the International Conference on Cataloguing Principles, further discussion at the international level appeared to be necessary in the light of several developments which had taken place. Comments and queries on the Paris Principles had been received. The Library of Congress had experimented with a 'shared cataloguing' programme. Mechanization was being applied to cataloguing procedures. The idea was becoming increasingly acceptable that national bibliographies needed to be regarded as having a second function, that of voluntary contributions to a world bibliography, and as such needing to be in as great conformity with each other as possible. Accordingly, having set in motion the specific projects proposed by the Paris conference, IFLA's Committee on Cataloguing turned its attention to implementing Resolution VII, which asked that 'consideration be given to the possibility of supplementing the Statement of Principles by the addition of a certain number of further points on which international agreement may be possible'. By that time a clear need had been recognized for international agreement on what information, apart from the heading, should be given in a catalogue entry, in what manner it should be presented, and how the separate parts should be designated.

A study of the content and arrangement of the information held in entries in a group of representative national bibliographies was made for Unesco and IFLA by Michael Gorman in 1968. It formed a working paper at the International Meeting of Cataloguing Experts (IMCE) held in the following year at Copenhagen.[30,31] The meeting was organized by IFLA, again with financial support from the Council on Library Resources. This time the participants were limited in number and were in effect a working party. Three sessions were devoted to discussions of an international standard for the descriptive content of catalogue entries. It was agreed that the description should be designed to be of use in both catalogues and national bibliographies and also that it should give all the information required in library records and elsewhere in the control and handling of books, including a note of the binding and the International Standard Book Number. All the elements were to be presented in a standardized form except the exact transcription of the title. A small working party was set up to draft the standard, and in a very short time, within two years, the draft was available for comment. In the light of comments made the text was slightly amended and issued in a definitive edition as *ISBD(M): international standard bibliographic description for monographic publications* (1st standard ed. London: IFLA Committee on Cataloguing, 1974). It was reissued in a slightly revised form in 1978,[32] and as a revised edition in 1987.

A preliminary note to the 1978 edition defines its purpose as primarily

> to aid the international communication of bibliographic inform-
> ation. It does this by (i) making records from different sources
> interchangeable, so that records produced in one country can be
> easily accepted in library catalogues or other bibliographic lists in
> any other country; (ii) assisting in the interpretation of records
> across language barriers, so that records produced for users of one
> language can be interpreted by users of other languages; and (iii)
> assisting in the conversion of bibliographic records to machine-
> readable form.

The elaborate punctuation used in the ISBDs, as exemplified in reference 32, which is an exact transcription of the 'recommended catalogue entry' (prepared as British Library cataloguing-in-publication data) shown on the verso of the title leaf of *ISBD(M)*, is really a code which identifies parts of the entry as an aid to interpreting entries in a language which is unfamiliar. For example, the sequence 'space, oblique stroke, space' separates the title statement from the author statement and also the edition statement from the statement of editorship of that edition; in the imprint the sequence 'space, colon, space' separates the place of imprint from the name of the publisher; in the collation, the sequence 'space, semi-colon, space' separates the pagination from the size; each separate element of the entry is divided from the element which follows it by the sequence 'point, space, dash, space', or by indention. The code also performs some of the identifying functions necessary within an automated record.

Other IFLA working groups have prepared similar standards for the description of serial publications, audio-visual (non-book) materials, cartographic materials, printed music, older printed books, component parts and computer files.[33-39] In order to arrest the development of the inconsistencies between the standards (already conspicuous in the two first published), a general guide was necessary to lay down the principles to be observed in making special provisions for particular materials. Such a general standard, *ISBD(G)*, was published in 1977, with annotations to assist in making connections between it and the specialized guides.[40] Revision of the underlying theory of the general principles necessitated the revision of *ISBD(M)*, and also of *ISBD(S)*, both of which had first appeared in 1974. A record of the work done on ISBDs and an evaluation of their application has been written by Eva Verona,[41] and a full bibliography up to 1980 has been published.[42]

The provisions of *ISBD(M)* did not differ greatly from those of the Anglo-American cataloguing code. The second edition of *Anglo-American cataloguing rules (AACR2)* is fully compatible with those ISBDs which had been promulgated before its own completion, including, of course *ISBD(G)*.

UNIMARC

At the IMCE Henriette Avram had made the point that economy of machine time was a prime factor in requiring a fixed order of elements. Machine recognition of elements in the bibliographical description, made possible by a standard sequence, standard symbols and standard punctuation in the printed or typewritten records, would save the cost of the skilled work of editors, who needed to be cataloguers with training in computer work. Bochum University Library supported this argument by reporting on its own experience in using tapes from the *Deutsche bibliographie* and the *BNB*.[43] In a later paper Avram again stressed the difficulties that arise in automating library records when standardization is lacking.[44]

Although most countries base their MARC structure on the international standard format (ISO 2709),[45] which is itself a generalized derivative of the MARC II record structure (developed in the Library of Congress from the original MARC record), there remains a lack of uniformity between records, necessitating adjustments when the records are used by agencies other than the one which produced them. Particular problems reside in the differences of function between a national bibliography produced independently of a national library and one produced as a continuation of such a library's catalogue. Inconsistencies between national cataloguing codes, the lack of a single subject-control system (such as might be provided by a universally applied classification scheme), and the variety of national languages used to designate subjects and to annotate entries also present difficulties. The variety of national scripts causes further complications; an 'exotic' appearance hinders reading, transcription tables vary from country to country, and not all required forms are included among the symbols of the ISO and equivalent BS character set, although extensions to that are being published.[46-50]

In order to minimize differences in those parts of the MARC entry which are not subject to local necessity, as are vernacular and subject requirements, *UNIMARC: a universal MARC format* has been agreed, and published by IFLA, to standardize such components of the entry as content designators, and thus render one-to-one conversion codes between individual biblio-graphic agencies unnecessary.[51] It follows the format structure of ISO 2709. In theory, each national MARC format will be converted into UNIMARC format for sending out inform-ation. Each receiving agency will convert the UNIMARC format to its national MARC format for use in its own database. In fact, UNIMARC was received with little enthusiasm. National formats in Taiwan, Hungary, Japan and South Africa were based upon it; in 1978 ABACUS members agreed in principle to adopt it, but in 1983 they were still making conversions directly from MARC tapes received to their own versions of MARC. LC was, however, preparing a conversion program between US MARC and UNIMARC, which has since been completed. LC now offers its tapes in either US MARC or UNIMARC format. In 1986 other countries also converted part of their files to UNIMARC, and a new edition of the UNIMARC handbook appeared, providing rules for recording nonbook materials and taking account of revised ISBDs.[52]

Not only the circulation of those standards but also the face-to-face exchange between influential cataloguing administrators of ideas, explanations of national traditions and of current trends in authorship, modes of publication, and legal requirements have made co-operation easier and more acceptable.

During most of the 35-year period of IFLA's cataloguing activities reviewed above, it has been possible to keep in touch with what has been going on by means, first, of the irregularly issued *IFLA International Conference on Cataloguing bulletin* (later *Newsletter*) from November 1958 to March 1967, then of the Committee's *Newsletter* and from the beginning of 1972 by means of the regular quarterly publication *International cataloguing*.[53] The publication has enlarged its scope to include articles of interest to cataloguers whose acquisitions extend beyond those in a few western languages. Volume 3, 1974, for example, contains an article on Ethiopian names and another on the Chinese catalogue set up in one of its branches by the Toronto Public Library. The same issue contains a 'Chronology and bibliography' relating to the activities of the IFLA Committee on Cataloguing, and also 'A retrospective view' by Hugh Chaplin, who was the committee's first executive secretary and later its chairman.

Universal bibliographic control

In July 1974 the Committee's extended role was reflected in another change of name, to the IFLA International Office for UBC, after IFLA's call for universal bibliographic control

(UBC) had been voiced at its conference in Grenoble in 1973. The object of UBC had been stated thus by F.G. Kaltwasser: 'The information on a book should be produced as completely and correctly as possible at the earliest possible date. In the interest of speed, accuracy, and simplicity this should be done in the country of origin by the national bibliographies. The data should be made available in machine-readable form'.[54]

With that end in view IFLA initiated the seminal International Congress on National Bibliographies in 1977, as a result of which many new national bibliographies were begun and others revitalized. Progress made and experience gained during the ten years which followed that congress were reported to the National Bibliographies Seminar at IFLA's annual conference in 1987. (The collection of reports is due for independent publication by IFLA UBCIM Programme in 1988.)

UBC is, at the same time, a broader and a less overwhelming concept than Jewett's idea of a universal catalogue. On the one hand, the literate universe has greatly expanded since Jewett's day, and on the other, the means of recording and communicating the records of its literature have taken on an aspect then undreamed of. The user of the records has also changed. He is no longer the 'humble, patient and appreciative browser in the vast stores of information' presented by a large library catalogue.[55] He is the impatient researcher, manager, governmental or inter-governmental official, working in a pressing, competitive and international environment. The sense of urgency is reflected in a detailed working paper prepared by Dorothy Anderson, then Director of the UBC office, and presented on behalf of IFLA to Unesco's Intergovernmental Conference on the Planning of National Overall Documentation, Library and Archives Infrastructures, 1974.[56]

An annotated bibliography compiled by the International Office for UBC, *Standard practices in the preparation of bibliographic records* (1982), lists current standards and interpretive works.

In January 1987 the UBC Programme was merged with IFLA's International MARC Programme, under the name IFLA Universal Bibliographic Control and International MARC Programme (UBCIMP).

Standardizing work still to be done

Libraries and national bibliographies are not, as has already been noted, the only agencies which disseminate bibliographic information internationally. The specialized indexing and abstracting services and the information systems of the large intergovernmental organizations concentrated more on developing their own systems than on co-operating with other agencies, and as a result there is even less compatibility between their records, and between their records and those of libraries. (A comparison of the record structures of magnetic tapes produced by eight secondary services, including BNB, INIS and INSPEC, found that only four of them conformed closely to ISO 2709. BNB, using a MARC format, was, as was to be expected, one of the four.)[57] Concern among the scientific community over the hindrances thus caused to easy access to disseminated information resulted in the setting up jointly by UNISIST and the International Council of Scientific Unions' Abstracting Board (ICSU-AB) of a Working Group on Bibliographic Descriptions, which attempted to define a set of data elements that would constitute an adequate bibliographic citation for exchange without limiting the freedom of any organization to make additions to suit its own purposes, and to present a record format as defined by ISO 2709 in a way most suitable for indexing and abstracting services. The Working Group published a manual in 1974 for 'technical management and systems design staff in information centres, abstracting and indexing services, and libraries, to assist them in designing local systems in such a way that they can exchange files in either direction with other centres which have adopted the *Reference manual* format'.[58] Incompatibilities persisted, however.[59] (The UNISIST guide to standards for information handling lists more than 1,000 separate items.)[60]

Evidence of widespread concern among supplying agencies other than libraries was shown at two joint meetings of members of the Association of Information and Dissemination Centres (ASIDIC), the European Association of Scientific Information Dissemination Centres (EUSIDIC), the International Council of Scientific Unions-Abstracting Board (ICSU-AB), and the US National Federation of Abstracting and Indexing (now Information) Services (NFAIS). The first meeting took place in Washington in 1975, the second in England in 1978.[61]

The seemingly parallel streams bearing bibliographic information having its source in libraries and national bibliographies on the one hand and in the indexing and abstracting services on the other converged at a temporary infinity, as it were, in Taormina in 1978. Sponsored by Unesco and organized by UNISIST International Centre for Bibliographic Descriptions (UNIBID), in co-operation with ICSU-AB, IFLA and ISO, a symposium there brought together representatives from all sections of the 'information community' to discuss the nature and role of machine-readable bibliographic exchange formats. They expressed the hope of achieving greater agreement on the set of elements required uniquely to identify a document – the 'cataloguing' content – with allowances for the expansion of any section to suit the needs of a particular agency; the sequence and grouping of the elements; and the symbols used for identifying fields, subfields and recurrent specifications; together with commitment to the use of the relevant ISO requirements on carrier format, physical tape standards and character sets.[62]

At that meeting yet another committee was formed, a subcommittee of ISO's Technical Committee concerned with documentation, ISO/TC 46 Sub-committee 6: Bibliographic Data Elements in Manual and Machine Applications, and a number of recommendations were made, stressing the need for a broad basis for working committees, for urgency in their collaboration to produce a common exchange format which would include all desired elements and would be operationally tested before being officially promulgated, for definitions and procedural manuals to be prepared. Is it possible that the two bibliographic streams, like Alpheus and Arethusa, have met and for ever comingled in the happy soil of Sicily? Apparently not, but Hopkinson reports that the symposium 'went a long way towards halting the increasing polarization between the abstracting and indexing and national library communities'. He has described the international situation as at the end of 1983.[63]

To achieve agreed definitions and standard terminology is the object of several ISO committees. Since no science can develop without a corresponding development in its terminology, it is no surprise to find active committees of practicians concerned with the terminology of librarianship and documentation: IFLA's Committee on Terminology, FID's Technical Committee 46, in addition to the ISO committees. What is surprising is the continued division of labour and of outlook which has kept the vocabulary of 'librarianship' – the province of IFLA – apart from the vocabulary of 'documentation' – the province of FID. UNISIST has stepped forward as marriage-broker, with its INFOTERM bureau (see p.154). (Terminology is dealt with in greater detail in Chapters 9 and 10.)

All the work of international bodies such as IFLA and FID depends very largely on the intellectual contribution of individual librarians and libraries. Outside such bodies systems developed by national institutions have had a much wider application than at first envisaged. The Library of Congress's development of MARC has been extended or adapted for use in many other countries.[64] The successful venture of Cataloguing-in-Publication (CIP), instigated by the same library, is being copied elsewhere. LC transliteration tables are widely used in other English-speaking countries. The standard book number has become the international standard book number. Many specialized organizations (including commercial systems) distribute their printed and machine-readable indexes and abstracts throughout the world and support them by other bibliographic services. Large databases acquire their capital from smaller bases originating in different interests and different countries.

The overall pattern of bibliographic recording which is becoming evident is that of division of responsibility (for national bibliographies, special forms of publication, special subjects); the support by governments of bibliographic research as well as of everyday bibliographic activity; the enormous amplification of the powers of the human hand and eye brought about by automatic data processing; the potentiality for co-ordinating all the separate undertakings through bodies such as Unesco/UNISIST and the inspiration of enlightened self-interest.

References

1 *UNISIST guide to standards for information handling*; prepared by the UNISIST Working Group on Bibliographic Data Exchange; compiled by Erik Vajda. Paris: Unesco, 1980.
2 *International standard book numbering (ISBN)*. ISO 2108-1972.
3 Whitaker, D., 'International standard book numbering', *in Penrose annual*, vol. 63, 1970, 209 – 12.
4 F. H. Ayres (and others), *USBC (Universal Standard Book Code): its use for union file creation: a feasibility study for a national database.* London: British Library BSD, 1984.
5 *International standard serial numbering (ISSN)*. ISO 3297-1975.
6 American Society for Testing and Materials [and] American National Standards Institute, *Standard recommended practice for use of CODEN.* Philadelphia: ASTM, 1976.
7 Wall, R. A. and Wilson, C. W. J., 'Codification of periodical titles: a note on ASTM CODEN versus standard serial numbers', *Library Association record,* 75(5), May 1970, 188 – 90. (8 references)
8 'NFAIS standards survey', *NFAIS newsletter,* 24(2), April 1982, 1.
9 *UNISIST newsletter,* 10(4), 1982, 51 – 2.
10 *World guide to library schools and training courses in documentation.* Paris: Unesco, 1981; supplemented by Grolier, Eric de, *Register of education and training activities in librarianship, information science and archives.* Paris: Unesco, 1982. (Notes specialized activities and grants for study, particularly for the benefit of nationals of developing countries.)
11 *Newsletter on education and training programmes for information personnel.* The Hague: FID, 1977 – (experimental nos. 1, 2, 3; vol. 1, no. 1 – , 1979 – . Quarterly).
12 Unesco/ICSU Central Committee on the Feasibility of a World Science Information System, *UNISIST: study report on the feasibility of a world science information system.* Paris: Unesco, 1970. (Synopsis 1971.)
13 *UNISIST newsletter,* vol. 1, no. 1 – . Paris: Unesco, 1973 – . (The quotation is from 4(4), 1976, p.8.)
14 Intergovernmental Conference for the Establishment of a World Science Information System, 1971, Paris, *UNISIST: final report.* Paris: Unesco, 1971.
15 'UNISIST: a forum', *Aslib proceedings,* 24(2), 1972, 111 – 22.
16 Koster, C. J., 'ISDS and the functions and activities of national

centres', *Unesco bulletin for libraries*, 27(4), 1973, 199 – 204. (4
references)

17 'Ten years of the International Serials Data System (ISDS)',
    International cataloguing, 11(1), 1982, 10 – 11.
18 International Serials Data System. *ISDS manual*; prepared by the
    ISDS International Centre; ed. by A. A. Mullis. Paris: The
    Centre, 1983. (Replaces the Centre's *Guidelines*, 1973.)
19 Vassallo, Paul, 'Introducing the National Serials Data
    Program', *in* IFLA Council Proceedings, 1973.
20 *Library of Congress information bulletin*, 33(11), 15 March, 1974,
    A-75.
21 Koops, Willem R. H. and Wieder, Joachim (eds.), *IFLA's first
    fifty years; achievement and challenge in international librarianship.*
    München: Verlag Dokumentation; London: Saur; Bingley,
    1977.
22 International Conference on Cataloguing Principles, 1961,
    Paris, *Report*. London: IFLA, 1963; reprinted Bingley, 1969.
    (Reissued, with new introduction briefly outlining the advances
    of the last 20 years, by IFLA International Office for UBC,
    1981.)
23 International Conference on Cataloguing Principles. *Statement of
    principles . . .* ; annotated edition, with commentary and examples
    by Eva Verona [and others]. London: IFLA Committee on
    Cataloguing, 1971.
24 *Names of persons: national usages for entry in catalogues.* 3rd ed.,
    compiled by the IFLA International Office for UBC. London:
    IFLA UBC Office, 1977. Supplement, 1980.
25 *Names of states: an authority list of language forms for catalogue entries.*
    London: IFLA International Office for UBC, 1981.
26 *List of uniform headings for higher legislative and ministerial bodies in
    European countries*; compiled by the USSR Cataloguing
    Committee. 2nd ed. rev. London: IFLA Committee on
    Cataloguing, 1979.
27 *African legislative and ministerial bodies: list of uniform headings for
    higher legislative and ministerial bodies in African countries.* London:
    IFLA International Office for UBC, 1981.
28 *Anonymous classics: a list of uniform headings for European literatures.*
    2nd ed., by R. C. Hewitt. London: IFLA International Office
    for UBC, 1978.
29 *List of uniform titles for liturgical works of the Latin rites of the Catholic
    Church.* 2nd ed. rev. London: IFLA International Office for
    UBC, 1981.
30 'Report of the International Meeting of Cataloguing Experts,

Copenhagen, 1969', *Libri*, 20, 1970, 105 – 32.

31 Spalding, C. Sumner, 'ISBD: its origins, rationale and implications', *Library journal*, 15 January 1973, 121 – 3.

32 In its 'recommended catalogue entry', this is:
ISBD(M): International Standard Bibliographic Description for Monographic Publications / International Federation of Library Associations and Institutions. – 1st standard ed. revised / [prepared by an editorial group, Chairman Eva Verona]. – London : IFLA International Office for UBC, 1978. – viii, 51p. ; 30 cm
Previously published: 1st standard ed., London : IFLA Committee on Cataloguing, 1974.
ISBN 0-903043-21-1 (paperback)

33 *ISBD(S): international standard bibliographic description for serials.* London: IFLA International Office for UBC, 1974. Rev. ed. 1987.

34 *ISBD(NBM): international standard bibliographic description for non-book materials.* London: IFLA International Office for UBC, 1977. Rev. ed. 1987.

35 *ISBD(CM): international standard bibliographic description for cartographic materials.* London: IFLA International Office for UBC, 1977. Rev. ed. 1987.

36 *ISBD(PM): international standard bibliographic description for printed music.* London: IFLA International Office for UBC, 1980.

37 *ISBD(A): international standard bibliographic description for older monographic publications (Antiquarian).* London: IFLA International Office for UBC, 1980.

38 *ISBD(CP): international standard bibliographic description for component parts.* Draft 5. London: International Office for UBC, 1981.

39 *ISBD(CF): international standard bibliographic description for computer files* (in preparation, 1987).

40 *ISBD(G): general international standard bibliographic description: annotated text.* London: IFLA International Office for UBC, 1977.

41 Verona, Eva, 'A decade of IFLA's work on the standardization of bibliographic description', *International cataloguing*, 9(1), January/March 1980, 2 – 9. (57 references)

42 *An annotated bibliography of the International Standard Bibliographic Description.* 2nd ed. rev. London: IFLA International Office for UBC, 1980. (Occasional papers no.6)

43 See reference 30 above.

44 Avram, Henriette, 'International standards for the interchange

of bibliographic records in machine-readable form', *Library resources and technical services*, 20(1), 1976, 25 – 35.

45 *Format for bibliographic information interchange on magnetic tape.* ISO 2709: 1973 (rev. 1981). (Identical with BS 4748. London: BSI, 1982.)

46 *Specification for the UK 7 bit data code.* BS 4730 = ISO 646. London: BSI, 1985. (123 control and graphic characters, i.e. letters, digits and symbols, with their 7-bit data coded representation.)

47 *Specification for extension of the Latin alphabet coded character set.* BS 6474:Pt1 = ISO 5426. 2nd ed. 1983.

48 *Specification for Greek alphabet coded character set.* BS 6474:Pt2 = ISO 5428. London: BSI, 1985.

49 *Specification for African coded character set.* BS 6474:Pt3 = ISO 6438. (60 characters for African languages.) London: BSI, 1984.

50 *Specification for extension of the Cyrillic alphabet coded character set.* BS 6472:Pt4 = ISO 5427. London: BSI, 1986.

51 IFLA Working Group on Content Designators, *UNIMARC: the universal MARC format.* 2nd ed. London: IFLA UBC Office, 1980.

52 *UNIMARC manual*; ed. by B. Holt, with the assistance of S. McCallum and A. Long. London: IFLA International Office for UBC, 1986. (First published in 1983 as *UNIMARC handbook*, ed. by A. Hopkinson and others.)

53 *International cataloguing: quarterly bulletin of the IFLA International Office for UBC*, Vol. 1, no. 1 – , January/March 1972 – . London: IFLA Committee on Cataloguing.

54 Kaltwasser, F. G., 'Universal bibliographic control (UBC)', *Unesco bulletin for libraries*, 25(5), September/October, 1971, 252 – 9.

55 Francis, Sir Frank, 'A reconsideration of the British Museum rules for compiling the catalogues of printed books', *in* Piggott, Mary (ed.), *Cataloguing principles and practice: an inquiry. . .* London: LA, 1954, 28.

56 Anderson, Dorothy, *Universal bibliographic control – a long-term policy, a plan for action.* Pullach bei München: Verlag Dokumentation, 1974. (88 references)

57 Wainwright, Jane, *Standards used by bibliographic tape services: a comparison.* London: Aslib, 1974. (OSTI report no. 5191. Includes 14 references and list of manuals used by each service.)

58 *Reference manual for machine-readable bibliographic descriptions*; prepared by the UNISIST/ICSU-AB Working Group on Bibliographic Descriptions, with the assistance of ICSU and ICSU-

AB member services; compiled by M. D. Martin. Paris: Unesco, 1974. (2nd rev. ed. by Harold Dierickx and Alan Hopkinson, 1981.)

59 Mackenzie-Owen, John, *Format incompatibility and the exchange of bibliographic information: a comparative study.* Paris: Unesco, 1976.
60 See reference 1 above.
61 Reported in *Bibliography, documentation, terminology*, 18(4), 1978, 208.
62 International Symposium on Bibliographic Exchange Formats, 1978, Taormina. *Towards a common international bibliographic exchange format?...*, ed. by H. Dierickx and A. Hopkinson. Budapest: OMKDK – Techno-inform; London: UNIBID, 1978. (Reported by H. Dierickx, *International cataloguing*, 7(2), 1978, 19 – 24. 15 references.)
63 Hopkinson, Alan, 'International access to bibliographic data: MARC and MARC-related activities', *Journal of documentation*, 40(1), March 1984, 13 – 24. (46 references) See also reference 64 below.
64 IFLA International MARC Programme. International MARC Project, *International guide to MARC databases and services: national magnetic tape and online services.* 2nd ed. Frankfurt-am-Main: Deutsche Bibliothek, 1984.

5
Descriptive cataloguing

The object of descriptive cataloguing

The primary object of descriptive cataloguing is to identify an item in a collection. Many of the criteria of descriptive cataloguing can be applied to several different media of publication; some are peculiar to a single medium and relate to the way its intellectual content is presented and how it is produced, or to its physical characteristics, especially those that may impose limitations on its use. The value of the description may be enhanced by giving additional information about the content or presentation of the work contained in the publication and its relationship to other presentations of the same work or to other works within the same bibliographic collection.

In the early days of libraries the name of the author and a summary designation of the matter were sufficient to identify a book within a necessarily limited collection and for a readership for whom the physical characteristics of the volume were more important than textual variations. To record simply *Musica Boecij* or *Boecius de consolatione*, together with the location of the treatise, was sufficient. The catalogue record changed with changing methods in the production, dissemination, collection and use of books. It was later adapted to describe the other media of communication that have been invented. It was also affected by the medium in which it was itself presented.

This chapter will take the printed book as a medium of prime importance to libraries which shares many characteristics with other media while remaining unique in possessing certain other features. It is the subject of the first chapter in *AACR2* devoted to a specific medium, that is, Chapter 2. Other media (apart from manuscripts), being not only much later additions to library collections but also less standardized in their own development, have not given rise to the same consensus as to their treatment. This is evident in the amount of revision accorded to the rules for non-book media in the consolidated second edition of *AACR2* and in the appearance to date (1987) of five drafts (but no definitive edition) of *ISBD(CP)* – which includes non-book materials – and also in the projected publication of a separate standard – *ISBD(CF)* – for cataloguing computer files.

Source of the description

The catalogue record, or entry, is based on the information which is printed on the book's title page, because it is the custom in printed books to bring together on the title page enough significant information to identify, or at least to characterize, the publication. The title of the book and the author's name indicate the particular work, that is, they provide a generalized appellation for a literary work which may appear in forms other than the original. An edition statement may indicate a particular version of the work. Further information about a version may be given by naming an editor, translator or illustrator who has in some way contributed to the version without, in most cases, taking away the primary responsibility for it from the original author. (An author is defined as the person primarily responsible for the intellectual content of a work.) The imprint shows where, by whom and when the version in hand was issued, information which not only helps to identify the book, but may also imply a local viewpoint and the status – learned or popular – and date of the text.

Manuscripts rarely had separate title pages. In printed books they became usual around 1480. A 1476 edition of Johann Mueller's *Kalendarium* is thought to be the first example of an ornamental title page. A border of acanthus leaves surrounds 12 lines of type which present the book, naming it and indicating its contents, saying that it shows the golden number (from which the date of Easter could be calculated), eclipses of the sun and moon and so on, and then follow the name of the author, Johann of Königsberg (Latinized as Ioannes Regiomontanus), the place and date of printing, and finally, in red, the names of the printers, Bernard Maler of Augsburg, Peter Löslein of Langenzenn and Erhard Ratdolt of Augsburg. The lines run

> Aureus hic liber est: non est preciosior ulla
> Gema Kalendario: quod docet istud opus.
> Aureus hic numerus; lune: solisqz labores
> Montrantur facile: [etc.]
> Hoc Ioannes opus regio de monte probatum
> Composuit: tota notus in italia
> Quod veneta impressum fuit in tellure per illos
> Inferius quorum nomina picta loco
> 1476
> Bernardus pictor de Augusta
> Petrus loslein de Lanencen
> Erhardus ratdolt de Augusta

Most other early printers used the title page simply to name the book. They appended their own names and the names of book-sellers after the text – hence the term colophon, meaning literally *summit* and by analogy the final touch to a piece of work – but gradually the information from the colophon was added to the title page. (The colophon of modern foreign-language publications should not be overlooked by the cata-loguer. It frequently supplements information given on the title page. In Russian books, for example, it gives the full names of authors and editors, and details of the edition.) Subsequently the wording on the title page was expanded to act as an advertisement for the book, as the title page of the *Kalendarium* had been, the title page sometimes being printed and circulated separately.

As an advertisement the title page introduced laudatory adjectives and phrases about the book and its creator, adding biographical information likely to commend him as an authority on his subject. The publisher's, or the printer's taste in display governed the layout of the title page. Our contem-porary taste for simplicity, and also for experiment, and the employment of book designers, have tended to restrict the wording on the title page itself, and to utilize other preliminary pages for the display of what is conventionally title-page information, sometimes using two facing pages to spread the title, sub-title, author's and publisher's names, and so on. The modern book jacket provides space for further information about the author and the book's contents.

A Joint Committee of the Publishers' Association and the Booksellers' Association of Great Britain and Ireland in 1929 'recommended and urged' (among other things) that a bibliographical note should be printed in a book indicating the status of a new issue of a work – whether it was a reissue or a new edition – and at what date it had last been revised. The Committee recommended that such a note should be 'printed on the back of the title page so that it might not be separated therefrom in rebinding'.[1] A brief statement of a work's publishing history, or part of it, may therefore be found set out on the reverse of the title leaf. That is also often the position of the date of first publication of a new work, and very often also of the copyright statement. By the provisions of the Universal Copyright Convention (UCC) international protection is given to new material published in individual countries after they have acceded to the UCC, provided that all copies of a work, from the time of its first publication, bear the symbol © together with the name of the copyright holder and the date of first publication. In Great Britain the right to this protection dates from 1957, when the 1956 Copyright Act came into force. Because reissues of a work first published before 1957 are not covered by the UCC, the © notice may apply to only part of a book, for example, a newly-published introduction. The provisions of the UCC and of UK and USA copyright law are briefly introduced and summarized in a pamphlet by Christopher Scarles.[2]

If a book is published in a series, the name of the series generally occurs on one of the preliminary pages. It may occur on the half-title, that is, the recto of a leaf which precedes the title page and gives a brief title of the book; alternatively the series name may be displayed on a separate page which constitutes in fact an advertisement for the whole series.

The parts of a book and their technical names are listed in Carter's *ABC for book collectors*[3] and in Glaister's more comprehensive work.[4]

Clearly, therefore, in modern books other preliminary leaves which set out traditionally 'title-page information' must be regarded as sources of data of equal validity with the title page itself. This has been recognized by the ISBDs and, following them, by the current edition of *Anglo-American cataloguing rules (AACR2)*, in all of which the sources from which it is permitted to take information for each area of the catalogue entry are listed in preferred order. (That the title page has been used to convey deliberately misleading statements is not unknown. Jacob Blanck quotes – among other bibliographic improprieties – the addition of the words 'second edition' and later 'third edition' during a certain book's *first* printing, in order to suggest that the demand for it was exceeding all expectations!)[5]

Other matter may precede the text of the work, such as a preface or an introduction or a table of contents, though the last is likely to follow the text in books printed on the Continent. The cataloguer should look at all of these. They may supplement information given on the title page (and any extension of the title page) or they may be important enough to be mentioned in the catalogue entry. For example, a preface may state that the text has been revised, or that it has been translated from a particular edition of the original, or it may itself be dated where the title page is not and so give a pointer to the book's probable date; an introduction may be an authoritative biographical or critical essay in its own right and may even merit its own catalogue record. Such preliminary matter is also a quick guide to the subject content of the book and its intellectual level.

Choice and sequence of elements of description

In preparing a catalogue entry, the cataloguer selects significant information from what is laid out before him in the book and presents his selection in a formalized manner. In a limited space and with limited typographical means he must convey the essentials of what the printer has *displayed*, using perhaps two or three pages and types of different founts and sizes.

Standard cataloguing practice consists of presenting formally a minimum number of separate statements which serve to identify and describe a publication and to make comparison possible with another description or another publication. A reader should thus be able to decide whether the book described in a catalogue entry would answer his needs because the catalogue description corresponded in essentials to a reference he had obtained elsewhere or because it indicated a book of suitable scope and presentation hitherto unknown to him. The accessions librarian should also be able to decide whether the book catalogued was the same as, or significantly different from, a book of which he had another catalogue description or a copy in hand.

The essential parts of a full catalogue entry for a modern book are:

1   the transcript of the *title*;

2   the statement of *primary responsibility* for the intellectual content of the work, which may need to be expanded to include the name of a secondary author, such as a translator or an illustrator;

3   the *edition* statement (which may include the name of an editor), which indicates the state of the text, as being, for example, as the author first presented it to the public, as it appeared after his own revision or updating, or after someone else's revision, as it appeared in a new setting-up of type, and so on;

4   the *imprint*, which names briefly the town from which the book is published, the publisher and the year of publication – information which may indicate point of view, level of scholarship, and timeliness or otherwise of subject matter;

5   the *collation*, which describes the book as a physical object, giving the number of its pages, the number and possibly kind of its illustrations and its height – partly as a help in recognizing it, partly as a help in assessing the suitability of its presentation, and also, if required, as a guide to the cost of rebinding it – and notes any accompanying material, such as an atlas or sound disc;

6   *the series statement* – if the book is issued as one of a series – which also helps to identify and characterize it;

7   any necessary *annotation*, which might take the form of a transcription of the book's contents list (a *contents note*, particularly when the book is a collection of writings by different people or on different subjects), or of an extension or qualification in the cataloguer's own words of information already given, particularly to explain the scope of a work or the readership for whom it is designed;

8 *the international standard book number* (ISBN) which is itself an identification code.

The parts of the entry and their sequence shown above are those required by the current Anglo-American code of descriptive cataloguing rules, *AACR2*, as set out in its first rule (1.0B). They are paralleled by the list of elements required in a catalogue entry by *ISBD(M)*, established there because they had been found to be common components – though not necessarily following the same sequence – in national bibliographies examined as a preliminary to drawing up the ISBDs. They are evident in any bibliography that aims to be more than a finding list.

In addition to the description of each individual book, the catalogue entry must carry a *heading* which determines its place in the catalogue and also signals a point of entry into the catalogue for the user. It is the known element from which a search in the catalogue can be begun. Any heading adopted must stand in a relationship with other headings such that the framework of the catalogue forms a coherent and logical whole that is apparent to the user.

Necessarily, since evidence of a book's existence within a library would be useless without any direction to lead the reader from the book's description to the volume itself, the book's location in the library must also be indicated, by means of its *press mark, shelf mark* or *call mark* or *number* – and within sight of the catalogue must be displayed a guide showing how to reach that location.

Author and title catalogues

Descriptive cataloguing, as opposed to subject cataloguing, uses as headings the proper names by which a book can be approached: its own name, that is, its title; the name of its author(s), and of any other person or body of persons closely connected with its genesis; and the name of the group, that is, the series, to which it belongs. For complete identification, the heading needs the amplification provided by the rest of the entry – if a title, whose? if an author, of which work? if a series, which member of the series?

Although an additional title entry has not always been made for works entered under the name of a known author, a number of investigations (summarized by Hamdy[6]) have shown that title entries fulfil a real need. Ayres finds that readers cite titles more accurately than authors' names.[7] An extreme view has been expressed by Domanovszky, who played a prominent part in the Paris Conference and in the discussions which followed it. He considers that intellectual responsibility (by which authorship is determined) is of little relevance to cataloguing, which should be concerned with statements on the book itself and not with the reasoning behind them. He says, 'So far as logic is concerned, it is the title to which priority must be assigned. A weighty reason for this is that virtually all books and works are provided with titles, while a great deal of them lack an author'.[8]

Indeed, responsibility for the intellectual content of a publication is often hard, or even impossible, to determine, but because of the uniqueness of people a personal name which is connected with a particular work tends to be the name most permanently associated with it.

Tracings

An indication that added entries are to be made under the title and any other name under which the book is likely to be sought is given in the final element of the entry, the 'tracings'. Tracings are a record of what other entries have been made for a publication beside the main entry. They take the form either of the exact wording which is to be superimposed as a heading on the uniform description, or of indications of specific parts of the entry, such as *Title* or *Series* where these are to be copied with no change from the form they take in the existing entry. If it is necessary to make any alteration to the catalogue entry after it has been filed – possibly to show a change in the book's location – or if the book is subsequently withdrawn from stock, all catalogue entries relating to the book must be found and corrected or withdrawn as the case may be, and for this the tracings enable the additional entries to be identified without further thought. Tracings may also be used by the cataloguer who prepares the main entry to show what additional entries are required, for example, how many duplicate copies of the unit entry are required and what additional headings must be set above the existing unit entry. The pattern of tracings on

Library of Congress printed cards is frequently followed. There one finds two series: the first, using arabic numbering, shows subject headings assigned to the book, the second, using roman numbering, shows added 'author' entries. The second series includes titles of books and of series as well as names of persons and corporate bodies.

As space restrictions have limited the matter of this volume to the generalities of cataloguing, the details of descriptive cataloguing – as directed by the Anglo-American code and as applied to various media – are not exemplified here. They are discussed and exemplified in the companion volume. The reader may find his own examples by looking at a selection of national bibliographies.

Catalogue format and presentation

The form of descriptive cataloguing chosen for *BNB* MARC tapes offers a sequence of unit entries beginning with the title of the publication (extended to include the name of the author, editor, etc.) above which any desired heading may be superimposed. The heading for the main entry is necessarily indicated. Such a form of unit entry was put forward in 1948 as the most suitable for international use.[9] Although serious attempts have since been made internationally to unify cataloguing practice it would still seem to offer libraries using a centralized cataloguing service the most easily manipulable entry. Uniformity of superimposed headings can be maintained within any system (e.g. the orbit of *AACR*) by recording in an agreed sequence main and added author headings as tracings on the unit entry.

Many different methods of reproducing catalogue entries are employed, the choice of any one method depending on the number of catalogues to be maintained and the degree of detail required in entering authors and subjects, the relative permanence of the catalogue, the means of reproduction available, and the restricted and private nature of the catalogue or its general use as a bibliography.

The format of my examples in later chapters will generally be that of an entry in a card catalogue because that remains a commonly required entry and because it can stand as a complete entity on its own. The layout devised to suit the physical limitations of the catalogue card standing vertically in a drawer has, in many catalogues, been carried over to other forms of presentation. This is perhaps inevitable when the same original copy is used by an agency for the production for different subscribers of both cards and film, but a standard layout more suited to the 'printed page' appearance within the frame of a microfilm reader or a visual display unit needs to be considered.

In any library the presentation of the catalogue is important. Its physical form, its placing in the library, guides to its use (both inside and outside the catalogue), the arrangement of the different sequences and the references incorporated with them, can all enhance the use of the library's collection, just as their neglect can discourage and turn away readers. How Anatole France must have suffered from his 'Monsieur Sariette'! Although M. Sariette spent all his time cataloguing and classifying the library's collection, says Anatole France, 'no one could find a book without his help, and far from being distressed by this, M. Sariette found in it a source of lively satisfaction'.[10]

The general arrangement of the catalogue should be explained in the guide to the library offered to every reader, and an explanation should be displayed beside the catalogue itself. Readers should be shown how to search under author, title and subject heading and how to proceed from the catalogue to the place in the library where the wanted publication may be found on the shelves or enquired after. The catalogue entry will provide a shelf-mark. Looking up from the catalogue the reader should immediately be able to see some directional sign which connects the symbols of the shelf-mark to a location in the library and also a sign which connects the place where he is standing to the place where he needs to be. This is a service which cannot be standardized, although visits to libraries will offer examples to be followed – or rejected.

Reviews of current practice have been made by the Royal College of Arts Readability of Print Research Unit,[11, 12] and as a result of the less-than-satisfactory picture which emerged, the Unit (now the Graphic Information Research Unit) has produced a practical handbook to help librarians achieve an effective system of library signposting and graphic displays.[13]

Where readers have access to an online catalogue, it is helpful to prepare a brief program that can be activated by catalogue users to show them how to proceed. First-time users of the Library of Congress computer catalogue are encouraged to type in the word TEACH, which calls up a program telling them what is in the catalogue, how to make author, title and subject searches, how to select terms, and how to have records displayed and printed.

References

1 Collins, F. Howard, *Authors' and printers' dictionary*. 10th ed., rev. London: O.U.P. 1956, 404 – 5.
2 Scarles, Christopher, *Copyright*. Cambridge: Cambridge University Press, 1980.
3 Carter, John, *ABC for book-collectors*. 4th ed., rev. London: Hart-Davis, 1966.
4 Glaister, Geoffrey Ashall, *Glaister's glossary of the book*. 2nd ed., rev. London: Allen and Unwin, 1979.
5 Blanck, Jacob, *The title-page as bibliographical evidence*. Berkeley: School of Librarianship, University of California, 1966, 8.
6 Hamdy, M. Nabil, *The concept of main entry as represented in the Anglo-American cataloguing rules. A critical appraisal with some suggestions: author main entry vs title main entry*. Littleton, Colo.: Libraries Unlimited, 1973.
7 Ayres, F. H., 'Author versus title: a comparative survey of the accuracy of the information which the user brings to the library catalogue', *Journal of documentation*, 24(4), 1968, 266 – 72.
8 Domanovszky, Ákos, *Functions and objects of author and title cataloguing*. Budapest: Akadémiai Kiadó, 1974, 37.
9 Ahlstedt, Valter, 'Unit cataloguing', *Libri*, 1(2), 1950, 113 – 70.
10 France, Anatole, *La révolte des anges*. Paris: Calmann-Lévy, 1914, 15 – 16.
11 Spencer, Herbert and Reynolds, Linda, *Directional signing and labelling in libraries and museums: a review of current theory and practice*. London: Royal College of Art. Readability of Print Research Unit, 1977. (Report No. 12).
12 Reynolds, Linda, *Visual presentation of information in COM library catalogues: a survey*. London: BLRDD, 1979. (BLRDD report no. 5472.) (Vol. 1 text, vol. 2 appendices showing examples from catalogues seen.)

13 Reynolds, Linda and Barret, S., *Signs and guiding for libraries*. London: Bingley, 1981.

6

Script and transcript I

Introduction

Increased contact with remoter parts of the world and the emergence of developing countries as producers of documents introduce to cataloguers scripts and languages with which they are unfamiliar but which they must learn at least to recognize and with which they must devise some method of dealing. Even the more familiar languages show differences of form and usage that cannot be ignored. It seems necessary, therefore, before going on to consider specific linguistic problems that confront cataloguers, to notice some of the changes undergone by languages, and the variety of forms used to represent them in writing, whether in their original script or in transcription. Names of persons and of places, in particular, are apt to appear in different forms, according to the source and the date of the documents in which they occur. The cataloguer must know when to suspect that other forms of presentation exist, and how to minimize the inconvenience caused by a multiplicity of forms.

This chapter points to some of the vicissitudes in the history of certain languages, which are offered as examples of what may befall a language. The following chapter describes in general terms how foreign-language materials have been assimilated into catalogues and considers the replacement of the characters used in writing a language by the characters of another script, and ends by drawing attention to some reference books on the identification, history and characteristics of particular languages and their scripts.

Linguistic changes

Ways of writing a natural language may change with a

country's fortunes, with pronunciation and vocabulary changes, and with speech habits as one dialect gains supremacy as a standard. Sometimes the changes are gradual and spontaneous, sometimes they are officially promulgated and may have political rather than philological motivation. A people's feeling for its own language goes very deep. The suppression of the right to use a native language, or the lack of official recognition for its use, is regarded as an unjust deprivation. The omission from the Universal Declaration of Human Rights of a specific safeguard for the language of a minority group within a state was seen to be such by the UN Commission on Human Rights during its first year's work. The Commission recognized that the Declaration's right to equal treatment before the law, the right to education, and the right freely to participate in the cultural life of the community were hollow promises unless governments provided 'adequate facilities in districts, regions and territories, where [minority] groups represent a considerable portion of the population, for the use of the languages of such groups in judicial procedure and for the teaching in state-supported schools'.[1] Even within the European Community governments are being urged to show greater recognition of minority languages. A report of the Council of Europe's Culture and Education Committee, published in 1980, has resulted in the appointment of a group of members of the European Parliament to consider ways of improving educational and cultural facilities for speakers of such languages.[2]

Any revival of nationalism tends to be accompanied by a resurgence of a native language which may have been suppressed or neglected. In the words (roughly translated) of the Danish writer N. F. S. Gruntvig:

Our mother tongue is the speech of our hearts,
The stranger's speech comes haltingly.
Alone our native words from tongue and pen
Can rouse a people from its lethargy.

We see it in the attempt to develop new words from Icelandic roots and suffixes rather than use American borrowings after Iceland ceased to be a colony of Denmark in 1944; in the recent enormous expansion of vocabulary in Hebrew; and in the suggestion of the World Sanskrit Conference in Allahabad that Sanskrit should again become the national language of India.[3] The Parliament of the newly independent state of Tanganyika, which became a republic in 1962, was addressed by the President in that year, for the first time, in Swahili, conferring on the native language the dignity of official status. After the union with Zanzibar to form the United Republic of Tanzania in 1964, renewed efforts were made to promote more widespread use of the language. A National Swahili Council was formed in 1967; schools were ordered to use the language for instruction in all subjects except English. Later (1974) the Prime Minister urged all national bodies to conduct their correspondence in Swahili, and the Organization for African Unity endorsed the use of Swahili as a national language throughout East Africa. Further south, the Zulu language is looked upon as an emblem of black nationalism, and riots have taken place against the enforced use of Afrikaans. Nearer home, the Irish language is taught as a compulsory subject in all primary schools in the Republic; there has been increased use and recognition of the Welsh language; and a creole language appears to be developing as a bond among Britons of Caribbean descent. It seems sometimes as though the symbol has assumed greater significance than the reality it represents. The Prime Minister of Canada, in a broadcast by the BBC in May 1977, spoke of the Québecois being willing to 'tear Canada apart' for the sake of language. Now, in Quebec Province, French has ceased to be one of the two official languages, as in the rest of Canada, and has become the only official language.

Changing political attitudes are shown also in official promotion of a second language. Russian must be learnt by Czechs, and until recently by Hungarians also. Thirty years ago Russian was taught in nearly all Chinese secondary schools, now the preference is for English. Scandinavia affords examples of quite dramatic changes in language use. In Sweden and Denmark Latin was used for learned writings until well into the 19th century. The University of Uppsala accepted its first master's thesis written in Swedish in 1839, its last inaugural dissertation in Latin in 1835. Kierkegaard's thesis, presented in 1841, was the first thesis written in Danish to be presented in the University of Copenhagen, although a century earlier Holberg had satirized the empty Latinity and sterile exercises of the university in his comedy *Erasmus Montanus*, in which the hero, a country lad named Rasmus Berg, comes home for the vacation and insists on being addressed as Erasmus Montanus and confounds the villagers with his – highly illogical – syllogisms. French was the polite language of the 18th century in Denmark, supplanted at court by German which lasted until the early 1900s. We therefore find Peder Lille, of Roskilde, writing as Petrus Parvus Rosaefontanus, Broby as Pontoppidan, and Kierkegaard's pseudonym Hilarius Bogbinder appearing as Buchbinder in a German translation of the work which he wrote under it.

Norwegian – an extreme case

Norway's experience may be taken as an extreme example of a deliberate attempt to establish a purely national language. It led to 'a permanent linguistic war being waged since 1830', to quote T. Støverud,[4] and to variant forms of the same language having official status. Støverud points to the length of the bibliography appended to Einar Haugen's account of the Norwegian language controversy as evidence of its fierceness and persistence.[5]

Norway had been freed from the domination of Denmark in 1814 and had acquired its own constitution and government (although until 1905 under the Swedish monarchy). The constitution specified that the business of the state was to be conducted in Norwegian, presumably meaning 'not in Swedish', since the country's written language then was the same as that of Denmark. Its spoken language consisted of the various local dialects.

Poets and nationalists, such as Henrik Wergeland, called for 'an independent written language', and introduced Norwegian syntax and vocabulary into their writings. Ivar Aasen synthesized dialect words and terms of speech into a new language which he called *Landsmaal* (language of the country) as opposed to the Dano-Norwegian, later called *Rigsmaal* (national or standard language). Books were written in the new language, government committees were set up to regulate and advise on it, laws were passed giving it official status and making its teaching compulsory in schools – for which standard word lists were published[6] – and a dictionary of *Nynorsk* (as *Landsmål*, with its overtones of 'peasant language' had been renamed) began publication in 1950.[7] A new dictionary of *Bokmål* (as Riksmål had become) was also published, recording a greater Norwegianizing of the language in vocabulary and spelling.[8] (Some changes in spelling may be noted above.)

Both forms of the language must still be studied in primary and non-technical secondary schools, and school textbooks must be published in both versions at the same time and at the same price. By law at least 25% of spoken radio and television programmes must be in *Nynorsk*. The textbook norm is recommended for use in 'official' broadcast programmes. Public controversy no longer rages but partisans of *Nynorsk* continue to hold meetings and several writers continue to use *Nynorsk*, especially for writing poetry. In the mid-1980s about 15% of national imprints were in Nynorsk. Popular songs are frequently written in *Nynorsk* or in dialect. For instance, more than half (133) of the individually named songs in a discography prepared by Støverud – *Norwegian viser* (unpublished) – are in *Nynorsk*.

Spelling reforms

The successive language reforms have, of course, resulted in the appearance of Norwegian literary works in various spellings and linguistic forms. Haugen illustrates the changes in spelling and word forms in use between 1900 and 1962 by presenting a passage from a folk tale as it appeared in seven successive editions. The title alone shows changes varying from *Manden som skulde stelle hjemme* (The man who was going to stay at home [to mind the house], of the 1899 edition, when the orthography was essentially Danish, to *Mannen som skulle stella heime*, of the *Nynorsk* version of 1938.[9]

Place names have also been changed in confirmity with the revised spelling rules. A large number were changed in 1917 and 1918, and on 1 January 1925 the capital city repudiated the name of the Danish king who had rebuilt it after the fire of 1624 and resumed its medieval name, Oslo. After the reform of 1938 was promulgated the city of Oslo changed nearly 300 street names, mostly to replace the Danish common-gender suffix -*en* by the feminine -*a* in *gata* (street) and the Danish *torv* (market) by *torg*.

The change from *aa* to *å* in all three Scandinavian languages presents more of a problem to librarians. Even the Scandinavians have wavered in deciding where to file the new letter. In 1948 the letter *å* was established as the *last* letter of the Danish alphabet, in spite of protests that the most reasonable sequence would be *a, aa, å, b, . . . z, æ, ø*. The most recent Danish filing rules retain *å* as the last letter of the alphabet (*a-z, æ, ø, å*), dragging the double *a* with it.[10] The Norwegians agree with the Danes but the sequence of the Swedish alphabet is *a-z, å, ä, ö*. The *Dictionary of Scandinavian biography*, on the other hand, ignores diacritical marks and files *æ* as *ae*, *å* and *a* as *a*, *ø* and *ö* as *o*. The Danish *aa* and *å*, and the *Nynorsk* and *Bokmål* spellings are used as found.

Other countries also have had officially promulgated spelling reforms, Russia, for example, in 1918, Portugal in 1916, the Netherlands several times during this century. The Russian reforms of 1918 were obligatory. They simplified spelling by eliminating certain letters and changing others when they occurred in specific positions. It was not until 1956, however, when Cheshko's rules were published, that a comprehensive statement of accepted orthographic usage became available. As the editor of the English translation puts it, Cheshko presented 'the first complete and authoritative codification of orthographic rules to be made since the reforms of 1918'.[11] It followed general discussion in the journals of areas of uncertainty, and its contents were confirmed by the Academy of Sciences of the USSR. The Lisbon Academy of Letters published its official and definitive simplified vocabulary in 1940.[12] Taylor's Portuguese-English dictionary lists spellings which may be encountered in earlier publications, with their modern replacements.[13]

In Ireland the Translation Section of the Houses of the Oireachtas supervised the production of a standard work on Irish grammar and spelling which appeared, in a wholly Irish text, in 1958.[14] In Greece and Cyprus the variety of accents introduced into Greek by Alexandrian philologists in the first century BC are no longer thought necessary, and from 1982 only the acute accent remains in use – officially, if not always in practice – and that is used to indicate stress on words with two or more syllables or to avoid ambiguity between a few mono-syllabic homographs. The spelling of Netherlandic (which we call Dutch when it is spoken in the Netherlands and Flemish when spoken in Belgium, although it is the same language) was revised and simplified in 1947 and a joint Netherlands/Belgian commission has been working towards conformity in both orthography and usage.

Other efforts are being made elsewhere to standardize usage, particularly of technical terms, in what is basically the same language spoken in different countries. Brazil accepted the Portuguese reforms, with minor variations, in 1943, although usage is not identical in the two countries, and dictionaries vary. Malaysia and Indonesia (which has adopted a form of Malay as 'Indonesian', repudiating the 'colonial' Dutch as well as the local spoken dialects) have established a committee which is trying not only to standardize spellings and reduce multiplicity of meanings but also to produce standard terminologies for the sciences, technologies and professions. A conference on Arab co-operation in terminology was held in Tunis in 1986, with the object of creating a methodology for the development of terminology and of organizing co-operation in producing Arabic translations and thesauri. These are not light tasks. Thinking of one's own language and its development overseas, it is easy to appreciate the ambivalent attitude one has towards it.

English

Deliberate but unofficial efforts to stabilize spelling and usage in England began to be made almost as soon as books printed in English first appeared. Among the books chosen for their impact on the mind of Western man displayed at the exhibition entitled Printing and the Mind of Man (London, 1963) were three English-language dictionaries, the first being Samuel Johnson's *Dictionary of the English language*, first published in 1755. It ran to five more editions in the author's lifetime and to countless more – enlarged, abridged, illustrated, modernized, and with other languages – throughout the following century. Of it the exhibition catalogue says 'This is the most amazing, enduring, and endearing one-man performance in the field of lexicography. . . Johnson's endeavours to "fix" the English language once and for all, however, were nullified by Webster and shown to be delusive by the *Oxford English dictionary*.' Noah Webster, whose *An American dictionary of the English language* first appeared in 1828, is described as 'an ardent nationalist [who] aimed at severing linguistic ties with England. As his dictionary became, and has remained, the standard American dictionary, he has in fact succeeded in breaking the fetters imposed upon the English language by Samuel Johnson to the ultimate benefit of the living language of both countries'. The *OED* is described as 'the greatest treasure-house of any language in the world for its comprehensiveness as well as its scholarship'.

Authoritative grammar books and dictionaries have by now ensured a standard form of 'correct' spelling of English, without the passing of national laws. The standard spelling, however, is alleged to be the main reason why nearly a quarter of the children who leave our schools are classed as 'ineffective readers'. Parliament has been reluctant to promote spelling reforms, but official blessing has at last been given to the use in schools, as a monitored experiment, of the Initial Teaching Alphabet. This is an augmented Roman alphabet, of 44 letters, which assigns a symbol to each of the sounds used in speaking southern English. It was designed and promoted by Sir James Pitman, who based his choice and form of letters on alphabets proposed by his grandfather, Sir Isaac Pitman, and by the Simplified Spelling Society. Its object is not to supersede traditional orthography but to enable children to learn to read English through seeing the words printed with letters each of which is to be pronounced with the same sound whenever and wherever it occurs. After the children have acquired fluency in reading and mastered a sufficient vocabulary, they are introduced to the digraphs and anomalies of traditional orthography. It is not beyond conjecture that a revised alphabet of proven virtue might finally become the means of introducing spelling reforms into the English language, particularly as the language is now spoken by so many peoples with no emotional ties to, or indeed, knowledge of, its traditions.

Implications for cataloguing

From the foregoing examples it is clear that language dictionaries, biographical dictionaries, and encyclopaedias may hold
variant entries according to the date of publication, and so care
will be needed in using them. The date of publication may not
of itself be a reliable guide. Perhaps because they take so long
to compile and print, dictionaries and other reference works
may postdate spelling reforms but still adhere to earlier
practice. For example, Allen notes a number of dictionaries in
his Norwegian and Portuguese chapters which need to be
examined to ascertain which spelling norm is being followed.[15]

Where an official spelling reform has been promulgated, the
likelihood is that the revised spelling will predominate and that
older works will be republished with not only the text, but
possibly also the authors' names respelled. It may consequently
be necessary to change the established form of a personal
author's name or that of a corporate body in a catalogue
heading, making, of course, the necessary references from the
discarded spellings. The title proper must be copied from the
title page, but a note of any change of spelling from the original
would be required. If the change would affect the filing order,
a reference from the original would be necessary; if the number
of editions and other factors warranted it a uniform title would
need to be established.

Changes in written characters

Norway's linguistic changes were gradual and long drawnout.
Norway was a democratic country with universal education,
sure of its own nationhood and in a mood to argue about its
own institutions. In certain other countries political expediency
has imposed changes of a far greater order and immediacy. A
tightening of central control may give rise to the need for better
communications between the administration and the masses of
the people, which in turn may give rise to the need for an
increase in literacy and an expansion of education generally. In
some countries this need has led, not merely to simplification
of spelling, but to the complete replacement of a difficult script
by one judged to be simpler and better adapted to the
expression of new ideas.

Turkey

Where the degree of illiteracy is great such a change can be swift and relatively painless. With 90% illiteracy in Turkey, for example, it was easy to substitute the Roman for the Arabic alphabet – itself imposed when Turkey was annexed to Islam and not ideally suited to the expression of the Turkish language.

The substitution of the Roman alphabet in Turkey was ordered by a law of 1928, to become totally effective within 18 months, and was facilitated by allying the reform of the alphabet to a national campaign to promote literacy and general education. The design of the new alphabet, and hence its adoption, was made as simple as possible. Every letter was to be pronounced, and every syllable was to be pronounced as written. Twenty-three Roman letters were taken and, additionally, seven of them were modified. A cedilla added to c and s, for example, made single-letter representations of the sounds spelt in English as ch and sh. The undotted ı (which, with the dotted capital I is so awkward for other users of the Roman alphabet) was needed to represent the short vowel as in the English word *sir*, as opposed to a long or a short i sound.

The new Turkic Roman alphabet was one of Kemal Atatürk's most effective means of breaking with an unchanging order dominated by doctrinal traditions, enshrined in Arabic texts, and unreceptive to ideas from the contemporary western world towards which he wished to turn his peoples. (He dropped his own Arabic name Mustafa on adopting the surname Atatürk (Father of the Turks) when he made the adoption of surnames compulsory in 1934.)

Arabic-speaking countries

The Arabic language has been traced back to pre-Islamic sources. Modern printed Arabic is derived from cursive written forms and preserves the features of a handwritten script. Just as English handwriting assumed different forms for different functions, developing distinct business, secretary, humanistic and other hands, so written Arabic assumed different forms, but to a much greater degree. Calligraphy was the subject of much study, and particular styles were developed in Persia, India and other countries. Because its printed form

89

remains cursive most of the letters take a different form according to whether they occur at the beginning, middle or end of a word. The writing is from right to left, and no capitals are used. Letters are joined by short strokes and those which have tails lose them in initial and median positions, the dots serving to distinguish similar forms, but more stylish ligatures are often used. Thus the letter *nun* (= n) may be written ‫.....ﻧ‬ at the beginning of a word, ... ‫ﻨ‬ ... in the middle of a word, ‫ﻦ‬..... at the end of a word, and ‫ﻥ‬ when standing alone, as it must when it comes after any of the six letters which cannot be joined to following letters. There are 28 letters, which are all consonants, and *alif*, which may indicate a long *a* or a glottal stop. Short vowels may be shown by pointings above or below the consonants they follow, but are usually omitted in printed books, except for editions of the Koran.[16-19]

A dictionary described by Beeston as 'the only Arabic-English dictionary of any use to students of the modern language'[20] is that of H. Wehr, *A dictionary of modern written Arabic*, ed. J. M. Cowan (Wiesbaden: Harrassowitz, 1961).

Spoken Arabic varies greatly according to where it is spoken – a Baghdadi hardly understands a Moroccan. J. D. Pearson recalls that there are over 400 ways of spelling the name of the Libyan President, resulting from transcriptions of different spoken forms.[21] Written Arabic remains a bond between all Arabs. Many proposals have been made to reform the Arabic script, the most practical being those which reduce the number of letter forms. 'Unified Arabic', for example, proposed a single standard form for each letter, no matter where it occurs in a word. Based on cursive Nashki calligraphy, the letters are easily recognizable, though it is questionable whether a piece of printed text remains elegant. There is, however, little enthusiasm in Arab states to alter the script which, according to tradition, was used even in the lifetime of the Prophet for setting down the sacred text of the Koran – and was, in the words of Sourdel-Thomine, 'the instrument of materialization and transmission of a message identified with the Divine Word', so that the script itself acquires a kind of consecration.[22] The Arabic script remains an outward symbol of Islamic unity. A change to a Roman script is patently unacceptable either culturally or politically. As for being a bar to progress in this computer age, it is possible to program a computer to choose which of the four forms of a letter, or a logotype, is required, and to position diacriticals correctly, so that computer-aided typesetting can be achieved by striking a keyboard on which only one form of each letter is shown.[23]

USSR

In the Soviet Union the Federal constitution originally encouraged the use of vernacular languages in the federal and autonomous republics. Some of those languages possessed an indigenous alphabet, notably the three East Slavonic languages, namely Russian, Ukrainian and Belorussian, which were written in the Cyrillic script, and also Georgian and Armenian, each with its own script. The use of the Cyrillic script had been adopted by some of the peoples bordering on the Russian-speaking areas, such as the Komi, and the Mordvinians, and also by the Yakuts, who, although more distant and speaking a Turkic language, had had their language first transcribed and its first great dictionary compiled in Cyrillic characters. A Mongolian tongue and script were used by the Mongolian peoples, such as the Kalmyks and the Buryats. The Jews wrote in Hebrew characters. The Arabic script, as mentioned above, had spread with the Islamic conquest, and was used by many of the peoples of Central Asia and the Caucasus. At the time the Union was established 43 peoples had no written form of their language.

The Central Asian States used their new freedom to slough off the imposed Arabic script, and by 1930 a unified Roman script was in use by 35 peoples of the Soviet Union. It was called the Unified Turkic Latin Alphabet. Reporting to the Institut international de coopération intellectuelle in 1934, the spokesman for the Society for Cultural Relations between the USSR and Other Countries summed up as follows:

> La portée révolutionnaire et éducative du nouvel alphabet unifié est marquée par le secours fourni par lui aux masses travailleuses des peuples orientaux de l'URSS, qui ont banni les alphabets aristocratico-bourgeois médiévaux, tels que l'arabe, et les ont remplacés par un alphabet populaire, socialiste et moderne, adapté aux besoins des masses populaires, fondé sur les caractères latins et qui rapproche les uns des autres les peuples de l'Orient.

Et de cette façon c'est trouvée justifiée la phrase adressée par Lénine au camarade Agamaly-Ogly, président du Comité central pan-soviétique des alphabets nationaux: La latinisation, voilà la grande révolution de l'Orient.[24]

But it could not be an independent revolution, and only ten years elapsed before the Roman was replaced by the Cyrillic script and the Soviet Central Asian states were in 1940 brought within the unifying influence of a common 'Russian' system of writing.

For by the end of the 1930s, by which time a degree of literacy had been generally achieved, the Russian language, with its modern administrative, social, economic and scientific terminology, had become the main vehicle of communication throughout the USSR, and the second language of all educated non-Russian people. It continued to be written in Cyrillic characters. To facilitate the use of Russian and to emphasize the unity of all the peoples, notwithstanding their indigenous traditions and cultures, Cyrillic alphabets were introduced to replace the recently adopted Latin alphabets. (Publications of all kinds still appear in more than 60 national languages within the Soviet Union.) Thus at present in the majority of states in the USSR the written form of the language makes use of the Cyrillic alphabet, although naturally the sound values of the different letters are not invariable, and some letters have been modified to represent sounds not present in Russian.

Exceptions are the three Baltic states of Lithuania, Latvia and Estonia, formally annexed by the USSR in 1940, and the Karelian (Finnish) Republic, all of whose use of the Latin alphabet was well established at the time of their entry into the Soviet Union. Latin characters had been banned in Lithuania by the Imperial Russian government after a Polish insurrection in 1863. Their use was restored in 1904. In the meantime books had been printed in Cyrillic characters. Three other peoples whose national alphabets have embodied a literature which goes back many centuries (but is not shared with any other peoples) also keep their individual alphabets: the Armenians, the Georgians and the Jews.[25]

China

The situation in China at the beginning of this century was somewhat similar to the situation in Russia, in that few people were sufficiently well educated to read the country's literature. Written as it was in characters derived from early pictograms, many of which over the centuries through assimilation of sounds and dropping of final consonants had come to sound alike and hence needed to be seen to be understood, literary Chinese had become an artificial language. Although in its written form it could be recognized and used by all educated people throughout China, the Chinese language had many dialects and often could not be understood if read aloud. The speech of different regions was incomprehensible to speakers from other localities so that to effect mass education and achieve linguistic unity it was essential to proclaim one language the national language. Just as the dialect of southern England gradually became accepted as 'standard English',[26] the speech of the Peking region, spoken by many throughout northern China, was becoming recognized as a standard educated language, with a standard pronunciation. It was natural, therefore, that when China became a republic in 1911, *guan hua* (official, court language, what we call Mandarin) ceased to be the language of only part of the country (although a large part containing two thirds of the population) and of administration and became the national language, being officially so designated in 1932, and made a compulsory study in all elementary schools. It was also strenuously promoted by broadcasts on its proper pronunciation and by propaganda.

The written form of the language has grown more colloquial, as have most literary languages in this age of informality and of the broadcast word, and it has become known as 'the generally-understood language'. It is, however, tedious to write. The original, prehistoric, engraved pictograph had at various times been modified, cumulatively to such an extent that the 'object' of the representation had been lost. The resulting ideograph had been combined with others, and supplemented with yet others for their phonetic, not semantic, content, as an aid in identifying a word. In spite of recent simplification of the characters, a different complication has been added, in that modern spoken Chinese, in order to prevent confusion caused by homophonous monosyllables, has often combined synonyms – as we jocularly differentiate 'funny-peculiar' and 'funny-haha' – which must be set down in writing as two word-representations instead of one. For speedy understanding of a written text there must also be a more explicit grammar than was required by the old literary convention.

Literary Chinese has made use of about 40,000 different characters, each one representing some particular idea. Of these characters about 2,000 are in very common use, and about 6,000 in frequent use. (The Oxford University Press has 6,000 in its Chinese 'ship'.) Each character is pronounced as a monosyllable. This does not imply that the Chinese ear, subtle though it is to detect tonal inflexions, can distinguish several thousands of monosyllables, only, of course, that many characters must have the same sound. Peking speech has about 400 monosyllables with which to express all the characters used. The group beginning with the sound represented by our letter *f*, for example, may be written for English readers as fa, fan, fang, fei, fen, feng, fo, fou, fu. The number of syllables is, however, increased fourfold in use, because each monosyllable can be spoken with four different inflexions, or tones, as we might, for example, vary the vocal inflexions in saying the word *yes*, and each different inflexion gives the monosyllable a quite different meaning. (Some dialects have more than four tones.) Even so, many homophones remain. Creel points to the sound *yi*, in a single one of its tones, as being represented by 89 characters in a small dictionary.[27] Hence comes the difficulty of understanding a passage read aloud and remaining unseen by the hearer, and the need for adding modifiers, to show in which sense a word should be understood. Moreover, literary Chinese has no parts of speech distinguished as such, although certain words function only as nouns, adjectives or verbs. Even they have no means of showing case, number, voice or tense. Where the same ideogram represents several aspects of an idea, as, for example, a single logogram represents the verb 'to have', the noun 'possession', and the adjective 'rich', the idea alone is presented. The word that expresses it takes the grammatical status we should give it according to the position of its logogram in relation to the other logograms in the sentence and by its required meaning. Also characteristic of classical writings are a number of stylistic conventions and an abundance of references to previous classics of the literature. A sentence may thus be verbally rendered, and 'literally' translated, quite correctly, in a number of ways, using a variety of grammatical structures. Clearly, to become a means of communication for the masses, the written language had to be much simplified and made more explicit, notably by giving it some recognizable grammatical structure.

The written forms of the characters also needed to be simplified – calligraphy is time-consuming. Even to learn the characters for such everyday terms as 'grain' and 'harvest' could cause the uneducated peasant much time and agony. It is not surprising that great enthusiasm greeted government schemes, promulgated in the late 1950s, for simplifying a number of characters (230 in the first list), and for further efforts to standardize the spoken language. How the characters were simplified by deleting redundant parts of antiquated symbols and by using phonetic compounds is shown in Tao-tai Hsia's *China's language reforms*.[28]

The standard form of the printed Chinese character is based on *kai shu* (model script), for which a determined sequence of prescribed brush, or pen, strokes is obligatory. Hsia and the Chicago manual mentioned earlier[29] show how the 15 individual strokes are made and how they are applied to build up the characters. It is essential to be able to identify the strokes used in building up a character because many dictionaries depend for their arrangement on the number of brush strokes assumed to be used in making each character. As soon as one can recognize the individual strokes and know, for example, that a 'square' component is made with three strokes (not four), it is not very difficult to count the strokes in a printed character.

For languages which are written using an alphabet, the simplest way of presenting to the enquirer a list of words of which he does not know the meaning is to arrange them in alphabetical order. The alphabet is brief and its sequence is fixed. It is therefore easy to learn. There is no fixed sequence for Chinese characters and if there were it would be too long to memorize. Chinese word lists have been arranged according to various classification schemes, so that characters which express ideas assignable to particular categories have been grouped together. Yet other lists have been arranged according to pronunciation. But for the reader encountering an ideogram for the first time neither meaning nor pronunciation is likely to be known. Such a reader must have a means of locating a character in a dictionary using only the datum which he has, and that is the form of the character itself.

The formation of the character therefore has been used as the basis of arrangement in most Chinese dictionaries since the time of the classic Chinese dictionary known as the *Kang Xi dictionary*, published in 1716 in the reign of the Emperor Kang Xi. This dictionary divided each composite character into its class element, called a 'radical', and the remaining components. Thus the character for 'water' might be separated from the combination of strokes which completed a composite character to give the idea of 'river', 'wave', 'wet' or 'wash'. The radicals, of which there are 214, are arranged as class headings in a sequence determined by the number of strokes needed to make up each radical. Each radical is given a running number. There are, for example, six radicals in the group of single-stroke characters, numbered 1-6, 23 in the group of two-stroke radicals, numbered 7-29, 11 in the group of nine-stroke radicals, numbered 176-186, and so on. It is necessary to be able to recognize the radicals (not all of which are true etymological roots like 'water' in the above example), and to know the running number which has been assigned to each. Within a dictionary, characters containing each radical are subarranged under the radical according to the number of additional strokes required to make the completed character. Many dictionaries also have an index of characters arranged according to the total number of strokes in each character, which can lead the lost searcher to the correct radical.

A Chinese-English dictionary may arrange the radical headings in the alphabetical order of their Roman-alphabet transcription, as in Giles's dictionary,[30] where the sequence runs A, AI, AN,...YÜN. The dictionary begins with a list of radicals, with, against each, the dictionary-entry numbers at which it will be found. The Radical Index which follows shows under each radical the composite characters which have that radical as part of their composition. They are grouped according to the number of extra strokes which must be added to the radical to turn it into the sought character. To the left of each character Giles puts the number of such strokes, to the right the number of the entry in the dictionary where the character will be found, as it might be 4 [character] 2526. At entry 2526, under the radical transcribed as chu, is shown the sought character together with other characters with which it may be found in a text. Each such phrase is translated.

Some more recently devised filing sequences are based on assigning arabic numerals to each character, but these again depend upon the formation of the character.

A dictionary which offers considerable help to the novice is one prepared by the staff of the Institute of Far Eastern Studies at Yale University.[31]

Japan

Similar help is given to those struggling with Japanese in A. N. Nelson's dictionary,[32] and in Arthur Rose-Innes's dictionary.[33]

Writing in 1944 Bodmer describes modern Japanese writing as:

> a mixture of two syllabic scripts and a formidable battery of Chinese characters. The syllable signs represent the sound values of the affixes and particles, the ideograms are used for the core of an inflected word. Thus the Japanese pupil has to learn two syllabaries...together with about 1,500 Chinese characters. Educated Japanese acutely realize their handicap... Consequently there is a movement to introduce the Roman alphabet.[34]

The Japanese appear never to have developed an indigenous script, but to have used the Chinese ideographs for their own writings from the earliest times. They did, however, many centuries ago, devise a cursive, and slightly later also a square, form of 70-odd Chinese ideographs which correspond when spoken, in Japanese pronunciation, to the sounds required in speaking Japanese. The *kana*, or syllabaries, thus derived, unlike their Chinese originals, represent not ideas but the pronunciation of the elements of the Japanese word, each

97

graph representing a single syllable, either a vowel alone or a consonant followed by a vowel, or the one final consonant *n*. The *kana* may supplement the Chinese characters, which are still in use, or may even be used alone to represent the Japanese word in full. In his article under 'Japan – Language' in the *Encyclopedia Americana*, 1972, R. A. Miller shows a facsimile of a modern Japanese text in which Chinese ideograms, giving the basic meaning, are combined with Japanese *hiragana* (cursive form of *kana*) representing grammatical particles and inflexional endings, and intermingled with *katakana* (the square form of *kana*) to transcribe European loan words. The simpler, square *katakana* is used especially for such transcription and also for teaching children to read – and for sending telegrams. The use of the *hiragana* is more widespread.

The movement to adopt the Roman alphabet lost momentum. Instead, the difficult shapes of many of the *kanji* (the Chinese ideograms) have been simplified, and a basic minimum of characters recommended. The Ministry of Education issued in 1946 a list of 1,850 'current characters', obligatory in writing official documents and found adequate for newspapers, magazines and most general books. The first 881 characters on the government list are now taught in elementary schools as the foundation of reading and writing. The language remains complicated.

Africa

Almost all of the languages mentioned in this chapter have an impressive written literature and their existence is universally known. There is, besides, a whole continent whose language map remains tentative. David Dalby says: 'Notwithstanding its relatively low population, Africa displays a greater degree of linguistic complexity than any other continent'.[35] He has identified between 1,250 and 2,100 languages in Africa (depending on the criteria used to distinguish individual languages). Three quarters of them can be assigned to one or other of two language families – or, as he prefers to call them, 'areas of wider affinity' – in the Northern area Hamito-Semitic, in the Southern area Niger-Congo. His language map of Africa shows the distribution of 'home languages' that is, those used as first language in the home.

The study of African languages affords a noticeable example of terminological variants typical of a discipline in its exploratory, descriptive stage, augmented in this instance by variety in phonetic transcription. Dalby says, 'The natural complexity of the African language map has been compounded by the multiplicity of names applied to individual languages in the literature. Parallel usages of linguistic names, ethnic names, topographical names and foreigners' names have been further multiplied by variations of spelling, both scientific and popular'. He has preferred to use the speakers' own name for their language, when this has been known, in an attempt to standardize a single nomenclature. Alphabets in use for the different African languages are shown in the Appendix to Dalby's *Thesaurus of African languages*.[36]

The bulk of printed publications in Africa are in Arabic, Swahili, and the languages of the various colonizing countries, although publications in the local languages are becoming more frequent. The Nigerian national bibliography for 1966 listed 14 vernacular languages in which publications might be found. The 1980 volume lists texts in about half-a-dozen, with Hausa, Yoruba, Efik and Igbo predominating.[37] Government departments in Tanzania now issue many publications with texts in both English and Swahili.[38] The current national bibliographies of the English-speaking countries of Africa have been described by S. Bankole.[39] In Somalia independence and a subsequent revolution led to the adoption in 1972 of Somali as the sole official language of the state and of a new national orthography using Latin characters. An alphabet for writing Somali, a Hamitic language, had been invented in the early 1920s, called *Far Soomaali* (Somali writing) or *Cismaaniya*, after its inventor Cismaan Keenadiid. It has been described as 'a very efficient orthography' but it 'suffered from the great disadvantage of having completely different letters from any known script, thus requiring a vast layout in terms of printing machinery and typewriter keyboards and involving additional educational problems when teaching any of the world languages'.[40]

In tracing the development of the new orthography and the modernizing of the language, Andrzejewski, whose own studies contributed to the movement and from whom the above quotation is taken, writes:

> it may seem strange that it took independent Somalia twelve years
> to decide to make Somali the national language and to introduce
> an orthography, especially when it is realized that all Somalis
> speak the same language. The reasons for the delay were political:
> the conflicting views on the choice of a script were so violently
> expressed by the public that it became a dangerous issue involving
> bitter polemics, demonstrations, and the possibility of violence on
> a major scale.

The new script was regarded as 'anti-Islamic and likely to
foster European cultural domination'. The pattern is familiar.
In fact the decision to adopt a new orthography using a Roman
script was announced in the President's speech at the parade
ground on 21 October 1972 during the celebrations of the third
anniversary of the revolution. The announcement 'was accompanied by the dramatic gesture of discharging masses of leaflets
with the new alphabet, and patriotic slogans written in it from
helicopters which hovered above the assembled crowds.
Opposition was overcome mainly by persuasion and skilfully
generated enthusiasm, with only occasional cases of coercion'.

The public soon discovered that the new orthography was
easy to learn and to use, and Somali began to replace the
foreign languages which had previously been used in government, business and education. The oral literature in Somali is
also now being written down and published. In fact, Somalia
has rapidly become a literate country.

As in Norway, a Language Commission had been set up (in
1960) entrusted with finding the best way of writing the Somali
language, and as in Norway, textbooks were prepared, using,
in this case, the three main scripts under consideration. The
script finally chosen has no diacritics or special letters. It uses
the letter 'c' for the voiced fricative 'ain', generally represented
in romanizing Arabic (with which the script used in Somalia
had something in common, reflecting an affinity with the
Arabic language) with a single inverted comma, and the letter
'x' for the voiceless fricative usually represented by an 'h' with
some diacritical mark above or below the letter. Some digraphs
are used, and long vowels are indicated by doubling the letter
for the sound. In the list of bibliographic references at the end

of his article, Andrzejewski spells authors' names as they will be found in the publications cited, with references from the new form as he has used it in his text. Thus the older romanized form Omar Osman Mohamed has now become Cumar Cismaan Maxamed; Hussein M. Adan has become Xuseen M. Aadan. The implications for cataloguers are spelled out in another article by Andrzejewski.[41]

C. G. Allen informs me that several of the African languages have suffered changes in their spelling, none so striking as in Somali, though they sometimes involve changes of alphabetical order.

The selective examples described above give some idea of what may happen, for reasons political, nationalistic, religious or educational, to languages and writing, and hence not only to the vernacular literature but also to the nomenclature of persons, texts and everyday life. To the task of identifying the language and script of documents which come into a collection are added complications of collating for cataloguing purposes what may be virtually the same text presented in different scripts or languages, or different states of the same language, and in reconciling conflicting forms of the same proper names.

To every reader his book. But how, in a library containing books in different languages and different scripts, can every reader locate his book? The following chapter refers to some of the ways in which librarians have attempted to escape the curse of Babel.

References

1 United Nations, *Yearbook...1948/1949*, 543 – 4.
2 *The Guardian*, 17 October 1980, 6, and 10 February 1983, 7.
3 *The Times*, 10 February 1970.
4 In a lunch-hour lecture (unpublished) given at University College London, on 3 March, 1970.
5 Haugen, Einar, *Language conflict and language planning: the case of modern Norwegian*. Cambridge, Mass.: Harvard U.P., 1966. (The bibliography is even longer in the Norwegian translation published in Oslo by the Universitetsforlaget in 1969.)
6 Norsk Språknemnd, *Ny laereboknormal 1959, Bokmål, regler og*

ordliste. Oslo: Kirke-og Undervisningsdepartementet, 1959.

7 *Norsk Ordbok: Ordbok over det norske folkemålet og det nynorske skriftmålet*; utg. av Det Norske Samlaget; hovudredaktór, Alf Hellevik. Oslo: Det Norske Samlaget, 1950 – . (Vol. 2, 1978, brings the alphabet to Flusken.)

8 *Norsk Riksmålsordbok*; utg. av Trygve Knudsen, Alf Sommerfelt & Harold Noreng. Oslo: Ascheburg. 1937 – 57.

9 See reference 5, 316 – 23.

10 Balling, Egil, 'The new Danish filing rules: reasons for variations from the ISO principles', *International cataloguing*, 3(4), October/December 1974, 4 – 5.

11 Cheshko, Lev Antonovich, *Russian orthography*; trans. by T. J. Binyon; ed. by C. V. James. Oxford: Pergamon, 1963. (Originally published as *Pravila russkoı orfografii i punktuatsii*. Moskva: Uchpedgiz, 1956.)

12 Rebelo Gonçalves, Francisco da Luz, *Vocabulário ortográfico da lingua Portuguesa*. [Lisboa] Imprensa nacional de Lisboa, 1940.

13 Taylor, James, *A Portuguese-English dictionary*. Rev. ed. Stanford: Stanford U.P., 1970. (4th printing, 1975.)

14 *Gramadach na Gaeilge agus Litriu na Gaeilge: an caighdean oifigiuil*. Dublin: Stationery Office, 1958.

15 Allen, C. G., *A manual of European languages for librarians*. 4th corr. imp. London: New York: Bowker, 1981.

16 Pearson, J. D., 'Languages of Asia, with special reference to the Islamic world', *The indexer*, 11(2), 1978, 63 – 7.

17 Article entitled 'Arabiyya' (= 'Arabic language and literature') in *Encyclopaedia of Islam*. New ed. prepared by a number of leading Orientalists. Leiden: Brill; London: Luzac, 1960.

18 Article entitled 'Khatt' (= 'Writing') in *Encyclopaedia of Islam*. New ed. Vol. IV. Leiden: Brill, 1978.

19 Mitchell, Terence Frederick, *Writing Arabic*. Oxford U.P., 1953 (reprinted 1978).

20 Beeston, A. F. L., *The Arabic language today*. London: Hutchinson, 1970, 112.

21 See reference 16 above.

22 See reference 17 above, 113.

23 Tracy, Walter, 'Arabic without tears', *Penrose annual 68*, 1975, 121 – 6.

24 Institut International de Coopération Intellectuelle, *L'adoption universelle des caractères latins*. Paris: 1934. (Dossiers de la coopération intellectuelle), p.174.

25 Matthews, W. K., *Languages of the USSR*. Cambridge: C.U.P., 1951, 72.

26 George Orwell notes 'even the *Daily Worker* is written in standard South English' (*The road to Wigan Pier*, 1937).

27 Creel, Herrlee Glessner, *Literary Chinese by the inductive method. Vol. 1. The Hsiao Ching.* 2nd ed. Chicago: Univeristy of Chicago P., 1948, 4.

28 Hsia, Tao-tai, *China's language reforms.* New Haven, Conn.: Yale University Far Eastern Publications, 1956 (reprinted 1966).

29 See reference 27 above.

30 Giles, Herbert, *A Chinese-English dictionary.* 2nd ed. London: Quaritch, 1912.

31 *Dictionary of spoken Chinese*; compiled by the staff of the Institute of Far Eastern Languages, Yale University. New Haven, Conn.: London: Yale U.P., 1966.

32 Nelson, Andrew Nathaniel, *The modern reader's Japanese-English character dictionary.* Rev. ed. Rutland, Vt.; Tokyo: Tuttle, 1966.

33 Rose-Innes, Arthur, *Beginners' dictionary of Chinese-Japanese characters and compounds.* Cambridge, Mass.: Harvard U.P., 1944.

34 Bodmer, Frederick, *The loom of language: a guide to foreign languages for the home student*; arranged and ed. by Lancelot Hogben. London: Allen & Unwin, 1944, 439.

35 Dalby, David, *Language map of Africa and the adjacent islands.* London: International African Institute, 1977. (Map in 4 sheets. Scale 1:5,000,000, with enlarged insets. With memoir. Provisional edition.)

36 *A thesaurus of African languages: a classified and annotated inventory of the spoken languages of Africa, with an appendix on their orthographic representation*; ed. by Michael Mann and David Dalby. London: Saur (for the International African Institute), 1987.

37 *National bibliography of Nigeria.* Lagos: National Library of Nigeria, 1973 – . (Annual. Succeeds *Nigerian publications*, originally published by the University of Ibadan.)

38 *Tanzania national bibliography.* Dar es Salaam, 1977 – . Monthly, with annual cumulations.

39 Bankole, Beatrice Solape, 'Current national bibliographies of the English-speaking countries of Africa', *International cataloguing*, 14(1), January/March 1985, 5 – 10. (14 references, table.)

40 Andrzejewski, B. W., 'The development of a national orthography in Somalia and the modernization of the Somali language', *Horn of Africa*, 1(3), 1978, 39 – 45. (22 references.)

41 Andrzejewski, B. W., 'Recommendations for Somali entries in library cataloguing systems', *African research and documentation*, 22, 1980, 21 – 2.

7

Script and transcript II

What catalogues in Babylon?

Not only do the scattered peoples of the earth now speak between 4,000 and 5,000 different tongues, but, as the few illustrations above remind us, they also represent their speech by multifarious signs, some phonetic, some syllabic, some logographic, each alphabet or other set of characters having its own sequence and for the most part being too alien to be assimilated into any other set of characters. A glance at Ostermann's *Manual of foreign languages* will show the great variety of scripts in use for printed publications.[1]

Hans Wellisch has compiled tables of literacy and of book production in the major scripts, from which he estimates that the Roman script is known and used by about 1,000,000,000 people throughout the world. His figures for literacy – a wavering concept – place Chinese next, then Cyrillic, Devanagari, Arabic, and Hebrew, in that order. Book production in 1973 was made up of 71.6% titles in the Roman script (which accounts for more than twice the figure for all non-Roman scripts combined), 14.4% Cyrillic, 6.3% Japanese, 2% Chinese, 1.6% Devanagari, 1.3% Arabic, 1.3% Korean, and less than ½% for Greek, Thai, Hebrew, Burmese, and other scripts. It must be remembered that current production does not always match a vast earlier literature, as in Greek and Hebrew.[2]

In a monolingual country most libraries which cater for the general reader – and we are all general readers when not pursuing our own specialities – can provide in a single author-and-title catalogue and an alphabetical or classified subject catalogue an adequate guide to materials required in the language of the country, and any cognate languages likely to be widely known there. For the immigrant who may not be literate in the language of his adopted country, access to books in his own language and script must be through a catalogue which he can read. In Toronto, for example, a collection of Chinese literature has been provided, with its own catalogue in its own script, for the use of non-English – non-French-speaking Chinese immigrants.[3] Even after becoming literate in the language of his adopted country, the immigrant may wish to preserve that part of his native inheritance represented by its literature, and if his local library provides such literature, the reader's easiest access to it will still be through a catalogue which uses the script in which he expects to read the books – books which in any case are unlikely to interest the library's other readers.

In bilingual countries there is more likelihood of the general reader's having some mastery of the language which is not his vernacular, especially where, as in Canada, both languages are official languages of the country and of international status. For obvious reasons, where both languages are written in the same script, a single author sequence and a single, classified subject sequence (with an index in each language) are often found, as in Canada and South Africa.[4,5] There is, of course, no problem in interfiling words in English with words in French or Afrikaans. As the book production figures show, in developing countries, such as some of the Arabic-speaking countries of Africa, English or French is a necessary second language. Interfiling of the Roman and Arabic scripts is, however, if not impossible, at least arbitrary and unpredictable.

In countries like Yugoslavia, which has five languages of its own: Serbo-Croat, Slovene, Macedonian, Albanian and Hungarian, or the USSR (which has around 200 languages) – and even more so in India where several hundreds of indigenous languages are spoken – the general reader may be literate in only one language, and that language may vary from reader to reader.

The specialist may or may not need to read works in foreign languages. If his speciality concerns, say, a particular country or its literature, then he must be able to read texts published in that country and possibly other related materials in their original form. On the other hand, if his speciality is, say, Physics, provided that he is able to obtain translations of foreign-language material, the language in which a publication originally appears is of minor importance to him in comparison with the rarity of its subject matter or the standing of its author.

Hence, demands on the catalogue will vary from: What is available here and now that I am able to read? to: Is a work, which I must have, available in the edition I need, in this library? and: What is available on my subject or by a particular author, whether I can read it unaided or not? Similar questions are put, of course, to published abstracting journals and other bibliographies, whose citations lead sometimes to material that is immediately available in the searcher's own library, sometimes to further search in union catalogues as a preliminary to interlibrary borrowing.

Some solutions to the question of what catalogues to provide and how to organize them in libraries holding multi-lingual, multi-script collections are easily found by a commonsense appraisal of the needs of readers, and fortunately the scope of the problem is limited for most libraries. Some other solutions, adopted at a time when readership was confined to 'scholars', appear to depend on assumptions which, if valid when made, appear now to be open to question, particularly when practices adopted by large national and research libraries are automatically passed on to smaller libraries, whether in fact their needs are being met or not.

A separate catalogue for each language appears at first sight to be the ideal solution, until one realizes that, to take an extreme example, the library of the University of London's School of Oriental and African Studies would need nearly 400 catalogues!

Clearly the most onerous cataloguing decisions have fallen to those libraries which collect materials in many different languages and scripts, not for the information and recreation of speakers of the different vernaculars, but for record and in the interests of 'scholarship', which until recent years has lain primarily in the field of the humanities.

The *General catalogue* of the British Library integrates into a single sequence entries for such books as do not fall within the province of the Department of Oriental Manuscripts and Printed Books. For those excluded materials there are many separate catalogues, divided by language or language group. They include also indigenous languages of Africa, America and the Pacific.[6]

The *General catalogue* therefore incorporates entries for its accessions printed in the Roman, Cyrillic, and Greek scripts, and reproduces the half-uncials found in Irish books. Being a name catalogue, it also contains entries for translations and works written in western languages *about* writers whose original works are listed in one or other of the oriental catalogues, so that names of oriental writers must also find a place in the catalogue. The Bodleian Library does likewise, relegating books wholly in non-European type to the specialist oriental catalogues. Cambridge University Library incorporates entries for all except Chinese books into its general catalogue. The Library of Congress includes in its catalogues entries for books received in *all* languages and scripts. The catalogues of other libraries with extensive oriental collections are noted by Pearson[7] and Collison.[8]

In the New York Public Library, where more than half of the 300,000 volumes acquired annually by the research libraries are in languages other than English, and a quarter of those require non-Roman scripts for their description, an automated central system has been initiated which will eventually take in all its non-Roman accessions.[9]

How is integration into a single catalogue possible? And when accomplished, does it satisfy everyone?

Briefly, the answer to the first question is that integration is effected by representing characters of a non-Roman script by characters of the Roman alphabet. A romanized form of an author's name takes its place in the alphabetical sequence of main headings, but thereafter the description may continue in the original script, or partially in the original script. More briefly, the answer to the second question is No.

The *General catalogue* of the British Library, for example, establishes a secondary alphabetical file for titles in the original script arranged in the sequence of the letters of that script. Thus under the heading TOLSTOI (Lev Nikolaevich), in the category of entries headed 'Single works', appears the title

Анна Каренина which is followed first by editions in the original language, then by Translations arranged in the alphabetical sequence of the English names of the languages into which the work has been translated, then by Appendix, the term used to cover adaptations, and also references to related works. These entries are followed by the uniform title **Война и мир** for Russian-language editions, followed in turn by entries under *War and peace, La guerre et la paix, Krieg und Frieden,* and so on. The Library of Congress catalogue adopts a similar arrangement. On the other hand, all parts of the entry are romanized in cataloguing the City of Liverpool's International Library.

How the needs of readers have been met in some other libraries which hold multi-language, multi-script collections has been described in a series of articles in *International cataloguing*. Speaking of catalogue provision in the USSR, A. A. Khrenkova says 'One of the fundamental principles of cataloguing in libraries in the USSR is the description of a book in the language of publication and in the script characteristic of that language.' There may be some variation on this principle; for example, foreign-language publications printed in the Roman alphabet may all be located by means of a single catalogue, as may also all works in Asian and African languages, for which entries are made in Russian transcription.[10] The National Library of Singapore also finds it expedient to compile separate catalogues for materials in English, Malay, Chinese and Tamil.[11] Cataloguers in Delhi Public Library find themselves handling seven languages in five scripts. Each language has its own catalogue in its proper script.[12] The *Indian national bibliography* records publications in the 15 languages (including English) which the country's constitution recognizes as national languages. Ranganathan had suggested that the bibliography should be compiled in fascicules, each in a local script, within the region where the script was used, and then circulated. Each regional compilation could thus have provided a cumulative bibliography of works in its particular language and helped to preserve the use of the script.[13] The decision was made, however, to issue a single, centrally produced national bibliography, and to interfile all the entries in a single, classified sequence, using the Dewey decimal classification. (Some bibliographies have additionally been issued in local scripts.)

Joel Downing has explained the difficulties of publishing such a national bibliography.

> No one press could be found in 1958 [when the *Indian national bibliography* came into existence], or even at the present time, with the capability of setting material in the different scripts representing those [15] languages. Consequently the original designers of *INB* decided to romanize entries for those books in non-roman scripts so that all the entries could be understood readily by librarians and others who possessed the ability to read roman script.[14]

The decision can only be regarded as the lesser of two evils, since setting up the type was slow and difficult and so was proof correction – for many entries the units to be set and corrected would be individual letters, not words or phrases. Inevitably, the *INB* lost currency. Downing, whose advice on reorganizing the *INB* had been sought by the Indian government, suggested retaining the original design, but adopting more up-to-date methods of compilation, including phototypesetting and the use of current editions of *AACR* and Dewey, and of ALA romanization tables (see pp.126-7), 'so that at an appropriate point in the future the exchange of machine-readable records would be possible'.

In the *Indian national bibliography* publications under each class number are arranged by languages, so that the reader can see all that is available, choose among the publications he is able to read, and note what other publications he may need further information about. It may be remembered that the notation of the Colon classification was expanded by Ranganathan to make the 'book number' which uniquely identified a volume in a library, and that the first element to be added to the class number was the symbol for the language in which the book was written. Other classification schemes can have their notation similarly expanded. (Book numbers are more fully described on p.180.) The MARC record also provides a field for language identification.

Transcription

Many of the languages with which we are acquainted are written in the Latin, or Roman, alphabet. They assign, for the most part, similar sounds to the same letters, sometimes adding diacritical marks, like the French acute and grave accents, the German umlaut or the Spanish tilde, to increase the range of distinct sounds represented, sometimes relying, as we do in English, on the position of a letter in a word and its juxtaposition with other letters, and on our knowledge of the word's etymology, to ensure the correct pronunciation. Certain other languages are written in a script the characters of which have been specially designed to represent the sounds peculiar to that particular language, as the Cyrillic script, although derived from the Greek alphabet, represents the sounds of Russian. Yet other languages, like the Chinese, are written in a non-phonetic script, the symbols of which represent not sounds but concepts.

A national script has some of the same emotional appeal as a national language – witness the revival in Ireland of the use of the half uncials of the *Book of Kells* in spite of the long break in their transmission! It may also symbolize religious, racial or national unity – witness the persistence of the Arabic script, and the suppression of the Unified Turkic Latin alphabet in the Central Asian states of the USSR, where greater 'Russianization' was hoped for by imposing a Cyrillic script that should be common, with minor variations, throughout the greater part of the Soviet Union.

The adoption of a single, standard, phonetic writing system in place of the world's multifarious systems would certainly facilitate international communication, and proposals for such a universal alphabet have been made.[15] However, the number of separate characters needed to express subtle distinctions of sound essential to the phonetic representation of some languages and the unfamiliar forms that some of the characters would need to take would have material disadvantages. In addition, the mass of literature already existing in the different scripts and the labour of transcribing it, together with the various political, religious and patriotic influences at work, make the adoption of such an alphabet extremely unlikely in the foreseeable future.

110

In the meantime a way must be found of incorporating words written in an exotic script into a sequence written in a native script, as, for example, the names of Russian authors into an English library's author catalogue. It is not possible to interfile two scripts, maintaining the sequence of letters proper to each alphabet and at the same time placing the individual letters of one alphabet in an undisputed position in regard to the letters of the other. A method must be devised of representing the letters of the foreign script by those of the home alphabet. This substitution of familiar letters for the unfamiliar is called transliteration.

A distinction is made between transliteration and transcription. 'Transliteration' can properly be used only for the representation of the *letters* of one alphabet by the letters of another, that is, there must be two alphabets to begin with. Writing down the *sounds* of one language using the letters normally used for writing another language and giving them the sound values they would normally have in that language is 'phonetic transcription'. Similarly, representing logograms by letters of an alphabet is 'syllabic transcription', not transliteration. *Transcription*, literally copying out in writing, comprehends both transliteration and phonetic transcription.

Transliteration hitherto has predominantly been an attempt to change a script in a non-Latin, or non-Roman, alphabet into a form that can be incorporated into a text in English and other languages written in the Roman alphabet. Hence the term 'romanization', which applies equally to transliteration and to phonetic transcription, and so is a convenient word to denote the transfer of exotic typography to the Roman alphabet. The British Standard on typeface nomenclature (BS 2961: 1967) deprecates the use of 'Roman' except to mean a typeface. The term 'Latin', it says, 'should be used to distinguish the letter-forms used in Western Europe from others, e.g. Cyrillic, Arabic, etc., which are referred to in the industry as "exotics" but would be more conveniently referred to as "non-latin"'. BSI has, however, circulated specifications for the 'romanization' of Japanese and Chinese, thereby being inconsistent with itself but conforming to what appears to be general English-language practice. On balance, 'Roman' and 'romanization' seem to be the better terms. Indisputably the

Romans stabilized the letters of the alphabet in the form which they still have, both as a set of letters and as a vertical style of lettering on which certain typefaces were later patterned. Historically 'Roman' applies to both uses, but one use is not likely to be mistaken for the other, whereas to 'Latinize', say, a Russian word might imply either transliteration or translation. In addition, it is convenient and unequivocal to refer to that set of Roman-alphabet letters (possibly with additions and modifications) which is used for writing a particular language as 'the Latin alphabet', 'the English alphabet', 'the Danish alphabet', and so on.

Ideally transliteration would be a letter-for-letter substitution which could be automatically made and automatically converted again to the original, serving equally well for transcription from a Roman into a non-Roman script, without thought for the *sound* of the letters in either of the scripts – the exotic or the transcriber's own. In practice, however, this ideal relationship is rarely achieved, being impeded by the demands and inadequacies of both sound and symbol. Early systems of transliteration were made in Europe in the pursuit of Biblical scholarship and consequently scholars had no need for transcription from a modern script to the archaic script on which their studies were based. Until recent years and attempts at universal bibliographic control, concern has stayed with romanization for the benefit of the western world, without consideration for the reciprocal need to convert the Roman alphabet to other scripts.

An early consideration of the problems involved in transliteration was presented to the Asiatic Society of Calcutta in 1788 by Sir William Jones, the jurist and orientalist, who proclaimed a common ancestry for all Indo-European languages.[16] His *A dissertation on the orthography of Asiatick words in roman letters* finds that 'our English alphabet and orthography are disgracefully and almost ridiculously imperfect, and it would be impossible to express either Indian, Persian or Arabian words in roman characters as we are absurdly taught to pronounce them'. He rejects the introduction of entirely new characters to represent non-English phonemes, but does use five diacritical marks, the apostrophe, and a number of digraphs, and recommends modifying some of the English sounds in favour of the sounds of some Continental alphabets, adapting, for example, from 'the Italian orthography, which of all European systems approaches nearest to perfection', the long 'i' sound, as in the Italian word *dice*. Using his own table of romanized representations of vowels, diphthongs and semivowels, consonants, and compounds, he gives examples of transliterations from Devanagari, Arabic, Persian and Hindi texts.

There are obvious advantages in having a close phonetic correspondence between the symbols which represent each other in the original language and in the language with which the transliterated form is to be used, but several factors make such a correspondence hard to achieve. Transliteration tables have in the main been drawn up by individuals, learned bodies with bibliographical interests, or national committees, all primarily concerned with the needs of speakers of their own language. Some of the symbols of the original script will stand for sounds which do not exist in the western European language, others will stand for sounds usually represented in the European language by digraphs or diphthongs. Whereas the Roman script has roughly 25 letters – not all European alphabets are identical – some other scripts have considerably more: Russian, for example, has 33 representing 39 phonemes (36 letters in the unreformed, pre-1918 alphabet), Georgian and Armenian each 38, Arabic 28 and three pointings to indicate the presence of short vowels. Semitic languages present an added difficulty in that they may be written with the short vowel pointings omitted. The vowels must be restored – an impossibility without some knowledge of the language – before a transliteration can be filed into a Roman-alphabet sequence.

This is not the sum of the problems which non-Roman scripts present. The individual symbols of certain scripts, such as the Chinese, represent, as has been said, not phonemes, but ideas, words or parts of words, they are not letters but logograms. Others, though phonetic, represent sounds already in combination, like the Japanese syllabaries. The situation is even further complicated by the fact that for practical purposes certain proper names, both personal and geographical, have been transcribed in a romanized spelling of a spoken form, sometimes altered to suit European habits of pronunciation. There may be more than one Europeanized form of such a name, because different transcriptions of the same word may result from local variations in pronunciation of the original language and also from variations in the letters used to represent the same sound in different European languages. The English heard and wrote *wadi*, the French heard and wrote *oued*. Arabic names may also appear in variant forms according to whether they are phonetically transcribed from the spoken form or transliterated from the written form for yet another reason. The two phonemes which make up the definite article *al* (sometimes written *el, il, ul*) may in certain sequences be assimilated to the sound of the following letter. Pearson explains how 'Abd al-Salām may come to be written 'Abdussalam.[17] A famous medieval Arab historian appears variously as 'Abd al-Rahmān ibn Muhammad called Ibn Khaldūn (British Library catalogue), Ibn Khaldoun (Bibliothèque Nationale catalogue), Ibn-Haldūn (Deutsche Bibliographie), Ibn Khaldūn (Library of Congress catalogue), Abderrahmán ben Chaldûn (*Enciclopedia universel ilustrada*), Abenjaldún (Ortega y Gasset), and Eben Caliduno (Italian title page). The name in full is made up of several elements and the choice of entry word has varied according to the library or other context in which it has been found – but that is another problem. Such variant transcriptions continue to be made.

Chinese
Chinese personal names require extreme caution if confusion is to be avoided. Relatively few words are used as surnames among the Chinese and some of these are differentiated from a trio of others only by their tones. Librarians are not alone in fearing to create 'ghosts', or to confound two persons under one name, as the following *cri de coeur* from the *Guardian* shows:

> Most newspapers use a degenerate form of the old Wade-Giles system [of transcription of Chinese logograms], with all the apostrophes and diacritical marks left out. Thus Chun, Ch'un, Chün and Ch'ün all come out as Chun. The Chinese Government has adopted, for use within China, a system of romanization that avoids this confusion. It distinguishes between Zhun, Chun, Jun and Qun. If we cannot use the pristine Wade-Giles system (and

that would be a compositor's nightmare) why not adopt this system? It would have to be a concerted decision: The *Guardian* (for instance) could not make this great leap forward independently...moreover we are dependent on our sources.[18]

The Wade-Giles system to which the *Guardian* refers is based on a system of transcription devised by Sir Thomas Wade for his *Peking syllabary*, 1859, and revised for his textbook for learning Chinese.[19] With slight amendment it was used by Herbert Giles in his Chinese-English dictionary of 1892.[20] It has since been modified by the dropping of certain syllables which do not conform to the pronunciation of modern Chinese and of some diacritical marks, four of which were originally used.

The Chinese government first promulgated a system of romanization in 1928, called *Gwoyeu Romantzyh*, in which the four Mandarin tones which show the particular meaning of a monosyllable were incorporated in the spelling. Thus the names indicated by Wade as t'ang$^{1-4}$ were written tang, tarng, taang, tanq. Government interest did not, however, stop there. In 1952 a Research Committee for Reforming the Chinese Written Language was set up, with the task of simplifying the Chinese characters (which had been in use practically unchanged for 4,000 years) and also of studying schemes for a phonetic alphabet. A phonetic alphabet based on the Latin alphabet was adopted in 1956. A revised form of this alphabet, called *Hanyu pinyin* (Chinese spelling) was presented to the fifth session of the first National People's Congress in 1958, who endorsed the government's policy of romanizing the written language, *Guoyu* (national language), and approved *Pinyin*.[21] The tones inherent in the orthography of Gwoyeu Romatzyh are represented in Pinyin by accents, as *mā, má, mǎ, mà* and *ma* (a neutral form is sometimes required). Pinyin was designed only as a system of romanization, to be used for transcriptions of documents in transactions with the outside world. It was not intended to supplant the existing system of writing in China. Its use was more formally imposed by an official decision to use Pinyin in all diplomatic documents, passports, export catalogues and other publications for use outside China from 1 January 1979. It now completely supersedes the earlier official systems. It was to Pinyin that the *Guardian* referred. After the official ruling on its exclusive use from 1979, the *Guardian*, in common with other papers, decided to follow the lead given by Reuters and to use the new romanized spelling of Chinese names. The revised forms Beijing and Deng Xiaoping now supersede the familiar Peking and Teng Hsiao-p'ing.

The uses to which Pinyin is now put have been summed up by Legeza as:

1 to give the pronunciation of Chinese characters (as a kind of phonetic annotation to the Chinese script);
2 as an aid in teaching and learning common speech;
3 as a common basis on which various national minorities may create their written language;
4 in transliterating names, scientific terms;
5 to help foreigners learn Chinese;
6 as an aid in compiling indexes;
7 to transform the Chinese written language into a phonetic language.[22]

László Legeza's *Guide to transliterated Chinese* from which I have just quoted (vol.1, p.12) begins by saying that the Chinese language has been more of a barrier than the Great Wall itself and adds that there are more than 50 major sinological romanized systems alone, for which no comparative tables have hitherto existed. His *Guide* has been compiled so that 'both specialists and non-specialists can easily convert a transliterated form of a syllable from a modern system into another modern system, from an archaic into another archaic, and from an archaic into a modern without the use of the Chinese character itself, *but not from a modern system into an archaic*' (p.8). The first volume lists currently used romanized systems, the Chinese phonetic system and the Russian Cyrillic system, and two outdated systems, Sin wez and the 1956 Pinyin, for converting the 407 syllables which cover all possible mono- and/or polysyllabic word-combinations in the modern Peking dialect. Volume 2 covers out-dated European systems and volume 3 is planned to cover non-romanized systems in some oriental languages. The author gives a brief description of each system, and indicates the languages in which it is used.

He notes five currently used systems in English. To this number must now be added Pinyin, adopted by the British Library Department of Oriental Manuscripts and Printed Books for cataloguing all books required after 1965. It was also adopted for use in *BUCOP...New periodical titles*, from 1964 onwards, because periodicals published in mainland China frequently bore the Pinyin transcription on the title page, in conjunction with the title. A similar presentation on title pages of scientific and technical books has led to the use of Pinyin in modern scientific and technological libraries. Its use in recently published western atlases and gazetteers, such as the 1980 edition of *The Times atlas of the world*, should also be noted. The inclusion of a Cyrillic system in Lászlo Legeza's first volume and his projected third volume are a reminder that romanization is not the only form of transcription in use in the modern world. The Russians need to present Chinese originals in Cyrillic characters, as in their Asian language catalogues, Arabs and Japanese need transcriptions of Russian names, Indians need to represent one Indian alphabet by another Indian alphabet, and so on.

In China, as has already been said, Pinyin does not replace the Chinese characters in general usage. Alain Peyrefitte quotes Chou En-lai as saying: 'How wise the Vietnamese were to adopt the Roman alphabet so long ago, when the number of people who knew the ideograms was infinitesimal!' It had facilitated the education of the masses in Vietnam, but the Chinese had waited too long. By the 1950s too many people had become attached to the old way of writing and the services of those people were essential for the further spread of education. In addition, there were so many other changes of a more urgent nature to be made at that time that this particular reform was deferred till later. Peyrefitte points out that, equally, the time was not yet ripe for such a reform. Not until the speech of the people was truly one language could that language be given a standard phonetic alphabet. (Broadcasts, listened to by millions, on the proper pronunciation of the common language were among official attempts to standardize usage.) Until a common speech should unite all the people, the one tie which bound them together, namely the ideographic writing, could not be broken. To break it would be to

117

Balkanize China.[23]

Meanwhile, Pinyin is being used in China similarly to the way the romanized alphabet was used among the mountain peoples of the Eastern Soviet states, for teaching Chinese to minority groups to whom it is a new language and for writing down minority languages which had hitherto no script, and also for transcribing foreign words adopted with foreign technological inventions. We may compare the first of these applications with our own use in primary schools of the Initial Teaching Alphabet.

The use of Pinyin as a complete replacement of the existing logographic scripts would, it is argued, render all Chinese literature inaccessible. Unlike the older Turkish literature which is being reprinted in new editions in the Roman alphabet, Chinese literature simply transcribed in a romanized form would be incomprehensible or would need to be studied, as we study Latin, to become accessible. To become readily understood its homonyms would need to be replaced by modern vocabulary, and grammatical additions taken from the spoken language would need to be inserted. The literature would indeed be 'translated' much more drastically than we translate Chaucer for a wide modern audience. According to Guo Moruo (president of the Academy of Sciences and a vice-president of the Permanent Committee of the National Assembly), however, the change to romanization will surely come.[24]

But just as computerization and photocomposition can simplify typesetting in Arabic, so it can revolutionize methods of printing in Chinese characters. To quote Peter Large (*Guardian*, 28 August 1980) 'Chinese newspapers are still produced by manually picking out each bit of type: the printers roller-skate (literally) along rows of cabinets... It still takes about thirty hours to get one edition of the *People's daily* into type.' The revolution proposed (by Monotype) is for the operator to compose each character by striking keys representing single strokes or combinations of strokes on a keyboard containing only 238 components, the average number of keystrokes per character being 2.7. Other companies are also working on the reduction of the number of keys required for computer keyboards.

118

Japanese

Traders and missionaries to Japan used the Roman alphabet to represent phonetic equivalents of the *kana* (see p.97), and it is the system of romanization devised by an American missionary, James Curtis Hepburn, for his dictionary of Japanese and English, first published in 1867, that has become the most widely used – now with slight modifications to the original. Official Japanese systems have been devised: around 1900, *Nippon-siki*, and in the late 1930s, *kunrei-siki*. The latter combined elements of both Hepburn and *Nippon-siki*, and was subsequently, in 1954, reaffirmed as the government's preference. The Japanese systems differ from the modified Hepburn system in reflecting the theoretical pattern of the syllabaries, rather than the actual pronunciation, where a difference exists.

Attention has been drawn to confusion which can be introduced by romanization. In the case of Japanese names a warning has been given always to transcribe the full name when using the romanized form. It arose from the examination of author indexes to certain periodicals. As we have seen, names written in ideograms are frequently homophonous, and therefore when romanized look alike. Since Japanese personal names have only one forename the practice of some author indexes of giving forename initials only when transcribing *kanji* names can lead to the collection under a single name of articles written by different individuals. The cumulative author index of *Nuclear science abstracts of Japan* was examined to see how many of the names there fully spelled out would still be differentiated if the forename were represented by the initial only. Fully spelled names of 5,289 authors for 7,552 articles were found. With initials only used, the number of authors appeared to be reduced to 3,972 – a grave inconvenience in a highly specialized field of study.[25]

Romanization standards

As a matter of necessity, individual libraries with large oriental and Slavonic collections, cartographic institutions, postal services and other organizations dependent upon the identification of names and the exchange of information worldwide have evolved their own systems of romanization and are now

increasingly concerned to promote the adoption of standardized transcription schemes.

The International Congress of Orientalists has shown a
perennial interest in the subject. At its 11th Congress in 1897
a committee was set up to draft an international system of
romanization, but no agreement could be reached on the
proposals it presented to the 13th Congress in 1902, at which
a resolution was passed that national systems should be set up.
The Congress in 1971 included a seminar on international
standards in orientalist cataloguing among whose concerns
were, still, spelling and transliteration. They remain matters of
concern. A glance at the *Union catalogue of Asian publications* will
show how far off we are from even a national common
practice.[26] The catalogue, a finding list of oriental material
held in 64 British libraries, records, in one alphabetical
sequence of authors' names, holdings in all languages in Asia
outside the Soviet Union and those published in Arabic or the
Ethiopian languages in North Africa. There are some 66,000
entries, of which the general pattern is: author's name
romanized, title in original language and script, transliterated
title, translated title, pagination, imprint, holding libraries.
The catalogue has been produced in book form by
photographing card catalogue and other entries sent in by the
contributing libraries. The editor comments: 'It is the
exception rather than the rule for the name of the author of a
vernacular work to be reported in exactly the same form by two
different libraries' (p.ix). He has therefore had to impose
romanization from a single set of tables in order to bring under
one heading all the works of a particular author. As he points
out, variant transcriptions may have already been printed on
English-language title pages before they reach a library, but
since those transcriptions are simply variant phonetic
renderings in the English alphabet of a single original form,
there is good reason for adopting in such a case, as does the
Union catalogue, a standard English form of the vernacular
name. Thus all the spellings of Banerji will be brought together
as one surname under this standardized form. Naturally the
catalogue contains references from other spellings. The
compiler has also thought it useful to comment on some of his
solutions to problems encountered and to give advice on

120

alternative approaches if the reader does not find, either as entry or as reference, the form he is seeking. Similar problems had already been encountered in compiling the *Index Islamicus*[27] and were to recur in compiling the index to the second edition of the *Encyclopaedia of Islam*.[28]

The International Organization for Standardization (ISO) has published recommendations for the transliteration of Arabic, Hebrew, Slavic Cyrillic, and Greek characters into Roman-alphabet equivalents.[29-32] But until the need for conformity is seen to be urgent – which it undoubtedly is – they remain merely recommendations, to be followed or ignored according to local decisions.

Arabic

The ISO system for the romanization of Arabic characters is similar to the recommendations put to it by BSI[33] and the Association française de normalisation (AFNOR).[34] The British standard differs from it only over an additional letter used for a non-Arabic sound, the French reprints the essentials of the ISO recommendation. The standardizing bodies' recommendations, however, postdate the use of schemes applied in certain influential publications. The scheme printed in the *Encyclopaedia of Islam* is naturally favoured by orientalist scholars, although they are not unanimous in their use of it. Many libraries follow forms found in the LC catalogues, on which the American standard is based.[35]

Hebrew

There remains much controversy over the romanization of Hebrew, for which no British standard has been promulgated. The American standard contains an alternative system designed with computer typesetting in mind. It has 27 characters, acceptable for a display device having a limited character-set and is said to be easy for the user to memorize.[36] The ANSI scheme for computer use has been applied to the catalogue of the large Hebrew collection in the New York Public Library.

Cyrillic

Five Slavonic languages, Croatian, Slovenian, Czech, Polish and Sorbian, use phonetic roman alphabets.

Although Serbo-Croation is a single language, spoken by Serbians of southern and eastern Yugoslavia (the former kingdom of Serbia, with Belgrade as its capital), and by the Croats of the north of the country, two systems of writing are in use for it. As in other instances, the system adopted depended upon who did the writing. The Cyrillic alphabet, invented, it is said, by St Cyril to further the spread of Christianity in south-eastern Europe, was the writing system used by the Greek Church which converted the Serbians and to which they have adhered. The writing system of the Church became, with modifications, the writing system of the people. In the north of the country, Christianity was brought by the Roman Church, and the Roman system of writing used by its clerics was adopted by the Croats. Its use was reinforced by Venetian, and later, Austro-Hungarian rule. Closely related to Serbo-Croatian is Slovenian, spoken in the north-eastern corner of Yugoslavia and along its adjacent borders with Austria and Italy. It was not written as a separate language until the 16th century and not standardized until the 19th. A Latin alphabet is now in use, but earlier publications used Cyrillic.

Czech and Slovakian, although recognized as two national languages, have much in common. Czech had been written in a Roman script since the Middle Ages (Jan Hus reformed the Bohemian alphabet as well as the ideas of the Bohemian people). When a literature in Slovakian emerged in the 19th century, a Roman alphabet similar to the Czech alphabet, though not identical with it, was used.

Polish, another west Slavonic language closely related to Czech and Slovakian, has been written in a Roman alphabet since the Middle Ages, under the influence of the Roman Church. For a brief period in the 19th century while under the domination of Russia, only publications in Cyrillic were permitted after the insurrection of 1863. Although – perhaps because – Poland was so often fought over and partitioned, it has a considerable national literature.

Sorbian, spoken by only a small number of Sorbs (Wends) living near the eastern borders of Germany with Poland and Czechoskovakia, has little literature.

Although all the above-mentioned languages are related,

their phonetics differ somewhat, and as a result different adaptations of the Roman alphabet have been made, chiefly in modifications to the letters used.

In considering the romanization of writing systems which used the Cyrillic alphabet, it was natural to think of the three most important Roman alphabets used for writing Slavonic languages, and to put forward the alphabet used by the Croatians, known as *Latinica*, as the most suitable for the basis for transliterating Russian Cyrillic.

Latinica can easily accommodate the sounds of Russian, has fewer inflected letters than the other two alphabets, and had already been used in the 1890s for romanizing names in the Balkan Peninsula for military maps used in the Austro-Hungarian empire, and it is widely favoured, being the choice of the ISO, but it is not generally acceptable to English speakers. The use of 'the Latin alphabet of the Croatians' was proposed to the American Library Association in 1900 by a Committee on Transliteration of Slavic Languages as being the most suitable, but the Committee realized that certain of the letters written with diacritics were likely to prove unacceptable and proposed letter combinations as alternatives.[37] The alternatives were, in fact, accepted, and English-speaking committees have generally preferred the sound-values of English consonants and Italian vowels to represent an approximation to the sounds of non-Roman letters. The Croatian alphabet, offered again by the ISO in 1968, is no nearer general acceptance. The alternative use of the British standard is, however, permitted by the ISO standard, albeit reluctantly, to judge by subsequent proposals circulated, ISO DIS 9/2-1978 and DIS 9/3-1984.

The table overleaf shows variations between the International,[38] Library of Congress,[39] British,[40] and Soviet[41] official systems for transliteration from the Cyrillic alphabet as used for the Russian language. It also includes the letters preferred by the system approved jointly by the United States Board on Geographic Names and the (British) Permanent Committee on Geographical Names, which has particular importance for place names.[42] ANSI Z39.24 agrees with BS2979.

The French system[43] agrees with the International standard,

Cyrillic	ISO	LC	BSI	USSR	USBGN/PCGN
Ж	ž	zh	zh	zh	zh
Й	j	ĭ	ĭ	j	y
Х	h	kh	kh	kh	kh
Ц	c	t͡s	ts	c	ts
Ч	č	ch	ch	ch	ch
Ш	š	sh	sh	sh	sh
Щ	šč	shch	shch	shch	shch
Ы	y	y	y	ý	y
Э	ė	ė	é	è	e
Ю	ju	i͡u	yu	ju	yu
Я	ja	i͡a	ya	ja	ya

as does also the German[44] except for the letter X which it renders as ch. (Earlier German transcriptions may still be found, of course, as in Tschaikowsky and Tschechow.) The Library of Congress system uses the same letters (but not the same diacriticals) as the British standard, except for the last two Cyrillic letters shown, which are transcribed respectively as i͡u and i͡a. (The ligatures are necessary to show that the letter represented by the former is the single letter Ю and not the two letters И and У, and the letter represented by the latter is the single letter Я and not the two letters И and А, essential information for reconversion to the original. (The underlining of pairs of letters in some schemes for the romanization of Arabic serves the same purpose: t͟h for example represents ث and not ت and o.) A recent proposal for the transliteration of Cyrillic justifies a set of letter equivalents using neither diacriticals nor ligatures.[45]

The International standard includes also equivalents for Cyrillic letters which occur in Bulgarian, Ukrainian, Belorussian and Serbian. Giliarevskii has reminded us that of the 65 languages used by peoples of the Soviet Union which form the national publishing output only seven do not use the Cyrillic alphabet. Of those which do, 16 use letters which do not differ in form from those of the Russian alphabet and which may therefore be transliterated from the existing table. That leaves 42 languages which use Cyrillic alphabets containing letters which are additional to, or modified forms of, letters in the Russian alphabet. These languages have provided some of the material contributed by the Soviet Union to the *Index translationum* and it was seen to be necessary in preparing that material to establish stable transliteration tables for the neglected languages. The transliteration tables have been published in the hope that they would be adopted as standard bibliographical usage within the Soviet Union and also as the basis for an international standard, supplementary to the existing standard for Cyrillic alphabets.[46] A draft international standard is in fact under consideration.[47]

Chinese

Three more British standards for romanization have recently been under preparation, for Chinese, Japanese and Korean. The *Guide to the romanization of Chinese*[48] notes how widespread is the use of the (modified) Wade system for place names in library catalogues and in English-language publications generally. 'In the fields of documentation and publication its position is paramount in English-speaking countries and throughout Europe (except France and the USSR), Asia and Latin America.' (I notice that Peyrefitte[49] has used it in preference to the system promulgated by the École française d'Extrême-Orient. His name index includes also two variant transcriptions, that of the École and Pinyin.) The BSI *Guide* concludes, however, 'There is no evidence that either Wade or Pinyin will, in the near future, supplant the other in international and Chinese usage. In these circumstances, it seems clear that no useful purpose would be served by adopting either of these systems as the sole basis for the British Standard.' What the *Guide* does, in fact, is to print conversion tables for the two romanized systems, first Wade to Pinyin and then Pinyin to Wade. The increased use of Pinyin in publications coming from China since the beginning of 1979 and the decision of the Library of Congress to continue using the Wade-Giles system increase the need for references between the two systems.

Japanese

The BSI specification for the romanization of Japanese warns: 'Unrestricted application of the system, as with any other

125

system, requires that the romanizer possess a detailed knowledge of the language in its modern and historical written forms'.[50] The Chinese characters encountered in a Japanese text are to be transcribed according to their *kana* values, which presupposes a correct reading of the words presented in the Chinese characters. Only the *kana* appear in the specification. The committee which prepared the specification were of the opinion that the long-established Hepburn system was still the one best suited for use in the English-speaking world. They therefore recommend the adopting of the 'modified Hepburn' system, with one exception concerning the transcription of syllabic n – the only consonantal ending to a syllable in Japanese. The specification prints tables of correspondence showing the *hiragana* and *katakana* characters with their alphabetical equivalents. For guidance on capitalization and word division the reader is referred to the Library of Congress's *Manual of romanization, capitalization, punctuation and word division for Chinese, Japanese* and *Korean*.[51] The Library of Congress also, of course, bases its transcription on modified Hepburn. The American National Standards Institute worked closely with the British Standards committee and has produced a standard in complete agreement with theirs.[52]

The BSI circulated a draft guide to the romanization of Korean as BS/RD 6505 in 1982.

The warning given in the specification quoted above and the presence of pages of notes and instructions which accompany several of the LC romanization tables all point to the need to become familiar with a language and its script if one is to use romanization tables to give an accurate and consistent rendering of a language. Nonetheless, the crude approximation which some acquaintance with non-Roman scripts and their Roman equivalents can provide is not without its uses.

Library of Congress romanization tables

The Library of Congress is included among the standardizing bodies because, like its other practices, the practice of romanizing non-Roman scripts in order to make access to the whole collection possible through an author and title catalogue in a single sequence is followed by many other libraries, as are also LC's methods of romanization.

Since the passing of the Act of Congress (see p.15) which made the Library of Congress responsible for acquiring and cataloguing books from all over the world on an unprecedented scale, the need for stabilizing and publishing a widely accepted system of romanization for all non-Roman scripts has been recognized as acute by the Library and work has progressed unremittingly. Revisions of the romanization tables, agreed by ALA and LC (the more recent ones by the Canadian Library Association also) are published in the Processing Department's bulletin *Cataloging service*.[53] The ALA has agreed to publish in book form all romanization tables approved jointly by ALA and LC. It might seem that standardization of transliteration practices is well on the way to accomplishment. But is it?

Standards but no standardization
An investigation by Hans Wellisch into romanization methods used by libraries with large collections of material in scripts other than their national script confirms that the LC schemes are the most widely used. Libraries' own schemes have second place, except for Cyrillic scripts (where the LC scheme predominates, followed by the ISO scheme and then that of the *Prussian instructions*). Even so, Wellisch comments, the overall rate of application of LC conversion tables to non-Roman scripts (except the logographic ones)

> hovers around 40% only. In other words, there is no romanization scheme for alphabetic non-Roman scripts which is used by a clear majority of the world's libraries with documents in non-Roman scripts. If we consider also the romanization practices of abstracting and indexing services which form a huge segment of universal bibliographic control tools, there is even less uniformity, since it is known that these services do not use LC schemes to any degree, and most of them prefer to employ their own schemes.[54]

Reviewing cataloguing policy in the light of the adoption of *AACR2*, the Association of Bibliographic Agencies of Britain, Australia, Canada and the United States (ABACUS) discussed concerted action on romanization. They concluded:

> Although there are certain attractions to converting to ISO romanization standards in 1980, LC's findings to date show that most libraries prefer ALA/LC romanization tables. NLC

[National Library of Canada] uses the ALA/LC tables for English and ISO for French. NLA [National Library of Australia] uses the ALA/LC tables consistently, and BL has adopted the ALA/LC romanization for Cyrillic. For Hebrew there are strong proponents in the US of a version of the ANSI standard, which is not ISO-compatible. The general feeling is that major changes in any library's standards are to be shunned until the more pressing problems of adopting *AACR2* are solved.[55]

The British Standards Institution decided in 1983 to withdraw from participation in ISO work on transliteration, considering that schemes in use were already sufficient. Existing British standards will be maintained if there is a demand for them.

In *AACR2* itself the ALA/LC romanization tables are used in examples in which romanization is called for because of the known preponderance of libraries which use the ALA/LC schemes in those countries most likely to use *AACR2*. It is expected, however, 'that authorized translations [of the code] will, in examples, substitute romanizations derived from the standard romanization tables prevailing in the countries or areas for which the translation is intended' (*AACR2* 0.13). There is also a reminder that the examples in the code are illustrative not prescriptive.

Signposts in Babylon
Meanwhile the cataloguer and the catalogue user must be prepared to recognize the same word in various different guises. To the unavoidable variations resulting from political change which may translate or transform a name, and from official spelling reforms which may give rise to different spellings of the same word in publications emanating at different times from the same country in the same language, must be added the scholars' and librarians' various renderings of the same original word. The use of different systems of transcription may result in the same original characters appearing in different romanized forms in publications emanating not only from different countries but also from different organizations and individuals within a single country and even from a single library at different times, where successive specialists have preferred different systems or where non-specialists have been insufficiently wary.

The difficulty of properly identifying persons becomes acute when material from different sources is being assembled for a bibliography. Magda Whitrow has described some of the problems encountered in compiling the cumulative bibliography from 50 years' issues of *Isis*, a periodical devoted to the history of science in which the critical bibliographies ranged in time over all historical periods and were culled from original sources in all languages in which the documentation of science exists.[56] In addition to confusion caused by the use of more than one system of romanization for a single language is the trap for the unwary set by phonetic renderings of foreign names, such as Mişel for Michel in Turkish, and **ПЕРРО, Ш** for Perrault, Ch. and **ЧИЛСОН, МАЙКАЛ** for Wilson, Michael in Russian catalogues.

How to minimize the inconvenience caused by the existence of multiple transfigurations of the same word? As our codes of cataloguing have always directed, references are made from alternative forms to the one chosen for a heading, so that the reader can be assured of finding the cataloguer's choice of heading at least at his second attempt. But why is it not general practice to include in the guide to the library a note of the romanization tables used, and as a supplement to it a set of the tables so that the reader who has frequent traffic with the catalogue can anticipate the romanization and find his required entry at the first attempt? The British Library's *Reader guide, no. 3* shows both its own Cyrillic transliteration (for use with the *General catalogue* printed volumes) and LC transliteration (for use with currently produced catalogues.) When our catalogues are all online, alternative forms of name can be linked without the reader's being aware that his spelling may be a variant from the official one, and so he *will* find the required entry at the first attempt.

The advantages of romanization – to consider the most familiar aspect of transliteration as used in those catalogues whose predominant script is the Roman – are claimed to be the following. A single author/title catalogue can assemble the records of a library's entire collection. Records of all versions of a work are assembled at a single heading: texts in the original language in their various editions and in translation together with commentaries and criticisms in any language or script, as in the *Union catalogue of Asian publications*. Once romanized, the record of a publication issued in an exotic script can be treated like the majority of entries in the catalogue. It may be found, and the work it records retrieved, by an intermediary between the book and the reader who is quite unacquainted with the original script and the original language. In the wider context of the exchange of bibliographic information between different agencies, a single romanized form of identification would be of immense value.

Against these claims must be set the following drawbacks. Readers seeking a text in a non-Roman script will often have, on paper or in their minds, the original form of the heading they are seeking. They are not helped by a rendering in the Roman script. The reader and the intermediary must agree on the romanized form to be sought, and that, as I have already stressed, is neither invariable nor self-evident. Much literature which appears in a non-Roman script is not translated: the labour of transcription is therefore wasted. The argument that universal bibliographic control is advanced by transcription is weakened by the diversity of transcription schemes used even for the conversion to the Roman alphabet, to which must be added conversions to other alphabets. That words are the only necessary symbols for identification of documents is no longer true. For modern publications the ISBN and the ISSN form unique identifiers which can be used by machines, and for some purposes, such as checking serial publications, in the absence of machines.

Transcription is of course necessary. The names of people and places on the other side of the world must be accessible when they are needed. For those who do not read a foreign language, works in that language do not exist if not in translation and rendered in the script of their own tongue. The works of Leo Tolstoy (Lev Tolstoi), the teachings of the Koran (Qur'ān), the thoughts of Mao Tse-tung (Mao Zedong) must be findable in a recognizable form in a primarily English-language catalogue, no matter how their authors wrote their names or titled their books in the original languages. Arguments for standardization of romanization and other conversion tables remain pressing.

Equally cogent are the arguments for making, not a single

catalogue incorporating transcribed headings for works in vernacular scripts, but a number of specialized catalogues, each drawn up wholly in its own script. Hans Wellisch concludes that:

the choice lies between a continuation of the present practice of wholesale romanization which creates bibliographic chaos under a thin veneer of apparent order, at steep costs for the operators and with small or non-existing benefits for the users, and a system that is demonstrably less costly (because several stages of conversion are eliminated) and offers increased benefits to the users (which constitute an indirect cost reduction).[57]

Sumner Spalding, whose long experience in the Processing Department of the Library of Congress and whose long involvement with the Anglo-American cataloguing rules lend authority to his judgement, is of the same opinion.[58] Having called romanization 'a can of worms' and the universal catalogue (so far as author and title entries are concerned) 'a snare and a delusion' benefiting only the filer, he recommends separate catalogues for each writing system. 'The alphabetical subject catalogue is the catalogue in which the concept of universality has real significance', he says. (He might have included the classified subject catalogue.) He goes on to suggest adding a symbol for each non-Roman writing system (or language) to the subject heading for each publication. This would automatically group together, first Roman-alphabet records, then non-Roman, by system (or language), each system being subarranged according to its proper sequence. (The same effect is produced in the classified arrangement of the Indian National Bibliography – see p.109.)

For names originating in non-Roman forms for which romanized forms are required as subject headings, Spalding gives criteria in order of preference: 1) an established form in English-language reference sources, editions and translations; 2) the form already established in the catalogue; 3) the form resulting from romanization according to a) the ISO system (where one exists) or b) the LC/ALA system. References would, of course, be made from alternative transcriptions. International conformity would not be required here, says Spalding, because the field is confined to the English-language, subject-heading system. (He writes 'system' in the singular!)

For translations and added entries in the general author catalogue and for musical compositions, Spalding proposes the same criteria as for the subject catalogue. References to the forms used in the general catalogue should be provided in the non-Roman-script catalogues.

As Spalding points out, and as I have indicated in the preceding chapter, countries which do not use the Roman alphabet do not force other scripts into a transcribed form in their own script. Why should we? 'Romanization', it has been said, 'is an insult to the language and literature of another country'.[59] Given the emotions evoked by a native language and script, one is inclined to agree, reserving transliteration for those cases where to leave it unapplied would render information inaccessible.

Some general works of reference

In addition to particular citations already made, the following works give a more general introduction to the study of languages and scripts for practical purposes.

The beginning of the use of letters and their adoption and development in different forms for writing in different parts of the world and the resultant alphabets are described by David Diringer in his *The alphabet: a key to the history of mankind* (3rd ed. New York: Funk and Wagnall; London: Hutchinson, 1968, 2 vols, Vol. 1 (473p) text; Vol. 2 (452p) illustrations.

Marcel Cohen's *La grande invention de l'écriture et son évolution* (Paris: Imprimerie nationale: Klinesieck, 1958, 3 vols) traces the development and use of writing in vol. 1, gives references, notes and index in vol. 2, and a sheaf of illustrative plates in vol. 3.

Les langues du monde, par un groupe de linguistes sous la direction de A. Meillet et Marcel Cohen (Nouvelle édition, Paris: Centre national de la recherche scientifique, 1952. Réimpression 1964, xlii, 1297p. in 2 vols) gives some history of each language, its main characteristics, where it is spoken and for which languages its alphabet is used. Bibliographies are also given.

Georg F. von Ostermann's *Manual of foreign languages for the use of librarians, bibliographers, research workers, editors, translators and printers* (4th edition, New York: Central Book Co, 1952) was compiled from the author's experience as Foreign-Language Editor in the US Government Printing Office. For each language the alphabet (or script) is shown. For many of the languages an indication of the pronunciation of each symbol is given and, where relevant, a generally accepted transcription into the Roman alphabet. (Since the work was published there have been changes in some of the scripts and transcriptions, so that the tables do not necessarily reflect current practice.) There are also notes on the language, its syllabification, accents, articles and a modicum of grammar, and tables which give the vernacular names for the cardinal and ordinal numbers, months, days, seasons and the generic words for the units of time.

More up to date is Kenneth Katzner's *The languages of the world* (London; New York: Routledge and Kegan Paul, rev. ed. 1986, 376p), which shows languages and scripts and the countries where they are used.

C. G. Allen's *A manual of European languages for librarians* (London; New York: Bowker, in association with the London School of Economics, 1975, 4th corrected impression 1981, 803p) has, as its name implies, been designed specifically to help librarians who must arrange, catalogue, or use books in languages unfamiliar to them. It is restricted to European languages, but they are given fuller treatment than by Ostermann. The languages are grouped by families: Germanic; Latin and Romance; Celtic, Greek and Albanian; Slavonic; Baltic; Finno-Ugrian; Others (Maltese, Turkish, Basque and Esperanto). A pattern of exposition is followed for each language: a specimen passage followed by general remarks on the language; bibliolinguistics – a detailed analysis of the use of the language on title pages of books and in periodicals, followed by a glossary – and a grammatical section comprising essential information, and where necessary warnings, on the alphabet, phonetics and spelling; articles; nouns; adjectives; numerals; pronouns; verbs; adverbs; prepositions; conjunctions; particles; word-formation.

Another work written for librarians is Gregory Walker's *Russian for librarians* (2nd ed. London: Bingley, 1983, 120p). Its 'Russian course' and 'Notes on cataloguing' bring in vocabulary likely to occur frequently in the front matter (and colophon) of Russian texts, and a section on Soviet publishing practice is augmented with notes on acquisition and lending, and a list of bibliographies and reference works. Among his list of Russian-English dictionaries Walker recommends as 'the standard work for general use' *The Oxford Russian-English dictionary* (Oxford: Clarendon Press, 1972). The English-Russian volume, ed. by P. S. Falla, appeared in 1984.

Handbook of oriental history, by members of the Department of Oriental History, School of Oriental and African Studies, University of London; edited by C. H. Philips (London: Royal Historical Society, 1951, 265p) gives notes for each area – the Near and Middle East, India and Pakistan, South-East Asia and the Archipelago, China, Japan – on romanization of words, formation of personal names and titles, geographical names, calendars and systems of dating, and dynasties and rulers.

African languages: a guide to the library collection of the University of Virginia, by Mary Alice Kraehe, Cristina W. Sharretts and Christine H. Guyonneau (2nd ed. Charlottesville, Va.: University of Virginia Library, 1986) lists dictionaries, grammars and teaching materials by language families.

Hans H. Wellisch's *The conversion of scripts, its nature history and utilization* (New York; Chichester; Wiley, 1978, 500p) is a long and thorough examination of the subject, with a good index and bibliography.

A. J. Walford and J. E. O. Screen have compiled a *Guide to foreign-language courses and dictionaries* (3rd edition, London: Library Association, 1977, 343p). The book covers most European languages and Russian, Arabic, Japanese and Chinese, assembling for each language notes on courses, textbooks, audio-visual materials, and dictionaries. The University of Exeter, in its series 'Exeter tapes', has produced a number of sound cassettes for learning foreign languages.

Dictionaries of all kinds are included in Wolfram Zaunmüller's *Bibliographisches Handbuch der Sprachwörterbücher: internationales Verzeichnis von 5600 Wörterbüchern der Jahre 1460-1958 für mehr als 500 Sprachen und Dialekte* (Stuttgart: Hiersemann, 1958, xvi, 495p).

Walford's *Guide to reference material* (4th ed. London: Library

Association, 1980-6, 3 vols, is more selective and more recent. Dictionaries which explain and translate the vocabulary of individual subjects are distributed throughout the volumes according to the subject, language dictionaries being in volume 3.

References

1 Ostermann, Georg F. von, *Manual of foreign languages for the use of librarians, bibliographers, research workers, editors, translators, and printers.* 4th ed. New York: Central Book Co, 1952.

2 Wellisch, Hans H., *The conversion of scripts: its nature, history and utilization.* New York; Chichester: Wiley, 1978, 232-45.

3 Kishibe, K., 'Cataloguing books in Chinese', *International cataloguing*, 3(1), 1974, 4.

4 Elrod, J. McRee, 'The two-language collection with the bilingual reader', *International cataloguing*, 3(1), 1972, 6-8.

5 Musiker, R., 'Bilingual catalogues: a survey of South African practice', *South African libraries*, 30(4), 1963, 130-3.

6 'The catalogues of the British Museum: 1. Printed books', by F. C. Francis, *Journal of documentation*, 4(1), 1948, 14-40; '2. Manuscripts', by T. C. Skeat, *Journal of documentation*, 7(1), 1951, 18-60; '3. Oriental printed books and manuscripts', by F. C. Francis, *Journal of documentation*, 7(3), 1951, 170-83.

7 Pearson, J. D., *Oriental and Asian bibliography.* London: Lockwood, 1966, 164-234.

8 Collison, Robert and Moon, Brenda, *Directory of libraries and special collections on Asia and North Africa*, London: Lockwood, 1970.

9 Malinconico, S. Michael, 'Vernacular scripts in the NYPL automated bibliographic control system', *Journal of library automation*, 10(3), September 1977, 205-25. (21 references)

10 Khrenkova, A. A., 'The experience of libraries in the USSR', *International cataloguing*, 2(4), 1973, 7.

11 Siew, K. Y., 'Cataloguing the multi-language collections of the National Library Singapore', *International cataloguing*, 1(2), 1972, 7-8, and 1(3), 1972, 5-7.

12 Mehta, J. C., 'Problems in Delhi Public Library', *International cataloguing*, 2(1), 1972, 5-6.

13 Wells, A. J., *in S. R. Ranganathan, 1892-1972: papers given at a memorial meeting on Thursday, 25th January, 1973*; ed, by Edward Dudley. London: LA, 1974, 13.

14 Downing, Joel C., 'The Indian National Bibliography – its

present state and future prospects', *Library resources and technical services*, 28(1), January/March 1984, 20-4.

15 Aurousseau, M., *The rendering of geographical names*. London: Hutchinson, 1957, 96-104.
16 Jones, Sir William, 'A dissertation on the orthography of Asiatik words in roman letters', *in The works of Sir William Jones*. London: Stockdale, 1807, vol. 3, 252-318.
17 Pearson, J. D., 'Languages of Asia, with special reference to the Islamic world', *The indexer*, 11(2), 1978, 65-6.
18 *The Guardian*, 29 November, 1966.
19 Wade, Sir Thomas, *Yü-yeñ tzǔ-êrh chi. . . a progressive course designed to assist the student of colloquial Chinese*. London: Trübner, 1867.
20 Giles, Herbert, *A Chinese-English dictionary*. 2nd ed. London: Quaritch, 1912.
21 *Reform of the Chinese written language*. (Six speeches by Chou En-lai and others.) Peking: Foreign Language P., 1958, 60.
22 Legeza, Ireneus László, *Guide to transliterated Chinese in the modern Peking dialect*. Leiden: Brill, 1968 – . (To be completed in 3 vols.)
23 Peyrefitte, Alain, *Quand la Chine s'éveillera*. Paris: Fayard, 1972, 153.
24 See reference 23 above, 154.
25 *Library science abstracts*, 6, November/December, 1970, abstract No. 70/2514 of Japanese original.
26 *Union catalogue of Asian publications, 1965-1970*; ed. by David E. Hall. . . at the School of Oriental and African Studies, University of London. London: Mansell, 1971.
27 *Index islamicus: a catalogue of articles on islamic subjects in periodicals and other collective publications*; compiled by J. D. Pearson and others. Primary sequence 1906-1955. 4th printing 1978. Four five-yearly supplements. Continued by *The quarterly index islamicus*, 1977- . Cumulated five-yearly. All published by Mansell, London.
28 Pearson, Hilda M., 'The encyclopaedia of Islam and its index', *The indexer*, 13(1), April 1982, 33-5.
29 International Organization for Standardization, *Transliteration of Arabic characters into Latin characters*. 1984. (ISO 233).
30 International Organization for Standardization, *Transliteration of Hebrew characters into Latin characters*. 1984 (ISO 259).
31 International Organization for Standardization, *Transliteration of Slavic Cyrillic characters into Latin characters*. 1986 (ISO 9).
32 International Organization for Standardization, *International*

system for the transliteration of Greek characters into Latin characters. (ISO/R843 1968.)

33 British Standards Institution, *Transliteration of Arabic characters*. (BS 4280: 1968. Reissued 1983.)

34 Association française de normalisation, *Translittération des charactères arabes en caractères latins*. (FD. Z no. 46-002).

35 American National Standards Institute, *American national standards system for the romanization of Arabic*. New York: ANSI, 1972.

36 American National Standards Institute, *Romanisation of Hebrew*. New York: ANSI, 1975. (pp.14-15, keypunch-compatible transliteration style.)

37 *Cataloguing rules, author and title entries*; compiled by committees of the Library Association and of the American Library Association. English ed. London: LA, 1908, 72.

38 See reference 31 above.

39 Library of Congress. Processing Department, *Cataloging service bulletin*, 119, Fall 1976, 63.

40 British Standards Institution, *Transliteration of Cyrillic and Greek characters*. 1958 (BS 2979); and *'British' system for transliteration of modern Cyrillic*. 1959 (BS 2979C). Both reissued 1983.

41 Gosudarstvennyi Komitet Standartov Soveta Ministrov SSSR, *Transliteratsiya russkikh slov latinskimi bukvami*. 1971. (Gost 16876-71)

42 United States Board on Geographic Names, *Romanization guide*. Washington, D.C.: The Board, 1972.

43 Association française de normalisation. *Translittération des caractères cyrilliques slaves*. 1971. (NF 46-001)

44 Deutsche Normenausschuss. *Transliteration slawischer kyrillischer Buchstaben*. 1962. (DIN 1460)

45 Steyskal, George C., 'A plain-letter romanization for Russian', *Library resources and technical services*, 24(2), Spring 1980, 170-3.

46 Gilîarevskiĭ, R. S. and Krylova, N. V., 'Transliteratsiîa bibliograficheskikh opisaniĭ na îazykakh narodov SSSR latinskimi bukvami' ('Transliteration of bibliographic entries in the languages of the USSR with letters of the Latin alphabet'), *Sovetskaîa bibliografia*, 5(63), 1960, 37-44. (Translated into French, together with the Royal Society's animadversions on Cyrillic transliteration, in an article: 'La translittération des caractères cyrilliques à propos de deux articles récents', *Bulletin des bibliothèques de France*, 6(6), 1961, 279-92.)

47 International Organization for Standardization. *Transliteration of alphabets of non-Slavic languages of the Soviet Union using Cyrillic characters*. 1974. (ISO/DP 2805)

48 British Standards Institution, *Guide to the romanization of Chinese*. BSI, 1978. (PD 6483; under revision, 1987)
49 See reference 23 above.
50 British Standards Institution, *Specification for the romanization of Japanese*. BSI, 1972. (BS 4812; reissued 1983. An international standard is also under consideration – DIS 3602)
51 *Cataloging rules of the American Library Association and the Library of Congress: additions and changes 1949-1958*. Washington, D. C.: LC, 1959, 47-57.
52 American National Standards Institute. *American national standard system for the romanization of Japanese*. ANSI Z39. 11. 1972.
53 Romanization tables developed in LC, reviewed by ALA's Descriptive Cataloging Committee and currently valid, are printed in LC's Processing Department's bulletin *Cataloging service*, 118, Summer 1976. Some of the tables are reprints, having appeared in earlier issues of the bulletin, others are previously unpublished or revisions of previously issued tables. Further tables appear in *Cataloging service*, 119-25, and its continuation *Cataloging service bulletin*, 1 – , Summer 1978 – .
54 Wellisch, Hans H., 'Script conversion practices in the world's libraries', *International library review*, 8(1), 1976, 55-84. (19 tables, 10 references, quotation, 66.)
55 Report of ABACUS meeting, March 1978 in *BLBSD newsletter*, 11, November 1978, 9.
56 Whitrow, Magda, 'The *Isis cumulative bibliography*, 1913-1965', *The indexer*, 13(3), 1983, 158-65.
57 See reference 2 above, 418.
58 Spalding C. Sumner, 'Romanization re-examined', *Library resources and technical services*, 21, Winter 1977, 3-12.
59 Moran, M. L., 'Further considerations on romanization: Saudi Arabia', *International library review*, 13(3), July 1981, 276-85.

8

Subject catalogues—introduction

Identifying the subject of a document

The perfect cataloguer is, of course, omniscient. The lucky cataloguer has the good fortune to work within the subject of his own preferred interest, but most of us have to handle, recognize and introduce to our readers a wide variety of topics, viewpoints and forms of presentation, and must draw on experience, skill in the use of reference tools, intuition and sheer lifemanship to help us bridge the gap between our ignorance and an acceptable indication of the author's intention and achievement. We cannot study a subject until we master it before venturing to assign to a book a place on the shelf or a heading in the catalogue:

> Imagine the whole, then execute the parts –
> Fancy the fabric
> Quite, ere you build, ere steel strike fire from quartz,
> Ere mortar dab brick!

Browning's Grammarian would have made an exasperating librarian! Gradually, with reading and experience, a practical mastery is acquired, and with specialization, if that can be indulged, a more satisfying skill. Students are often distressed by the superficiality which is imposed on them when they are asked to catalogue books on a variety of different subjects, many of them in fields quite unfamiliar, but it is necessary to enlarge one's view, to discern the relationships which link subjects and to acquire a certain dexterity with specialist nomenclature – in short, to accept cataloguing as a practical means to an end and not an end in itself, just as one takes the London Underground from Waterloo Station to Piccadilly without first studying transport engineering – but not without first taking a look at the map of the Underground system. Dictionaries and encyclopaedia articles are obvious resources for the preliminary mapping. Is one totally ignorant of medicine? Anatomy is discovered to be about the structure of the body, Physiology about its functions, Pathology about its illnesses, and so on – a rough drawing of boundaries that will make further exploration easier. To know the name of a thing is to wield some power over it. If one knows nothing of a subject then no signal, however rudimentary, is to be despised. Do the illustrations in a book on the production of nitrogen show a laboratory bench or factory machinery? The answer will point one towards Chemistry or Chemical Technology. Is the language of a book on railways that of Engineering or of Economics? Is the author of a book on the brain described as a professor of anatomy or as a professor of psychology? Does the introduction to a book say for what readership it was intended, for example, is a book on making clothes written for the home dressmaker or the garment trade? Is the ostensible subject of a book on the anatomy of apes the real subject, or was the author's purpose to show the evolutionary descent of man? The whole of knowledge can now be no one's province, but there is no need to let the limits of previous study for ever fence one in.

It would not have been difficult to assign a volume to a shelf in a monastic library. A new book of herbal remedies would take its place with half-a-dozen other books on Physick, and that would be that. A modern book on diet, however, might be addressed to the housewife, the hospital dietician, the student of human metabolism, the economist studying world food supplies. 'Physick' like other subjects has split up and its aspects have multiplied. In Maunsell's catalogue of 1595, 'Cookerie, which is Phisicke of the Kitchen' shows an early step in the division. The cataloguer must establish the specific subject of a book within its context, take into account the purpose for which it has been written, the standpoint of the author, the limitations of time and place within which the subject has been studied, and the intended readership. Much of this information can be gathered from the title page, the list of contents, the style and content of the illustrations, the name of the series in which the book is published, possibly in

140

conjunction with the names of other volumes in the series; perhaps a preface will explicitly state the author's purpose and the readership he had in mind. Obviously the title of a work is of prime importance in designating its content. Generally speaking, the title has been chosen to be memorable, unique or significant – qualities which do not necessarily support each other, nor do they have equal value in all kinds of writing. To be explicit and accurate a title may need to be long, which is no handicap for an article in a learned journal, but it becomes an immediate practical problem if it has to be lettered on the spine of a book: and the longer it is, the less memorable it is likely to be and the more chance it has of being wrongly cited.

Scientific terms, by definition, aim to be unambiguous. *A textbook of botany* declares itself to be presenting the basic facts about plants as living organisms, ignoring all other aspects, such as the horticultural or decorative. Other words have overtones, which the writer may deliberately make use of, notably in direct quotation, or which the reader may unconsciously supply. *Amurath to Amurath* will be significant only to those acquainted with the history of the Ottoman empire; even those potential readers the author has preferred to lure with a touch of mystery rather than writing baldly: *A journey through the Ottoman lands*. The title *Field crops* is likely to arouse expectations of barley and potatoes if read by an East Anglian farmer, of maize and soya beans if read by a farmer in Illinois. Names are not concrete things but abstractions. They suggest not only an aggregate of essential qualities but also a host of attributes that will be associated with them variously by different people according to their own experience of using them and finding them used. It is the cataloguer's job to interpret or to amplify the statement made by the author, to find the classification symbol or the subject heading that will place a work together with others on the same subject and that, read in conjunction with the bibliographic description, will enable the reader to decide whether the book will suit his needs or not. (The book has been used in this chapter as representative of all library materials.)

Few books that come into a library have a single, self-evident subject that can be summed up in a single word. The subject itself may be a more, or less, complicated amalgam of ideas than an unqualified word can suggest. In addition, the author may have imposed limitations on his exploration of the subject by choosing only certain aspects, or certain occurrences in time and space. The work will necessarily take some physical form, such as monograph, report, statistical tables. Its function in the library may also be relevant: is the book perhaps for reference only, or for relegation to a collection of historical, non-current material?

Formulae for subject analysis

PMEST

It is therefore a help to have some formula for subject analysis. One such formula is Ranganathan's PMEST (= Personality, Matter, Energy, Space, Time), where Personality is the thing which forms the real subject in its context, the object of the author's concentration, Matter the matter which may be connected with it, Energy the activity concerned, Space and Time the geographical location and historical period which have limited the extent of the study. Application of this formula identifies the categories, or facets (to use Ranganathan's own word), into which a subject may be divided, and pinpoints the specific topic within each of the facets. It thus produces a brief and formal statement of the subject of a book, beginning with the most concrete element and adding other elements in decreasing order of concreteness. A facet is left unfilled if its content is too diffuse to be meaningful or if it is considered to be irrelevant. For example, a book on making glass-fibre lifeboats might be analysed thus:

Personality	Matter	Energy	Space	Time	Form
Engineering	Plastics	Construction	–	–	–
Shipbuilding	Glass-fibre				
Lifeboats	reinforced				

The Space and Time facets have been left blank, the construction being unaffected by geographical location and the interest being presumed to be contemporary.

A history of steamships in the 19th century (written from the engineering point of view) might be analysed:

142

Personality	Matter	Energy	Space	Time	Form
Engineering	–	History	–	1801-1900	–
Shipbuilding					
Steamships					

Building the 'Great Eastern' might be analysed:

Personality	Matter	Energy	Space	Time	Form
Engineering	Iron	Construction	Great	1850s	–
Shipbuilding			Brit-		
Steamships			ain		
'Great Eastern'					

The assumption here is that a monograph is the expected medium. The form facet has therefore been left blank. All other media are to be designated, as periodical, film, etc. (In descriptive cataloguing 'monographic' has assumed the meaning of printed material in the form of 'books, pamphlets and single sheets' (*AACR2*, rule 2.0A), and 'non-serial publications' (*ISBD(M)*, p.vii). Thus an encyclopaedia, which may be about everything, because it is conveniently described by the same rules as those for monographs, is included under the same term. In classification and subject cataloguing a distinction is made.)

Personality, Matter, Energy, Space and Time are very general concepts, which require a frame of reference and complementary subdivision if they are to be of practical use in subject analysis. Time and Space correspond easily to accepted geographical and chronological distinctions. Energy may represent a physical activity, such as 'construction' above, or a mental activity, a consideration of the subject from a particular point of view, as 'history' above. Matter may need to be further categorized as being of a certain kind or with certain characteristics, as 'Plastics, *reinforced with glass-fibre*'. Personality begs a very large question. The specific subject may be a kind of thing, a species of a genus, such as a steamship singled out from the class of ships, or, to take another example, a bricklayer singled out from the class of building workers; or, as in the *Great Eastern* example, it may be a unique member of a class of things.

Most definitions in common discourse assign a particular thing to its class and go on to say what is the difference between it and the generality of things with which it has been classed: its shape, purpose, behaviour and so on. Another frequently used kind of definition indicates a larger whole of which the thing being defined forms a constituent part, as semantics is that branch of philology which deals with meaning. Thus the specific subject of a book may be a particular variety of a thing, as an oak is a kind of tree; or a part of a thing, such as the root system of a tree or the retina of an eye; or a property of a thing, such as the flammability of a fabric. Always the whole, or possessor, must be identified first and assigned to its context.

The context, or frame of reference inferred in the examples above, is a structure consisting of the generally accepted broader disciplines, so that, for example, Engineering has been regarded as a manifestation of Personality although clearly, as a verbal noun, the word Engineering must imply a concept of energy. Within the narrowed context of the subject statement, the formula PMEST reveals the roles of the different ideas in their relationship to each other. Since its first use in the Colon classification in the 1930s, Ranganathan has elaborated the formula, responding to the increased demands of documentation and to the work of others interested in classification, such as the Classification Research Group. He gave a very clear exposition of the use of PMEST at a seminar held at Rutgers University in 1964.[1]

PRECIS

Another method for arriving at a brief statement of the content of a publication, which brings to the fore the real subject, is that designed by Derek Austin as a prior requisite to establishing a PRECIS index string. Austin's analysis requires a preliminary division of topics into Entities and Activities. Analysis of a compound subject may reveal more than one entity or activity. The subject of the book by D. J. Foskett entitled *Classification and indexing in the social sciences* is analysed as *Entity*: social sciences; *Activities*: 1) classification; 2) indexing. Each entity may be qualified as being of a particular kind, or it may be part of a larger entity. *How to look after your Siamese* is analysed as *Entity*: Cats – *kind*: Siamese; *Activity*: care. *Assigning subject headings in a dictionary catalogue* is analysed as *Entity*: catalogues – *kind*: dictionary – *part*: headings – *kind*: subject;

144

Activity: assigning. The correct relationships between all identified separate concepts must be established. Parts and properties of entities are subordinated to the entities to which they belong, or to the parts of entities, if it is the parts they qualify.

The functions of the entities (each with its own property or part, where these are present) are identified as being the agents (subjects) or patients (objects) of the activities. The 'key system', or real subject, is judged to be the object of a transitive action or the subject of an intransitive action. (The term 'system' is used as a reminder that any one thing is an integration of related parts which function together to make the thing what it is, as, for example, a hand (an entity) is made of bones and blood and muscles and nerves, etc., interacting in such a way that a hand is created.) Thus *Machines for testing gas-turbines in aircraft* might be analysed as *Entities*: 1) machines; 2) aircraft – *part*: turbine – *kind* (of part): gas-driven; *Activity*: testing. Machines are the agent of the testing, the turbines the patient, so the key system is aircraft gas-turbines. (A fuller description of PRECIS and its methods of analysis is given on pp.206-14.)

A good introduction to the principles and practice of subject analysis can be found in Mills's[2] and A. C. Foskett's[3] textbooks. General recommendations on how to examine documents, determine their subjects and select indexing terms are given in a British standard.[4] Procedures for identifying subjects with the specificity appropriate to various situations have been summarized by Coates,[5] Foskett,[6] Langridge[7] and Vickery,[8] who also show examples of the entries produced.

On not being misled

Not all books have such self-evident subjects as those used here as examples. Without dividing a general subject, an author may concentrate on one aspect of it, such as the historical or legal or terminological. Both the classified and the alphabetical subject catalogues allow such books to be kept together and distinguished from books on other aspects by employing 'standard subdivisions' or qualifiers, as, SCIENCE – History; PUBLIC HEALTH – Law and regulations; BOTANY – Nomenclature.

It is easy to give a false value to words occurring in a title which are identical with names of aspects or of common sub-divisions singled out to be specified in subject arrangement, that is, to classify the words and not the meaning. *What research tells the coach about swimming* is a book on coaching swimmers, the techniques advocated being based on the findings of investigations into human physiology and the dynamics of objects propelled through water. *A directory of graduate research in chemistry*, on the other hand, tells what *research* is being carried out and where and by whom. Research as such is part of the subject of the second book, but not of the first. Similarly, a book entitled *The study of poetry* may be concerned with what it is in poetry that can be studied, how that study can be carried out, to whom it is of value, and so on; whereas *A study of English lyric poetry* is the writer's considered opinion of the subject. *Studies in Victorian poetry* is a book of *essays* about Victorian poetry – study as an activity is not the author's concern.

A single publication may deal with two distinct subjects, in which case both may need to be shown in the subject catalogue, although only one subject can claim the book on the shelf. *Rhododendrons and azaleas* may be analysed thus: 1) Rhododendrons : cultivation; 2) Azaleas : cultivation. Two subjects may not be so simply related, however, as merely by co-existence within a single treatise. *The Common Market and economic development in Great Britain* is not about two separate subjects within the general sphere of economics; it is about the effect that one has on the other. The real subject is the British economy and what is likely to happen to it when it is faced with wider markets, demands for different commodities, etc. This conclusion can be arrived at by looking for the implied activity and assigning to the entities the roles of agent and patient they play in regard to it. *Activity*: influence; *Entity*: 1) Common Market (agent), 2) Great Britain economic conditions (patient, thence key system). Clearly information on an aspect of the Common Market which has been judged to be subordinate to another subject must not be hidden from potential users because a book can stand in only one place. Some entry in the catalogue – a secondary subject entry, reference, or index entry – must represent the secondary subject.

It may be found in analysing the subject content of a book that the subject which appears to be the most concrete is not necessarily the real object of the author's concern. J. Z. Young, in writing about the reactions of his octopus to certain stimuli, is describing his use of the octopus to find out about primitive nervous systems, about how the brain works and not about the behaviour of octopuses. All other 'guinea-pigs' are equally a medium for some specified inquiry. Places, likewise, which may constitute the subject of historical and descriptive works, may in other works be only elements of minor importance, not so much qualifying a subject as simply limiting its extent to manageable dimensions. A survey of why and how individuals live alone may be undertaken in Earl's Court because that is a district of London richer in bed-sitters than, say, the town of Retford, and though the survey throws light on some aspects of London life, its real object may be a sociological study of loneliness. Similarly, the effect of closing a coal-pit on the community it has sustained may be studied in a single mining village, but the locality is merely the study area and not the study itself.

Within any one library the nature of the collection and the demands of the readership are likely to create a bias to which the cataloguer must submit. *Prospects of opencast mining in Snowdonia* may be attracted to Investment in a financial library, to Pollution in a library of environmental studies. The most pertinent question in assigning its subject is: why did the library acquire the book? Studying out of a library context, in the unreal situation of a school of librarianship, the student lacks a clear answer to such a question, nor can he, as Savage suggests, in a very lively little book on classification, take the book to the shelves and see where it looks at home.[9]

Thus, in seeking to specify the subject of a document, considerations may have to be taken into account which qualify the whole subject, such as the author's point of view, or the geographical area or time span covered by the study, or the special interest of the library acquiring the document.

Forms of presentation
The way a subject has been presented is also pertinent to the use of the resultant document. Essays or papers in a symposium treat a subject selectively but discursively; statistics are again selective but not expositive; a code is a series of practical

recommendations – each form has a readership that will not necessarily be satisfied with an alternative form.

Similarly physical form may affect use. A book may be read in the train, or at home, but a set of microfiches will have to be consulted in the library.

All the above qualifications – space, time, point of view, form of presenting the subject content ('inner form') and physical form of the published document ('outer form') – may be relevant and should be expressed, generally in that order, in extension of the subject statement.

Making known the identified subject

Such analysis does not necessarily yield the terminology or the verbal sequence required for insertion into any particular subject catalogue or index. But it does identify the subject. Equivalent class notation and subject headings or index entries are usually sought in a chosen classification scheme and authority list of subject terms.

Having regard to the needs of a general academic or public library, where readers expect to find an arrangement of books which corresponds broadly to the conventions accepted in dividing the universe into coherent areas for study and for publishing the literature designed to promote or record what has been discovered, such a framework as the one proposed above, based on the several disciplines, proves to be convenient and reasonably obvious. It conforms, in H. E. Bliss's phrase, to the 'scientific and educational consensus',[10] or, as Wyndham Hulme expressed it, it follows 'literary warrant'.[11] It is certainly true that access to the shelves is itself an education if the reader can survey the extent and the ramifications of his subject and at least some of the relationships between the parts. Using a classified catalogue he has the same facility, but, particularly with a card catalogue, it is less easy to take in the whole plan of the arrangement, although guides both outside and within the catalogue can show the sequence of subjects and some relationships between them.

A subject is displayed by grouping together the books which treat it similarly and separating them from other books which concern other subjects or the same subject in different aspects, and by ordering the groups in a logical pattern, which is repeated for other subjects. One pattern of proven utility is that which presents first the general subject treated generally, and proceeds through aspects of the general subject to its parts, treating each of the parts generally and particularly, and coming down by subdivision to the smallest parts of those parts. Because the sequence is linear and not even diagrammatic, the viewer must accept the need for continual juxtapositions of the tail of one subject and the head of another. But man is a classifying animal – simply to name is to classify – and an ordered sequence is the only one in which we can function. There are, of course, many acceptable orders.

Entries in the subject catalogue

In making a classified catalogue, the frame of reference will inevitably be the chosen classification scheme. In making an alphabetical subject catalogue the frame of reference will be that inferred from the list of subject headings used, although the subject analysis which must precede any search for terms may follow any appropriate pattern. As we shall see, the classified catalogue makes use of the full subject analysis to determine the point of entry of a subject in the catalogue and may also use the steps in the analysis to construct the alphabetical index which guides the reader to the file in classified order. The dictionary catalogue needs the analysis to determine the subject before assigning it a name, and also to provide a system of references from related subjects.

The two forms of subject catalogue most generally in use are, as I have already implied, the alphabetical subject catalogue, which indicates the subject of a publication by name at the head of each entry and arranges the entries according to the alphabetical sequence of their headings, and the classified catalogue, which denotes the subject of a publication by its classification symbol in the chosen classification scheme and arranges the entries according to the sequence of classification symbols. The classified catalogue is supplemented by an alphabetical index which leads a searcher from the name of his required subject to the notation in the classified sequence.

The entry in the subject catalogue must give a description of the publication being catalogued which is at least as full as the description in the author catalogue. In the subject catalogue information is being presented to the reader concerning publications about which he may know nothing at all. If a library user looks up an entry in the author catalogue, he does so because he knows that some publication exists written by the author whose name he is looking under, and if he also knows the title he wants, often the only information he needs from the catalogue is where to find the book on the shelves.

But a reader using the subject catalogue is asking a whole series of questions, namely: Has the library any book or books on my subject? If so, whom are they by? When were they written? Are they presented in such a way that they will be useful to me at my present stage of knowledge of the subject? The reader thus needs to see the complete formal description of the book, and will often be grateful for an additional word or two of annotation.

The catalogue can also draw the reader's attention to subjects treated in parts of books, subjects which either do not form part of the predominant subject matter or which have particular importance for the users of a specific library – items relating to the locality or institution which the library serves are an obvious example. Such entries are called analytical entries. They can greatly increase the usefulness of a library's stock.

If the reader has access to the shelves, he can handle the books and make his selection after comparing the volumes themselves, which would probably be more satisfactory *if* all the books (and parts of books) could be placed physically together and not in different parts of the library and if no books were absent from the shelves because they were in use, or with the binders or in transit between one service and the next. In practice there tends to be multiple demand for certain books at certain times and it may happen that the most appropriate books for a particular use will *not* be on the shelves when a reader searches for them. If he has learnt how to use his library, he can identify the most helpful books from the catalogue and, if they are not on the shelf, can ask for them to be recalled for his use. In some libraries, either because of the size or value of their collections or because of the difficulty of supervising readers, the readers have no access to the shelves – apart from those housing the reading-room collection – and must therefore of necessity use the catalogue. The library staff,

150

particularly the subject specialist and the reference librarian, will also be assiduous users of the catalogue. If their questions can be answered speedily and recourse to the shelves for books which prove irrelevant prevented, the subject catalogue will be fulfilling another of its functions.

Who should make the subject catalogue?

It will be apparent by now that classification and subject cataloguing are basically the same operation. It is obviously an economical use of manpower to have new accessions handled only once by a single member of staff for both classification and subject cataloguing. Opinions vary, however, whether this task should be done by subject specialists or by cataloguers. In the University of East Anglia, for example, subject specialists were made responsible for book selection and bibliographic work within their subjects. They also classified and assigned subject headings to new accessions – work which constituted in the librarian's words, 'scholarship of no mean order' – although they did not make the catalogue.[12] In the University of Leicester, on the other hand, division of work based on subject specialization was replaced by a more functional arrangement, and 'valuable experience was gained in operating a centralized cataloguing and classification department, and a larger volume of current cataloguing and classification work was completed with greater economy and consistency than hitherto' and arrears of cataloguing were made up.[13] Perhaps, since so few people were involved in either case, it is a question here of personal commitment. In very large libraries, where language specialization is also pertinent, a certain amount of subject specialization is found among the cataloguing staff, who generally handle both descripive and subject cataloguing. Now that cataloguing within a particular institution is becoming more and more a process of identifying and amending entries distributed through a network, a centralized cataloguing department is becoming a practical necessity.

In reporting a survey of subject specialization in British university libraries undertaken in 1981, Woodhead and Martin conclude: 'With university income diminishing, subject specialization may become increasingly less feasible in future, and it seemed appropriate to record the situation before major changes occur, as indeed several of the replies in our survey indicated would happen. In retrospect, we may be seen to have been recording the high-water mark of subject specialization in British university libraries.[14]

References

1 Ranganathan, S. R., *The Colon classification*. New Brunswick, N.J.: Graduate School of Library Service, Rutgers, the State University, 1965. (Rutgers series on systems for the intellectual organization of information, vol. 4.)
2 Mills, J., *A modern outline of library classification*. London: Chapman & Hall, 1960.
3 Foskett, A. C., *The subject approach to information*. 4th ed. London: Bingley, 1982.
4 British Standards Institution, *British standard recommendations for examining documents, determining their subjects and selecting indexing terms*. London: BSI, 1984. (BS 6529)
5 Coates, E. J., *Subject catalogues: headings and structure*. London: LA, 1960.
6 Foskett, D. J., *Classification and indexing in the social sciences*. London: Butterworths, 1963.
7 Langridge, Derek, *Classification and indexing in the humanities*. London: Butterworths, 1976.
8 Vickery, B. C., *Classification and indexing in science*. 3rd ed. London: Butterworths, 1975.
9 Savage, Ernest A., *Manual of book classification and display for public libraries*. London: Allen & Unwin and LA, 1946.
10 Bliss, H. E., *A bibliographic classification*. New York: Wilson, 1940. (Page 21 points to Bliss's own use of the phrase and refers to the definitions and discussions in his two previous works: *The organization of knowledge and the system of the sciences* and *The organization of knowledge in libraries*.)
11 Hulme, E. Wyndham, 'Principles of book classification'. Six articles in *Library Association record*, vols. 13 and 14, 1911 and 1912.
12 Guttsman, W. L., 'Subject specialization in academic libraries: some preliminary observations on role conflict and organizational stress', *Journal of librarianship*, 5(1), January 1973, 1-8.
13 University of Leicester. Library. *Annual report 1971-72*.
14 Woodhead, P. A. and Martin, J. V., 'Subject specialization in British university libraries: a survey', *Journal of librarianship*, 14(2), April 1982, 93-108. (23 references)

9
Terminology

What it is and why it is important
Every activity has its own vocabulary which names the objects, materials and processes proper to it. The words of that vocabulary are taken from natural language, either as existing words or phrases to which an enlarged, restricted or biased sense is given, or as new words made up from the roots and affixes of natural language. In special cases ideas may be represented by letters or symbols, as in designating chemical elements.

When words or phrases are used with the meaning assigned to them in a specific context they are designated 'terms' and the whole set of terms proper to a particular activity is its 'terminology'. The idea of 'limitation' inherent in the etymology of the word 'term' remains. Even in common parlance, a 'term' is recognized as being a 'specialized word' – we speak of 'a term of address', 'a term of endearment', and our use of the word 'jargon' to denote the terms used by specialist practitioners amongst themselves is derived from that word's pristine sense of distinct language, as in Charles d'Orléans' roundel in celebration of the return of spring:

Il n'y a bête ni oiseau
Qu' en son jargon ne chante ou crie:
Le temps a laissée son manteau
De vent, de froidure et de pluie.

The development and control of the terminology of a science is as important as the progress of the science itself. Indeed, without an agreed terminology, permitting exact specification and unequivocal communication between scientists, there can be no progress. As Lavoisier put it, there is a threefold parallel:

the observed phenomenon of a science, the mental image of that phenomenon, and the word that calls up the mental image. It is impossible, he says, to improve language without increasing knowledge or to make advances in knowledge without progress in language.[1] I have referred in more detail elsewhere to the recognition by scientists of the importance of exact terminology once exact measurement and exact identification of substances became possible, and to the steps taken by chemists, biologists, electrical engineers and others to ensure its control.[2]

As the speed and spread of scientific discovery and technological invention have accelerated, so the need for unambiguous communication has grown, not only between individual practitioners of the various specialities, but also between organizations (many of which did not exist until recently) and between countries (many of which had little say in world affairs until recently). It has been realized that terminologies can no longer be allowed to evolve, like natural language with its receptiveness to alien forms and its wealth of synonyms, but must be controlled both in the use of existing terms and in the creation of new terms to express new ideas, and that standardization of terms in a single language and harmonization of terminologies between different languages are urgent necessities. This realization has led during the present century to the rise of a new 'science' of Terminology, having relations with Philosophy, Psychology, Linguistics and History, whose practical exercises furnish reliable sources for translators, interpreters, diplomatic draughtsmen, editors, writers and researchers, and, of course, cataloguers.

A seminal work is Eugen Wüster's essay on the general theory of terminology[3] which has given rise to a number of articles published in various journals devoted to the study of language, and particularly in the serials published by INFOTERM.

INFOTERM, the International Information Centre for Terminology, was set up by Unesco in conjunction with the Austrian Standards Institute in 1971 as part of the UNISIST programme.[4] INFOTERM's main function is to co-ordinate and publicize terminological activities throughout the world.[5,6] It collects and analyses terminological literature, stores and distributes information on terminology, arranges training sessions and seminars, publishes symposia, bibliographies, and, through a newsletter,[7] current news of work in terminology. A list of INFOTERM's publications up to 1981 is given in *Terminologies for the eighties*, a symposium which contains a special section on the history of INFOTERM's first ten years, its present organization and its plans for the future.[8] Universal co-operation has been made possible through the creation of a network – TermNet – of specialist bodies, one of which, the General Directorate for Terminology and Documentation in Ottawa, publishes *TermNet news*.[9]

The need for standardized terminology for use in scientific communication no longer requires stressing. The compilation and updating of glossaries by the British Standards Institution and the International Organization for Standardization attest its importance for technology and manufacturing. BSI publications in 1985 included glossaries of terms used in building and civil engineering, timber preservation, coffee and its products, and quality assurance. In the realm of international relations it is becoming more and more important to avoid misunderstandings by the use of unequivocal language, as, for example, among the 154 members of the United Nations.[10, 11] The economic and commercial value of standardized terminology is emphasized by the fact that the European Economic Community has asked the Gesellschaft für Information und Dokumentation GmbH, of Frankfurt, to prepare an inventory of all current thesauri which have appeared in at least one of the official languages of the Community, in any country. The information collected is to form a database on DIANE, with the purpose of providing a choice of appropriate documentary language, preventing the duplication of thesauri, and promoting standardization of different thesauri in the same subject field.[12]

Inconsistencies in terminology between different databases at best waste the time of the searcher who must turn from one set of instructions to another when searching different files; at worst they may lead to confusion and incomplete retrieval of data available. Ten years after they were originally voiced, A. R. Haygarth Jackson's complaints are still valid.

There is a need for consistent and controlled indexing vocabularies. Obviously those vocabularies need to be dynamic in order to accommodate changes and advances in knowledge but the end user would like the 'hard core of terms' to remain live for a reasonable period of time... The ease of interrogation of data bases on line would be greatly improved if there was some subject indexing compatibility between data bases and a means of vocabulary conversion, so that a single search query could be addressed to all data bases.[13]

The thesaurus

The vocabularies that are prepared for use in indexing and searching are currently termed thesauri. A thesaurus, in this context, takes its name from Roget's *Thesaurus*, a 'treasury' of English words and phrases, first published in 1852 and frequently updated, which lists words, not alphabetically as in a dictionary, but in groups according to their meaning, within an elaborate classification system. (An alphabetical list of all the words necessarily supplements the classified arrangement and leads to the numbered sections where each word will be found.) A modern thesaurus is generally confined to a single subject or to a group of related subjects. In form it is similar to the prototype in that it is an accumulation of words marshalled into classes or categories, supplemented by an alphabetical list, but its function is to restrict choice and to standardize usage. For any concept within a specified class or category, one term only is prescribed, though rejected terms may be shown and noted as such. If necessary, the precise meaning of the prescribed term is explained. The alphabetical list contains not only the preferred terms listed in the classified display but also synonyms and other rejected words. Hence, while terms accepted by the thesaurus can be checked in a specific context, at the same time access to the vocabulary of chosen terms is permitted through words not acceptable for use in bibliographies and indexes controlled by the thesaurus. Examples of the methods used by individual thesauri are shown in the following chapter.

Terminology an artificial language

A developed terminology is an artificial language. It has a core of terms which usage has sanctioned, whatever their derivation, a set of rules for forming new terms, and, often, a permanent authoritative body to regulate and guide its development and use. 'Impressionism', coined by a scornful critic in reference to Monet's painting entitled *Impression – sunrise*, exhibited in Paris in 1874, has become the accepted designation of a particular school of painting. Rutherford and Soddy reported in 1903: 'An atom of uranium breaks up spontaneously emitting an alpha-ray', and, after adjustment to recognize its true nature as a particle, 'alpha-particle' became an established term in radiation physics. 'Anode' and 'cathode', being less speculative, have more semantic content in their naming: anode, a positive electrode, from Greek *anodos* (ana + hodos, way up) and cathode, a negative electrode, from Greek *cathodos* (cat + hodos, way down).

In sciences and technologies where objects and processes are strictly definable the rules for the formulation of new terms naturally can be stricter than in fields of activity where ideas are more nebulous. In chemistry, for example, a substance should properly be named from a list of roots and affixes which, in combination, indicate its composition, as the name 'copper sulphate' is derived from lists of elements and affixes, the suffix '-ate' denoting a salt derived from the acid of the element, here sulphuric acid.

A systematic nomenclature illustrated by Botany

In Botany and Zoology international codes of nomenclature use the binomial system to identify each species, whereby a generic name is followed by a specific name, both derived from Latin forms, the former an accepted class name, the latter given by the writer who first publishes an acceptable description of the species, as the cabbage white butterfly is designated *Pieris brassicae*. Sub-species, varieties and cultivars (cultivated plants) may also be named by adding distinguishing elements to the binomial. (Cultivar names, from 1959 onwards, may no longer be latinized.)

Linnaeus (1707-78) first used the binomial system to regularize the naming of plants, individual species of which from the Middle Ages onwards had become known under a variety of names, Latin as well as vernacular. By fixing a single genus-species name, in an internationally recognizable form,

157

and rejecting all synonyms, Linnaeus made unequivocal naming possible, and, by reducing description to a method, he made identification possible from an economical but sufficient statement.

Biologists, of course, also use larger groupings, as Plant Kingdom, sub-kingdoms, divisions, classes, orders, families, tribes, and so on, although membership of those categories is not always fixed, as is the species within its genus. Botanists and zoologists use slightly differing technical terms, and traditional and modern names, like the classification systems, may vary. In printing, the convention is to use italics for genus, species and variety names, as *Chamaesyparis lawsoniana* and *Pinus mugo* var. *pumilo*, and to print the names of cultivars in Roman, enclosed in single quotes, as *Pinus mugo* 'Gnom'. The generic name, which is in the singular and with which the species name agrees grammatically when used adjectivally is spelt with a capital initial. The names of the larger groups are printed in Roman, with an initial capital. (For the correct representation of scientific names and symbols, the chapter entitled 'Science and mathematical books' in Judith Butcher's *Copy-editing* is recommended.)

Common nouns also are standardized and used methodically. For instance, Keble Martin describes the sweet violet under the name *Viola odorata* L. (the 'L.' indicating that the authorized binomial was fixed by Linnaeus), within the family Violaceae, as being 'a plant with stolons [= creeping stems which root at intervals]; leaves cordate [= heart-shaped]; petioles [= leaf stalks] with deflexed [= bent sharply downwards] hairs; stipules [= leaf-like appendages usually at the base of the petiole] glandular [= with lumps in or on them]; flower fragrant, blue-purple, April'.[14]

Similar methods of description have been adopted for commercial use, for example, for potato varieties. Redcliffe Salaman, speaking as chairman of the Potato Synonym Committee, said, 'We found over 200 aliases or synonyms of the one variety Up-to-date, most of which were equipped in the catalogues of the different dealers with different characters... A similar state of affairs was discovered in relation to every variety which at one time or another won popularity'.[15]

Having been purged of synonyms and subjectively attributed

qualities, potato varieties are now described by their botanical features – foliage ('habit'), stems, leaves, flowers, tubers, and sprouts – and by their agricultural features – reaction to disease, tuber diseases and virus diseases – as in the Potato Marketing Board's *British atlas of potato varieties.*

Even where synonyms have been eradicated from current use, their presence must be suspected in older literature, which may need to be searched under superseded terms. It must also be remembered that the same word may vary in significance according to the culture in which it is used, that is, the place and time of its occurrence. 'Family' in current English usage implies the nuclear family of parents and children; in current usage by Indians in England it embraces also parents' parents and siblings and their children; in *Joseph Andrews*, first published in 1742, Lady Booby uses 'my family' to mean 'my household'.

Ways must be found of guarding against misleading use of terms in catalogues and indexes, while at the same time providing access to verbal listings through 'non-preferred' terms. That ever-present problem is dealt with throughout the immediately following chapters.

A note on the terminology of librarianship

I would here add an admonitory footnote on the importance of controlling the terminology of librarianship. Flaccid terminology expresses loose thinking and we owe it to the development of our own discipline to keep a watchful eye on our own jargon, to avoid the use of imprecise vogue words and occasionally to submit our own preference to a generally accepted alternative. There is a British standard glossary of documentation terms which indicates the preferred term where more than one designation may be found in the literature.[16] L. M. Harrod's *Librarians' glossary* is more in the nature of a concise encyclopaedia.[17] Updated now to 1987, it defines or describes objects, techniques, corporate bodies and trade names which may be found in the literature of librarianship and related activities. The American norms are the updated *ALA glossary*[18] and the *ALA world encyclopaedia of library and information services,*[19] the primary aim of the latter being to provide facts for the comparative study of librarianship.

References

1 Lavoisier, A. L., *Traité élémentaire de chimie*. Paris: Cuchet, 1789. (Reference is to the Introduction.)
2 Piggott, M., 'Bibliography and the indexer: some notes on terminology', *in Bibliography and reading: a festschrift in honour of Ronald Staveley*; ed. by Ia McIlwaine, John McIlwaine, Peter G. New. Metuchen; London: Scarecrow Press, 1983, 83-105.
3 Wüster, Eugen, *Einfürung in die allgemeine Terminologielehre und terminologische Lexikographie*. Pt. 1 Text; Pt. 2 Figs. Wien; New York: Springer, 1979. (Schriftenreihe der Technischen Universität Wien, Vol. 8)
4 *UNISIST newsletter*, 2(1), 1974, 2.
5 *World guide to terminological activities*. 2nd rev. and enl. ed.; prepared by Magdalena Krommer-Benz. München; London: Saur, 1985.
6 *International directory of libraries and documentation centres in terminology*, compiled by Marie-Josée Cousineau. Ottawa; Vienna: INFOTERM, 1986.
7 *INFOTERM newsletter* 1-32, 1976-1982, published in *Lebende Sprachen* and, from 1977, in *International classification*, No. 33(3) – , 1984 – ; published independently by INFOTERM.
8 *Terminologies for the eighties*. München; London: 1982. (Section referred to, pp.19-116; list of INFOTERM publications, pp.69-84.)
9 *TermNet news*, Vol. 1, no. 1 – , March 1981 – . Ottawa: General Directorate for Terminology and Documentation, 1981 – .
10 Jastrab, Marie-Josée, 'Éléments pour une définition de la terminologie aux Nations Unies', *in World guide to terminological activities* (see reference 5), 258-63.
11 Arnold, D., 'United Nations terminology usage for the world community', *in World guide to terminological activities* (see reference 5), 264-9.
12 *FID news bulletin*, 34(9), September 1984, 67.
13 Jackson, A. R. Haygarth, 'What the large users expect from secondary services producers', *Aslib proceedings*, 28(10), October 1976, 347-54; (Quotations, 351-2.)
14 Martin, W. Keble, *The concise British flora in colour*, with nomenclature edited by Douglas H. Kent. London: Ebury Press and M. Joseph, 1965, pl.12.
15 Quoted in Cox, A. E., *The potato: a practical and scientific guide*. London: Collingridge, 1967, 22.

16 British Standards Institution, *Glossary of documentation terms.* London: BSI, 1976. (BS 5408; under revision, 1987)
17 Harrod, L. M., *Harrod's librarians' glossary of terms used in librarianship, documentation and the book crafts, and reference book.* 6th ed. compiled by Ray Prytherch. Aldershot: Gower, 1987.
18 *The ALA glossary of library and information science*; ed. Heartsill Young. Chicago: ALA, 1983.
19 *ALA world encyclopaedia of library and information services.* 2nd ed. Chicago: ALA, 1986.

10

Terminology in catalogues and indexes

Sources

Ingetraut Dahlberg's *International classification and indexing biblio-graphy* contains entries for some 2,300 classification systems and thesauri published between 1950 and 1982, on all manner of subjects.[1] *International bibliography of standardized vocabularies* lists glossaries put out by the various standardizing agencies. Begun by Eugen Wüster, its second edition appeared in 1979, and its publishers, INFOTERM, anticipate further updatings.[2]

INFOTERM's concern with terminology on a universal scale has already been mentioned. In Great Britain it is the policy of Aslib to acquire all significant subject-headings lists and thesauri in the English language and bilingual and multi-lingual publications with English as one of the languages. Lists of Aslib's holdings are published periodically.[3-5]

Aslib's holdings naturally include the lists of subject headings published by large libraries and research organiz-ations for their own use and for the benefit of other libraries and agencies which use, or contribute to, their catalogues or cataloguing and indexing services. The most widely used among libraries of such lists are the *Subject headings used in the dictionary catalogs of the Library of Congress (LCSH)*[6] and its simplified derivative *Sears list of subject headings (Sears)*,[7] used primarily in making catalogues, and *Medical subject headings (MESH)*,[8] used both in compiling *Index medicus* and in searching it in either its printed or automated form.[9] (*LCSH* is described in some detail in Chapter 12.)

The basic alphabetical list of terms in the more recently constructed thesauri is drawn from a previously set-out logical arrangement, such as the groups of categories in *MESH* or the complete classification scheme in *Thesaurofacet*[10] or the *Unesco*

162

thesaurus. [11] The faceted display indicates which hierarchical relationships are to be shown for any acceptable term printed in the alphabetical list. Such relationships are usually shown in the alphabetical list by adding immediately below each term 'broader terms' (BT) and 'narrower terms' (NT) drawn from the same hierarchy. Comparison between entries in the alphabetical list and the related section of the categorical or classified display helps the indexer to pinpoint the terms appropriate to the concept being indexed, and, where a conventional catalogue is being made, to select the appropriate references. Conversely, reference by the user of an index from a term sought in the alphabetical list to that term in its context in the display may lead to a more appropriate set of search terms.

One of the earliest fully worked-out thesauri was that prepared by the Engineers Joint Council, *Thesaurus of engineering and scientific terms (TEST).* [12] It naturally had an influence on the construction of subsequent terminologies. In addition to its use of BT and NT, the abbreviation RT (= related term) has frequently been adopted to indicate a relationship other than that between terms on different levels of the same hierarchy. For example, 'Screening' and 'Rejects' are reciprocally noted as related terms, one being taken from a category of activities, the other from a category of entities, the specific relationship being that between a process and its product. Terms commonly used as synonyms for a preferred term and terms more specific than a preferred term (referring generally to fringe topics) must appear in the list because they will be looked for by some users, but the fact that they will not be used as subject entries must be shown. Thus *TEST* enters 'Rules (instructions) USE Regulations' and 'Relevance ratio USE Information retrieval effectiveness'. That the preferred term is equivalent to, or includes, the meaning of the rejected term is indicated by the abbreviation UF (= use for) as 'Regulations UF Rules (instructions)'.

The inclusion of rejected terms is necessary because authors do not always use the terms preferred by the thesaurus and the indexer needs to be directed from terms in an author's text to the terms he should use in compiling his index. Their inclusion is necessary also because the index-searcher may not be aware of the preferred term, particularly if he is searching in a language which is not his own. A 'scope note', which defines a term – a definition not necessarily valid outside the thesaurus and its derived listings – has the same function of clarification. A new term arising in the literature will be assigned to its logical category, where its status in relation to existing terms can be determined. Relationships between terms in different hierarchies can be determined by seeking grammatical and logical correspondences, as, for example, between terms for an activity and for its product, as above, for the person or thing performing an activity, and also by drawing on familiarity with common usage. The BSI *Guidelines* for the construction of thesauri goes into the question of relationships and their signalling in some detail.[13] It also shows sample pages from thesauri, illustrating both alphabetical and diagrammatic display. Where no suitable thesaurus exists, one can be made to fit a particular purpose.[14]

The choice of terms in a thesaurus depends upon the areas of knowledge covered by the literature to which it is designed to give access and also upon the mode of access. Two recently constructed thesauri may serve here as contrasting models: the *UNBIS thesaurus*, which is the list of terms used in indexing and cataloguing documents relevant to the United Nations programmes and activities,[15] and the *Root thesaurus*, which has been developed by the British Standards Institution for the exchange of information on standards and other documents of a similar type.[16] Both thesauri are designed to index literature from all countries and potentially on all subjects, but the emphasis in the two corpora of literature is different: that controlled by the *UNBIS thesaurus* emphasizes the political, administrative, educational, economic, social and cultural aspects, primarily of human activities, whereas the literature of standards concentrates on the quantitative and qualitative, practical and technological aspects, primarily of materials and processes. Of the 17 main categories outlined in the *UNBIS thesaurus* one only is devoted to Science and Technology; of the 24 main categories of *Root* one only is devoted to Social Sciences and Humanities. This is a rough comparison because the meaning of terms in both lists can be modified by the simultaneous use of other terms, but the general bias of each list is evident.

Pre-coordinate and post-coordinate entry and retrieval
The modes of access for which the two thesauri are designed differ in that the headings, or descriptors, by which individual topics are recorded and retrieved are pre-coordinate in the one – *UNBIS* – and post-coordinate in the other – *Root*.

Pre-coordinate headings attempt to give a sufficiently complete summary of the semantic content of a document, or part of a document, by the use of a term taken from the thesaurus, qualified if need be by a subheading taken from a supplementary list of common modifiers appropriate to the literature. Thus, from *UNBIS* the following terms might be taken:

Protein-rich foods: developed and developing countries
United Nations: host country relations

Post-coordinate terms, or descriptors, on the other hand, name separate concepts which in total cover the subject of a document but which are not combined into a coherent statement like the *UNBIS* heading or like a PRECIS string. To designate the content of a document it may be necessary to assemble a number of such descriptors, which may subsequently, when an enquirer's search is being made, be sought individually, or as a set, or selectively (together with quite different terms), according to the searcher's needs. Thus from *Root*, assuming a subject which is an entity made of a specified material, such as Brick walls, two descriptors must be taken, here Bricks and Walls; where the subject is Electron tube amplifiers, the descriptors to be used are Amplifiers and Electron tubes.

The following terms may be compared to show both the bias of the thesauri and the different methods of applying descriptors.

From UNBIS	*From Root*
Warehouse management	Warehouses
	Management
Development planning : Africa	Economic development
	Planning
	Africa
Space technology : industrial	Space technology
applications	Industries

From *UNBIS*	From *Root*
Frozen fish : conditions of sale	Food Products
	Fish
	Frozen Food
	Selling
	Regulations
Protein-rich foods : developed and	Proteins
developing countries	–

(*Root* has a list of geographical names but so far the concept of 'Developed and developing countries' has not been present in the standards literature. As *Root* is expected to grow and to be applied in other contexts than those for which it was originally designed, it is possible that descriptors now apparently wanting will be included in a later edition.)

One of the most difficult decisions to make in establishing a list of descriptors for post-coordinate retrieval is the acceptance or rejection of a particular compound term. If a compound term is so familiar that readers will seek it without further thought, it would be perverse to divide it into its components. There is also the consideration that some component terms would be so general that they would have little value as search keys. *Root* has many compound headings such as Coal gas, Coal mining, Gaseous fuels, Fuelless energy sources.

The use of separate descriptors for post-coordinate retrieval began as an aid to mechanical searching for detailed information for which conventional subject headings, such as those used by the Library of Congress, proved inadequate.[17] Its development is described, with clear illustrations, by Hunter and Bakewell.[18]

Boolean formulae

A search can be made more precise by specifying not only terms designating wanted concepts but also by specifying terms to be excluded because they designate aspects of a subject not wanted in a particular search.

The relationships between the terms are expressed by symbols taken from Boolean algebra. George Boole was a nineteenth-century English mathematician and one of the founders of modern symbolic logic.[19] He used algebraic

166

symbols to express logical relationships and his pioneering work has been commemorated in the term 'Boolean algebra'.

Thus the *logical product* of two concepts, that is the overlapping of two separate concepts to make a *combination* of the two ideas, as in (to take another example) Coal mining in Yorkshire, is expressed by the mathematical symbol for multiplication, as Coal mining × Yorkshire. Mathematicians use also a full point to express multiplication or enclose each of the separate quantities in identical brackets.

The *logical sum* of two concepts, that is the presence of one *or* the other, is expressed by the plus sign. Coal mining in Yorkshire or Derbyshire would be expressed as (Coal mining × Yorkshire) + (Coal mining × Derbyshire).

The *logical difference* between two concepts, that is *the presence of one and the exclusion of the other*, is expressed by the minus sign. Coal mining, but not Coal mining in Yorkshire, would be expressed as Coal mining – Yorkshire.

All three symbols may be required to signify the presence of *either of two concepts, excluding*, however, *the area of their overlap*. Thus the concepts of Coal mining and of Yorkshire, but excluding the concept of Coal mining in Yorkshire could be expressed as (Coal mining + Yorkshire) – (Coal mining × Yorkshire).

The exact terminology used in retrieval would be determined by reference to the thesaurus used for indexing the collection searched. (If free-text searching is allowed, then a list of terms is still useful as a prompt.) Search strategies available are 1) broadening a search by changing the descriptor used to one designating a more comprehensive subject; 2) narrowing a search by seeking a less comprehensive term, or adding more qualifying terms; 3) covering related forms of terms having the same verbal root by using a truncated form, or, where this would introduce terms from unrelated subject areas having similar spelling, remembering to search also on related terms.

Pre-coordinate descriptors may also be used in automated databases and searched by full headings, main headings or qualifiers only, dates, and (if provision has been made for this) single words in headings. PRECIS, for example, was designed from the beginning for computer manipulation. The *UNBIS thesaurus* controls the computerized databases of the United Nations Bibliographic Information System.

Updating thesauri

Because terminology changes and, as Steiner puts it: 'In every fixed definition there is obsolescence or failed insight. . . The world can be other', the thesaurus itself must be hospitable to changes in terminology and in the denotation of words. Provision must be made for the insertion of new terms and for the restriction or enlargement of meaning of existing terms. The searcher must be warned when such changes have been made so that he does not ignore material recorded under previously used terms. The *ILO thesaurus*[20] warns of such changes by providing a History note (HN) which refers to past usage in its database. Two examples illustrate this practice.

RETURN MIGRATION
  BT MIGRATION
  HN Used from item 71955; for earlier items use the name
     of the migrants' home country with free text terms
     such as 'home' or 'repatria. . .' or a formulation such
     as 'Algerian' and 'Algeria'.

SLUM
  HN Used from item 29818; older items may be retrieved
     by using 'Poverty' with 'Urban' or 'Housing'.

The INSPEC thesaurus, beginning with its 1983 edition, notes the date of input (DI) of each term. Most terms go back to January 1973 when the first edition was published. Where relevant, a PT [= Prior Term] is signalled after a new term, so that documents indexed before the date of input of the new term may be sought under the superseded term.

Some of the older lists evolved with less control of their terminology and syndetic apparatus. A century ago Cutter's rules sufficed for indicating the subjects of monographs; today the subjects of some separately published monographs are so specific that a quite elaborate statement is needed to express them in the barest summary that will distinguish them from other subjects represented in the catalogue.

Subject cataloguers in the Library of Congress have tried to keep pace with the limitless expansion of the library's collections. Terms have been added to the list as new subjects were written about, the cataloguers endeavouring to choose the term which best expressed a new subject, was likely to be permanent, and was not at variance with established headings. It is easy to point to individual headings in *LCSH* which appear now to be ridiculous or even insulting, but most of them seemed unexceptional at the time they were taken from current usage.[21]

It is tempting when using *LCSH* or *Sears* to wish sometimes to replace a heading which appears to be 'old-fashioned' or 'not English usage' by a more appropriate term, but there are good reasons for not doing so, at least until all the implications have been taken into account. A catalogue aims to be a comprehensive whole made up of words, not petrified but certainly not proliferating in unseemly directions like a badly pruned tree. Within any individual piece of writing the author is at liberty to define his terms and then to use them in consistency with is own definitions. If he wilfully (or tendentiously) alters a meaning from that generally accepted in the field in which he is writing, he risks (or courts) misunderstanding, but if he takes his reader with him he can introduce nice distinctions which greatly add to clarity of expression. Within the Library of Congress catalogue, for example, restrictive definitions have been given to the words 'Precious stones' and 'Gems', by means of which the literature on mineralogical aspects can be separated from that of industrial and artistic interest. Where the collection of literature to be recorded is vast, many such arbitrary distinctions must be made, in addition to the differences, not always observed in colloquial use, which properly exist between terms for concrete entities and their study or exploitation, such as 'Shells' and 'Conchology', used to separate popular from scientific books. Under the term 'Gardening' *LCSH* explains in a 'scope note': 'Here are entered works on the practical operations in the cultivation of fruits, vegetables, flowers and ornamental plants'; under Horticulture, 'Here are entered works on the scientific and economic aspects of the cultivation of fruits, vegetables, flowers and ornamental plants'.

When establishing such headings in the catalogue itself, the cataloguer must ensure that the scope of a subject heading is made plain to the user, either by means of an explanatory note or through a reference. *LCSH*'s and *Sears*' *see* reference is, of course, the forerunner of the thesaurus's directive 'use', leading from an unused term to a used term. Their *see also* reference includes the thesaurus's more specific designations 'Narrower terms', 'Broader terms' and 'Related terms'.

The listing of references under a subject heading is required in order to show what a particular term denotes – and by implication what it does not denote – and to lead if necessary to a more appropriate term. When an established term in a list of subject headings is changed, all the related terms must be taken into consideration, as must also the possible occurrence of the term as a subheading to other entry words. The appendix to the 10th edition of *Sears* lists five pages of *see* and *see also* references which would need to be changed if the word 'Black' replaced 'Negro'. That replacement was in fact made in the following edition, in which the introduction states that 'terms considered by the editor to be sexist, racist or pejorative have been changed or eliminated. One exception is the heading "Man" which is to be used only in an anthropological and generic sense.' ('Man in space' has become 'Space flight'; 'Man power' has become 'Human resources'.)

To incorporate such changes in an existing catalogue has been an immense labour when it has had to be done manually. In an automated catalogue, provided that the constituent parts of an entry have been adequately coded, it is easy to run a program to effect the necessary alterations. Where, however, the introduction of automation has led to the 'closing' of a printed-book or card catalogue at a certain date and its continuation in computer-produced form, there could still be discrepancies between the old and the new, necessitating references from each to the other.

References

1   Dahlberg, Ingetraut, *International classification and indexing biblio-graphy*. Vol. 1. Frankfurt-am-Main: Indeks Verlag, 1982.
2   *International bibliography of standardized vocabularies*; initiated by Eugen Wüster. Prepared by Helmut Felber, Magdalena

170

Krommer-Benz, Adrian Manu. 2nd ed. München; London: 1979. (INFOTERM series 2).

3 Walkley, J. and Hay, B., 'An annotated list of thesauri held in the Aslib library', *Aslib proceedings*, 23(6), June 1971, 292-300.

4 Maccafferty, M., *Thesauri and thesaurus construction*. London: Aslib, 1977. (Aslib bibliography no. 7.)

5 Gilbert, V., 'A list of thesauri and subject headings held in the Aslib library [post-1970 publications]', *Aslib proceedings*, 31(6), June 1979, 264-74. (Updated in September and March issues of *Aslib information*.)

6 Library of Congress, *Library of Congress subject headings*. 9th ed. Washington, D.C.: LC, 1980. (Supplements are published quarterly and cumulated annually. A completely new edition is available quarterly on microfiche and film.)

7 *Sears list of subject headings*. 13th ed. by Carmen Rovira and Caroline Reyes. New York: Wilson, 1986.

8 National Library of Medicine, *Medical subject headings*. Bethesda, Md.: NLM. (Annual revisions)

9 Strickland-Hodge, Barry, *How to use* Index medicus *and* Excerpta medica. Aldershot: Gower, 1986.

10 *Thesaurofacet: a thesaurus and faceted classification for engineering and related subjects*; compiled by Jean Aitchison [and others]. Whetstone: English Electric Co, 1969.

11 *Unesco thesaurus*; compiled by Jean Aitchison. Paris: Unesco, 1977.

12 Engineers Joint Council. *Thesaurus of engineering and scientific terms*. New York: Engineers Joint Council, 1967.

13 British Standards Institution, *Guide to establishment and development of monolingual thesauri*. London: BSI, 1987. (BS5723)

14 Aitchison, Jean and Gilchrist, Alan, *Thesaurus construction: a practical manual*. 2nd ed. London: Aslib, 1987.

15 *UNBIS thesaurus: list of terms used in indexing and cataloguing of documents and other materials relevant to United Nations programmes and activities*. New York: United Nations, 1981. (Dag Hammarskjold Library Bibliographical series, no. 37.)

16 *Root thesaurus*. Vol. 1, Subject display; Vol. 2, Alphabetical list. 2nd ed. London: British Standards Institution, 1985.

17 Taube, Mortimer, *Studies in co-ordinate indexing*. Bethesda, Md.: Documentation Inc, 1953-6.

18 Hunter, Eric, *Cataloguing*. 2nd ed. London: Bingley, 1983.

19 Boole, George, *Mathematical analysis of logic*, 1847; and *Laws of thought*, 1854.

20 *ILO thesaurus: labour, employment and training terminology.* 2nd ed. Geneva: International Labour Office, 1978.
21 Berman, Sanford, *Prejudices and antipathies: a tract on the LC subject heads concerning people.* Metuchen: Scarecrow Press, 1971. (Reviewed by Lubetsky, Seymour, 'Politics and romance in subject cataloging', *Library journal,* 15 February 1972, 658-9.)

11

The classified catalogue and its indexes

Its uses and advantages

Early library catalogues were brief lists which recorded the books where they stood, or lay, either roughly grouped by subject in cupboards or presses, or set apart according to use at the altar or in the refectory. The books were almost invariably shelved before they were listed, a practice which continued into the eighteenth century. Fumagalli reports an early Vatican Library catalogue compiled from the shelves under the direction of Platino, appointed librarian by Sixtus IV, in 1475,[1] and sixteenth- and seventeenth-century catalogues, such as Naudé's catalogue of Des Cordes' library, bear witness to this method of compilation.

With fixed shelving in libraries it was essential to know in which of the parallel sequences, of which there were generally three – for large, medium and small volumes – to look for a desired book. The inventorial method of cataloguing repeated the three sequences, requiring the searcher to scan three groups of entries at any one heading. Librarians saw the inconvenience this caused but did not know how to prevent it. Rostgaard attempted to show at one place in the catalogue, instead of in successive groups, all the books the library possessed on a single subject by ruling a double-page opening of his catalogue into four columns, each for books of a different size, so that the parallel sequences might all be taken in by the eye at a single glance,[2] but this also had its drawbacks. In a survey of classification schemes used in German libraries, Kenneth Garside suggests that Jeremias David Reuss of Göttingen transformed the inventory into a true catalogue at the end of the eighteenth century. He 'laid down the fundamental principle that a book must be classified and then placed in its appropriate place on the shelves'.[3]

Once it had been accepted that a catalogue and a shelf register had different functions and should therefore be two distinct compilations, the catalogue became a much more flexible and helpful guide to the library. It could bring together descriptions of all the books and other materials on a particular subject, no matter where they were kept in the library. Indeed, in many large German libraries today a minutely classified catalogue is the reader's only – and essential – guide to the subject content of the collections. The reader has no access to the collections, a privilege which would avail him little, since the books do not themselves stand in classified order on the shelves but are arranged by running number within several different sequences of sizes, within a very broad subject grouping. The call number is thus quite different from the classification symbol, being composed of symbols to indicate 1) broad subject group, 2) size, 3) *numerus currens*, or accession number.

A single entry in the classified catalogue may be based on a unit entry for the item being catalogued. The unit entry, which may or may not include the author heading, is made an entry for the classified catalogue by the addition of the classification symbol, as

---

598.294	Reference
1969	folios
	598.294
	1969

British and European birds in colour / text by
Bertel Bruun, paintings by Arthur Singer. – Feltham :
Hamlyn, 1969.
    321p. : col.ill., 449 col.maps ; 30 cm.
    Bibliography: p.313-315.

The classification symbol (using the Dewey Decimal classification), being the primary filing element, has been placed in the top left-hand corner, and the location symbol in the top right-hand corner of the entry. It assumes a classified arrangement on the shelves, with large volumes in a separate sequence.

Different ways of showing the location of an item on catalogue entries may be seen in different libraries. The pattern followed above seems to be the clearest and most economical. For all entries, both author and subject, the filing element stands in the top left-hand corner of the entry – the author's name in the author catalogue, the classification symbol in the classified catalogue – whence the eye continues to move onwards in its normal reading habit to take in the description of the item. If the reader decides that he wishes to see the item described, he notes the call mark (or location symbol) which stands in the top right-hand corner of the entry. Thus, no matter which part of the catalogue the reader is consulting nor what kind of entry he stops at, the location of the item is shown in the same position, unconfused with any other data.

Not only does the classified catalogue bring together descriptions of books and other material on a single subject which may be widely scattered within a library, but it also brings together descriptions of books which include the subject within a broader context and of books which treat separately the different parts of the original subject. The classified order proceeds, in most schemes, from the comprehensive to the specific. Thus the reader, by looking at entries which precede those for the specific subject of his search, may find useful books which deal with his subject as part of a more inclusive subject, and by looking at entries which succeed those for the specific subject, may find more specialized works which make a relevant contribution to it.

The catalogue itself may, in fact, play a part in defining an enquirer's area of study, or in suggesting new lines of thought or approach. A reader ignorant of the resources of the library or vague about the way his subject has been treated in the literature is likely to approach the catalogue with only an approximate formulation of his real interest.

For instance, the reader who expresses an interest in Birds may select the following titles (here abbreviated for lack of space).

1	591.03 591.03
	1967 1967

1

591.03   591.03
1967   1967

A dictionary of zoology / by A.W. Leftwich . . . 1967.

2

591.51   591.51
1982   1982

Discovering animal behaviour / John Sparks . . . 1982.

3

591.525   591.525
1972   1972

Atlas of animal migration / Cathy Jarman . . . 1972.

4

591.525   591.525
1980   1980

Mystery of migration / Robin Baker . . . 1980.

5

598.0723441   598.0723441
1984   1984

RSPB guide to watching British birds / Peter Conder . . . 1984.

6

598.2525   598.2525
1983   1983

Bird migration / Chris Mead . . . 1983.

7

598.2924   598.2924
1985   1985

Birds of sea and fresh water / Karel Šťasný . . . 1985.

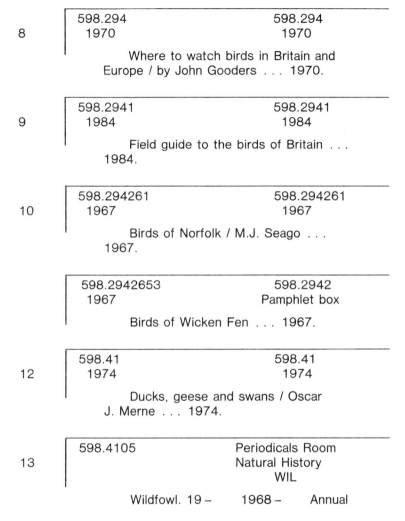

8	598.294 1970	598.294 1970
		Where to watch birds in Britain and Europe / by John Gooders . . . 1970.

9	598.2941 1984	598.2941 1984
		Field guide to the birds of Britain . . . 1984.

10	598.294261 1967	598.294261 1967
		Birds of Norfolk / M.J. Seago . . . 1967.

	598.2942653 1967	598.2942 Pamphlet box
		Birds of Wicken Fen . . . 1967.

12	598.41 1974	598.41 1974
		Ducks, geese and swans / Oscar J. Merne . . . 1974.

13	598.4105	Periodicals Room Natural History WIL
		Wildfowl. 19 – 1968 – Annual

The chosen titles suggest that the reader really wishes to study, not all birds, but migrant waterfowl in Britain, particularly those of East Anglia. The catalogue has suggested to him general works on animal migration and descriptive works on particular congregations of wildfowl in addition to the books limited to British aquatic birds. One of the haunts of serendipity is undoubtedly the classified catalogue. The verbal subject-heading catalogue, by pinpointing specific subjects and arranging entries according to the alphabetical sequence of their headings, lacks this immediate collocation and simultaneous presentation of related topics. Not all relationships can be shown at once in the classified sequence, however. Only the hierarchical divisions and collateral branches of a subject which have been given the status of a coherent class within the chosen classification scheme can be displayed at once. The embracing class which takes in the examples shown is zoology; hierarchical divisions are Aves (Birds) and Anseriformes (Ducks and Geese). Geographical and behavioural studies may be regarded as collateral divisions of zoology and of its hierarchical divisions. Other studies of birds which fall into classes separated from zoology must be sought elsewhere, within the classes to which they have been allotted in the scheme in use: birds as farm livestock within the class of Animal husbandry, birds in armorial bearings within the class of Heraldry and so on. Their place in the catalogue will be found by referring to the alphabetical subject index which the librarian will provide as a guide to the different class numbers which gather together entries for works on a subject in its different aspects.

There is one situation in which the classified catalogue is vastly superior to the alphabetical subject catalogue, and that is in a library which serves readers who do not all speak the same language. In Canada, for example, libraries collect publications indifferently in English and French, both officially recognized national languages, but not all readers are bilingual. An analogous situation exists in South Africa. The *Indian national bibliography* lists books in *14* different languages. The French-speaking Canadian, however, is not necessarily unable to read English, nor the Hindu unable to read Marathi or Tamil. If the alphabetical subject catalogue were used, two forms would be possible. Either a set of complete catalogues could be made, with subject headings for each in a single language, or selective catalogues could be made, each holding entries for works in a single language and having subject headings in that language. The first choice would be wasteful of the library's time, space and materials, the second would undoubtedly waste the time of those readers – and library staff – who could use material in more than one language or who might wish to obtain translations of available texts in foreign languages which appeared to be important. The classified catalogue can keep together entries for books in all languages, identifying a common subject by an unvarying symbol – the class mark – thus necessitating only one physical subject sequence. Reducing the subject catalogue to a single sequence does not, of course, do away with the necessity for making an alphabetical key to the class numbers in each major language, but separate alphabetical subject indexes will be smaller, easier to maintain and handle and much less costly than separate-language catalogues.

Arrangement in the classified catalogue

Entries in a classified catalogue are arranged in the sequence of the symbols used as notation in the classification scheme. Any addition to the symbols made by the classifier must be the subject of additional filing rules.

If the classification scheme in use provides no notation to distinguish individual members of a class, or if the scheme ceases to subdivide in any chain before the point desired by a particular library, recourse is usually had to alphabetical arrangement by name of subject. In order to place the more general works before the more particular, the unexpanded symbols will precede the supplemented ones, e.g. using Dewey, 780.92 [= Biography of musicians] precedes 780.92 Berlioz, which precedes 780.92 Delius, etc.

Many examples of expansion of the schedules to provide closer subdivision are shown in issues of the *BNB* from 1960-71 where alphabetical extension of a class mark follows an interpolated figure one in square brackets [1]. The supplementary schedules were published,[4] and the device was explained, with examples, in E. J. Coates' *Subject catalogues.*[5] However, time taken within a particular library to adjust a standard class mark, and subsequently to adjust one's search when using standard bibliographical tools, must be weighed against advantages gained by making local adjustments, and the fewer and simpler the adjustments can be kept the better. If a high degree of specificity in subject classification is needed it is wiser to choose a highly specific classification scheme to begin with.

Sub-arrangement by book number

Entries for more than one publication on the same subject, which have, of course, the same classification symbol, are frequently found arranged at the class number in alphabetical sequence of their authors' names. This convention is easy for the filer to follow and it facilitates the finding of an entry by a known author at a given place in the classification. It is used by the Library of Congress for shelf arrangement and hence in its shelf list.

Library of Congress call numbers consist in general of two principal elements: class number and author number, to which may be added as required symbols designating a particular work or a particular book. Based on a system devised by Cutter,[6] Library of Congress author symbols are composed of the initial letter of an author's name followed by Arabic numerals. They may be extended to distinguish different versions of a work and different copies held by a library. A guide to the application of such book numbers has been written by Donald J. Lehnus.[7]

Ranganathan has discussed the need for such extensions in his *Prolegomena to library classification*.[8] The whole of Ranganathan's 'book number' consists of notation to specify: 1) the language in which the publication is written; 2) the form of presentation if other than monographic; 3) the year of publication; 4) the second (third, etc.) book having the same class number, written in the same language and the same form and published in the same year; 5) the copy number (second, third, etc.); 6) the number of the volume as part of the work in question; 7) the number of any supplement; 8) a particular relationship, such as that of a criticism or an answer, which demands that the book in question be shelved immediately following the work to which it is related and whose class number it naturally takes.

Chronological sequence

Widespread though its use is, alphabetical arrangement by author's name within a single class mark is not, I think, the most useful arrangement. Most readers want up-to-date information when they first investigate a subject and the most recent bibliographical information when they try to keep up with the literature in their field. This they will find easily if entries in the subject catalogue are filed in date order, with the most recent coming at the beginning of each sequence. The date can be added to the class number to form the call mark, as in the examples on pp.176-7. Written as it is there, the significance of the lower line of figures is obvious.

If entries for books are filed in date order, with entries for the most recent publications presented first, readers with many differing requirements can be satisfied: to take the subject of hospital nursing, the enquirer who wants an overall view of nursing today, the student who wants to examine two or three textbooks, the teacher who wants to look over the latest acquisitions, the historian of the subject, and the reader who wants to know what treatment would have been given a patient at a particular period. In a rapidly developing subject, such as is computer science today, last year's textbooks may be out of date. If a file is not regularly weeded it should not risk impeding access to information on current publications because their authors' names occur at the end of an alphabetical sequence.

In a specialized research library last *month's* or last *week's* information may be out of date and a more precise statement of the date of issue will be needed for items from newspapers, reports, official statements, regulations, etc., in current awareness bulletins circulated internally.

In arranging subject entries for books, the date of publication of the edition in hand, rather than the date of the first edition is recommended. This will separate editions of the same work, but works are reissued because the ideas in them continue to be of interest, and the student would be deprived of valuable sources if the classics of his subject were not brought to his notice. It is the function of the author catalogue to bring together the various editions of the same work. A note of the date of the previous edition added to an entry would provide the reader willing to use another edition, if the latest were not available, with the requisite call mark.

Other interpretations of 'date' have been adopted. Sidney L. Jackson made a survey of the use of date arrangement under broad subject headings in 30 large American libraries[9] and Gilmore Warner has drawn up a set of rules for establishing the date sequence.[10]

Chronological arrangement of books and of subject catalogues is not new. Rostgaard advocated it in 1698.[11] Lund and Taube proposed classification primarily by period.[12] The Library of Congress classification scheme in some sections of its schedules segregates writings deemed to have only an historical value from more recent publications by allocating to them separate class marks.

Guides to the catalogue

Just as running heads in a manual or dictionary help the reader to find his way about and to stop at a wanted section, so the prominent display of the classification symbols in their sequence helps the reader to orient himself within the classified catalogue. The notation must, however, be accompanied by a translation into words, so that the searcher is reassured as he travels. Such signposts turn the cryptic symbols into comprehensible words, emphasizing the major divisions of the classified arrangement and showing how these have been subdivided into sections and sub-sections. The more comprehensive guides are followed by the tags which verbally identify the subjects of more specific class notation, in as much detail as is required to make the catalogue easy and encouraging to use. The 'feature headings' printed in the *BNB*, designed to be read in conjunction with superordinate headings, perform the same function. In a few libraries the class mark on each entry is interpreted in words above the descriptive entry.

In a card catalogue the label on the outside of each drawer which shows the inclusive classification symbols for the part of the catalogue contained in it, is, of course, the seeker's first signpost. He will have been directed thither by instructions on the use of the catalogues displayed in the library or printed in a handbook.

The alphabetical subject index

To show the reader what subjects and what aspects of those subjects are represented in a library's collection and to list them all together for the reader's perusal is the function, as has already been said, of the alphabetical subject index, without which the classified catalogue is gravely incomplete. It is the task of the alphabetical subject index to suggest to the reader at what point in the catalogue to begin his search and to indicate to him where to look for particular aspects of a subject which are scattered throughout the catalogue according to how they have been assigned by the classification scheme to the various branches of knowledge.

The physical form in which the index is presented is important. It is easy for the user to grasp how a subject has been split up by the classification scheme and to decide which lines to follow if all the entries under one heading can be seen together. This can be done if the subject index is presented in page form – in print, typescript, or computer printout, reprinted as necessary – or if it takes the form of a visible index displayed on a stand or a wall frame. An easy way of keeping up with insertions and deletions is to use a word processor to generate the index.

Chain indexing

A widely used method of constructing the index to the classified catalogue is the method called by Ranganathan 'chain indexing'.[13] For 20 years, until 1971, it was used by the *British national bibliography*. (References to *BNB* usage throughout this section necessarily refer to that period.) The use of chain indexing is also evident in the successive editions of the Dewey decimal classification. Dewey called his index a 'relative index' because it was not simply a list of unqualified terms referring to notation and hence to placings in the schedules which might or might not have been to the point; the context of each term was given so that the reader could find specified in the index any subject in its required relationship, and the notation attached to that entry would lead to the required aspect of the subject in the schedules. Although the method was in use, its rules had not been stated nor its separate steps set out in a systematic way. Ranganathan laid out the pattern and gave it a name, using the metaphor of a chain composed of individual, separable links.

Methodology

Chain procedure is very simple in its theory. Whether the index entry is to refer to a placing in the classification schedules or to an entry in the classified catalogue, the procedure is basically the same. Here chain indexing will be considered as the method for constructing the alphabetical subject index to the classified catalogue.

When a new accession has been assigned the class mark which approximates as closely to its specific subject content as the classification scheme in use allows, an entry denoting the specific subject is made in the alphabetical subject index, referring the searcher to the class mark at which the entry will be found. The index entry itself consists of the term which denotes the specific subject, followed by the term denoting the class to which the specific subject belongs, which, in its turn, is followed by the term denoting the next higher class in the hierarchy, and so on, each succeeding term denoting a more inclusive (broader) class, the line of terms being extended so far as is necessary to place the specific term in its context and to distinguish the relevant aspect from all the other aspects. Additional entries are then made under the name of each successive broader class in the same hierarchy of the classification, qualified as required by the name of *its* including classes, until the ultimate class has been given its index entry. Each entry refers to the class mark at which material on the named subject will be found. The metaphor's aptness is thus apparent. Each term is a link in the hierarchical chain. In a single entry the successive links form a brief horizontal chain; in the successive entries generated by a single class mark, each entry discards the link that corresponds to the specific subject, and corresponding entry word, of its predecessor, and thus unlinks a vertical chain.

It will be evident that the notational link which comes at the end of the class mark will correspond to the specific subject in any consistent sequence of subject subdivision, such as Science – Zoology – Vertebrates – Birds. If index entries are made methodically, beginning with the specific subject and continuing with the higher classes in order of increasing comprehensiveness, the links in the chain will be used, and discarded, from last to first, or from right to left when expressed as elements of the notation, giving such a sequence as:

Birds – vertebrates – zoology – science ... 598.2
Vertebrates – zoology – science ... 596
Zoology – science ... 591
Science ... 5

The process is not, however, entirely mechanical. A classification scheme such as the Dewey decimal or Colon, in which in principle – but in Dewey often not in practice – each step of the division is marked by the addition of another digit to the notation, encourages a mechanical approach, but inconsistencies in the schedules and in the 'number building' force the indexer to use his judgement. Moreover, there are frequent changes in the characteristic of division. If birds are to be grouped according to the localities where they are found, the characteristic of division ceases to be that of taxonomic zoology, which would go on with the genera and species of birds, and becomes that of geographical area. Whereas *Ducks* and *Birds of Great Britain* denote less inclusive classes than *Birds*, it is impossible to compare their specificity. Likewise, one cannot say that *Dictionaries* are more specific than *Zoology* – indeed one might think of them as being less concrete in that being a form of presentation of information they may be applied to any or all subjects whereas named subjects are constricted by their definitions. All aspects of a subject represented by a class mark must be shown in the index, but not necessarily all in the same way.

If we wish to apply chain indexing to the subject entries listed on pp.176-7, it will be necessary to look at the parts of the classification schedule concerned. The relevant divisions of the 19th edition of the Dewey decimal classification are shown overleaf.

Applying chain indexing mechanically to *A dictionary of zoology*, classed at 591.03, the following entries are obtained:

Dictionaries – zoology – zoological sciences –
  pure sciences   591.03
Zoology – zoological sciences – pure sciences   591
Zoological sciences – pure sciences   590
Pure sciences   500

Regarded critically, those entries are seen to be at once tautologous and inadequate. Zoology means 'the scientific

Selective excerpt from Dewey decimal classification, 19th edition, 1979

500	Pure sciences
570	Biological sciences
590	Zoological sciences
591	Zoology
591.03	Dictionaries [*From Table 1. Standard subdivisions*]
591.5	Ecology of animals
.51	Habits and behaviour patterns
.52	Specific relationships and kinds of environments
.525	Migrations
592-599	Specific animals and groups of animals
596	Chordata Vertebrata (Craniata, Vertebrates)
598	Aves (Birds)
598.07	Study and teaching
.072	Research
.0723	Descriptive
.07234	Bird watching (Add Areas notation 1-9 from Table 2 to base number 598.07234)
.0723441	Great Britain [*Table 2, Areas -41 British Isles*]
598.2	General principles and geographical treatment
598.21-.28	General principles (Add to base number 598.2 the numbers following 591 in 591.1-591.8)

598.2525 Migrations
598.29 Geographical treatment of Aves
.291 Treatment by areas, regions, places in general
.292 Special groupings
.2924 Water birds
598.293-.299 Treatment by specific continents, countries, localities
(Add area notation 3-9 from Table 2 to base number 598.29)

598.294 Birds in Europe
.2941 Great Britain
.2942 England
.29426 Eastern England East Anglia
.294261 Norfolk
.294265 Cambridgeshire
.2942653 Fenland
598.3-.4 Water birds
598.4 Anseriformes and related orders
.41 Anseriformes (waterfowl) Common names ducks, geese, mergansers, swans.

598.4105 Periodicals [*From Table 1. Standard subdivisions*] study of animals'. It cannot be anything but a science. The scheme itself presents a problem here. The notation 591 stands for general aspects of Zoology, having in fact the same significance as the original main class notation. The only number now in use under 590 appears to be 590.744, which is used for zoological gardens. The entries are inadequate because of two omissions. 'Biological sciences' – a 'centred heading' in the Decimal classification, designating a step in the hierarchical division which has not been paralleled by an addition to the notation – has been overlooked and left out of the hierarchical chain, and 'Animals' (suitably qualified), the name for the subject of study in Zoology, has not been offered as an alternative synonymous approach. Edited the entries become

Dictionaries – zoology	591.03
Zoology	591
Animals – zoology	591
Biology	570
Life – biology	570
Science	500

Applying the same procedure to the following three books in the list on p.176, we get

Behaviour – animals	591.51
Ecology – zoology	591.5
Migration – ecology – zoology	591.525
Habitats – ecology – zoology	591.52

'Zoology' is a necessary qualifier because the ecology and migration of plants will also be indexed, with 'Botany' as a qualifier.

The authority file

In order that index entries once made are not repeated unnecessarily, a record of them is kept, in classified order. Reference to this authority file shows whether a class number has already been used. If it has, and the specific subject of the document in hand is properly shown in the index entry, no index entries need to be made for it. If it has not, the authority file will show how far up the hierarchical chain entries will need to be made in addition to those for the specific subject. The authority file for the index entries made so far would consist of the following entries

500	Science
570	Biology
	Life – biology
591	Animals – zoology'
	Zoology
591.5	Animals – ecology
	Ecology – zoology
591.51	Behaviour – animals
591.52	Habitats – ecology – zoology
591.525	Migration – ecology – zoology

Continuing to make the index and its authority file for the remaining catalogue entries on pp.176-7, we get the following sequences shown overleaf. (Synonyms are bracketed. Unnecessary qualifying terms, such as 'Europe' after 'Great Britain', and also unsought entry terms, such as 'General principles', have been suppressed. Otherwise, automatic application of chain procedure has been followed. This gives rise sometimes to less than satisfactory index entries, which can be improved with editorial guidance as the subsequent comments indicate.)

The examples used in this chapter are very simple, but even so they have probably given rise to questions about the choice and form of terms, and to doubts as to the suitability of this method of indexing for more complex matter and for other schemes of classification.

Choice and form of terms

It is evident that editorial rules are necessary in formulating subject index entries. To enter the names of subjects in an index under exactly the same form as one might speak of the subjects in conversation appears at first sight to have much to recommend it, but in natural language a subject may appear under various names and various forms of the same name, according to the speaker and his familiarity with the subject and the context in which he is using it. He may speak, for example, of national archives, public records, documents, official papers, or even of inky blots and rotten parchment bonds.

Index entries

	Index entries	
5	Great Britain – bird watching	598.0723441
	Europe – bird watching	598.072344
	Bird watching	598.07234
	Research – birds	598.072
	Birds – zoology	598
	Aves	598
	Ornithology	598
	Chordata	596
	Vertebrates	596
	Taxonomy – zoology	592-599
6	Migration – birds	598.2525
	Habitats – birds	598.252
	Ecology – birds	598.25
7	Water birds – distribution	598.2924
	Distribution – birds	598.29
8	Europe – birds	598.294
9	Great Britain – birds	598.2941

Authority file

592-599	Taxonomy – zoology
596	Chordata
	Vertebrates
598	Aves
	Birds – zoology
	Ornithology
598.072	Research – birds
598.07234	Bird watching
598.072344	Europe – bird watching
598.0723441	Great Britain – bird watching
598.25	Ecology – birds
598.252	Habitats – birds
598.2525	Migration – birds
598.29	Distribution – birds
598.2924	Water birds – distribution
598.294	Europe – birds
598.2941	Great Britain – birds

10 Norfolk – birds   598.294261   598.2942   England – birds
    East Anglia – birds   598.29426   598.29426   East Anglia – birds
    England – birds   598.2942   598.294261   Norfolk – birds

11 Fenland – Cambridgeshire – birds   598.2942653   598.294265   Cambridgeshire – birds
    Wicken Fen – Cambridgeshire – birds   598.2942653   598.2942653   Fenland – Cambridgeshire – birds
    Cambridgeshire – birds   598.294265   Wicken Fen – Cambridgeshire – birds

12 Anseriformes   598.41   598.3-.4   Aquatic birds – zoology
    Ducks – zoology   598.41   Water birds – zoology
    Geese – zoology   598.41   598.41   Anseriformes
    Swans – zoology   598.41   Ducks – zoology
    Waterfowl – zoology   598.41   Geese – zoology
    Wildfowl – zoology   598.41   Swans – zoology
    Aquatic birds – zoology   598.3-.4   Waterfowl – zoology
    Water birds – zoology   598.3-.4   Wildfowl – zoology

13 Periodicals – waterfowl   598.4105   598.4105   Periodicals – waterfowl

Certain conventions are therefore followed, which, in standardizing the form of entries, make them easier to construct and to consult. In classifying a book, the cataloguer has already been obliged to determine its subject and the context in which the subject has been treated. He looks for the specific subject, the particular aspect of it which has been written about, any further qualifications such as that of time or place, and finally the form in which the material has been presented.

When we look up a subject in any alphabetical list we try to pick out from the phrase which we use to designate it the most telling word or words, which in most cases is the term denoting the most concrete part of the subject, the term that can apply to the least number of classes of things. As a rule the classification scheme has worked down from a general topic to more and more specific ones, so that an index entry compiled by writing down, first the term denoting the *final* element of the class number, and then in sequence the terms denoting each *upward* step, or division, of the classification, in fact, puts the most concrete term first and qualifies it with a series of increasingly general terms.

It is generally preferable to use a single noun for the leading element of an index entry if a single noun in common usage properly denotes the concept in question. The entries assembled under that word in the complete index then show readers at a glance all aspects of the subject designated, and allow them to choose the areas of the catalogue relevant to their enquiries, sometimes, in fact – as may happen when they are consulting the classified catalogue itself – suggesting the relevant lines of search. Single-word entry also minimizes the risk of separating entries for the same subject, and it simplifies the alphabetical arrangement. The subsequent terms in the entry are also formalized. Their relationship with the preceding terms is generally apparent without the use of prepositions. An index is, by definition, a pointing finger. The user, having used other indexes, expects it to be brief and to adopt certain conventions in order to be brief. Its rules of composition are quite other than those of a piece of sustained prose. Nevertheless nothing is more apt as a guide in compiling an index than Sainte-Beuve's requirements for writing prose:

'D'abord la clarté, et puis la clarté, et puis encore la clarté.'
In general, the plural form of the noun is used for discrete entities, both concrete and abstract, the singular for mass-words and general abstractions. That is, (to use Otto Jespersen's terms) 'countables' – those things of which the question as to quantity is 'How many?' – are plural, 'non-countables' – those things of which the question as to quantity is 'How much?' – are singular. This reflects common usage. The reader who asked, 'Where are the books on the Animal?' would sound unusual. The singular suggests an abstraction, the connotation of the word, whereas the plural suggests the concrete, the denotation, all the animals there are. A practical advantage follows the use of the plural form for discrete entities, in that the singular form may also be used when both forms of the word are normally used in different senses. Singular and plural may designate entirely different things, as Damage (injury in general) and Damages (compensation for injury); the collective and several, as Trade (business in general) and Trades (particular businesses); the aggregate and particular, as Baptism (a Christian sacrament) and Baptisms (recorded instances of that sacrament performed in a particular place); the abstract and concrete, as Honour (a moral quality) and Honours (visible signs of deference to that quality); an action and a related entity, as Building and Buildings. The use of the gerund is not recommended, however. Where possible the related word ending in -ion, -ment, -ure (and a few other suffixes) should be preferred, as Management rather than Managing. (PRECIS entries use the term Building construction.) A table summarizing the use of singular and plural nouns is set out in the PRECIS manual,[14] p.105. The following pairs of singular and plural terms show possible index entries.

Different entities
  Plant (= machinery)
  Plants (= vegetation)

Collective and several
  Drink – smuggling – crime
  Drinks – domestic economy

Activity and entity
    Painting (operation of applying paint to canvas)
    Paintings (canvases to which paint has been applied)

Abstract and concrete
    Income – economics
    Incomes – agriculture – economics

Particular and general
    Ear – man – physiology (special connotation)
    Ears – grain – crops – rate of growth

Many topics are designated in common usage not by a single noun but by a phrase, often made up of a qualifying adjective, or a noun used as an adjective, and a noun. Where changing such a phrase to a form beginning with a single noun would produce an ambiguous, astonishing or nonsensical entry, the existing phrase must of course be used as it stands, as these examples show:

English language
Juvenile delinquents
Mail order firms
Physical culture
Social work

When constructing the index, the cataloguer has before him the schedules of the classification scheme in use, and these offer him a set of terms for the index entry. Often the terms in the schedule will be usable as they stand; at other times the indexer will need to substitute a more appropriate term, possibly because the term found, when removed from its context in the schedule, is unsuitable as an entry-word, or because a standard term has been established which can be used as a qualifying term in many contexts. When a preliminary set of entries has been made the indexer must provide for the reader who looks up the topic under an alternative name. The indexer therefore makes entries also under synonyms and near synonyms, especially under the popular name where the classification scheme has used the scientific name, and under the name of the thing where the classification scheme has used the name for the study of the thing, as Chiroptera and Bats, Theology and Religion. Reference to a syndetic list of terms such as the

Library of Congress's list of headings used in the dictionary catalogues[15] is often fruitful, since the classification schedules do not show all the alternatives, neither can the cataloguer always think of them himself without prompting.

In an index it is better to make a second entry under a synonym than to make a see reference, as

| Meteorology | 551 |
| Weather | 551 |

rather than Weather *see* Meteorology, as the reader stands to gain in finding entries wherever he looks instead of only under the term preferred by the cataloguer. Where there are no subheadings the entry is actually shorter than a reference. Where, however, there would be very many entries under synonymous entry words, a reference is a necessary economy. A reference is also advisable for near synonyms that it is impossible to differentiate in all cases, or to differentiate usefully, although their definitions may be distinct enough; for example, the names used in referring to the British Isles. It seems preferable to use the name Great Britain and to regard it as synonymous with England, British Isles and United Kingdom, while keeping Ireland, Scotland and Wales as entry words for matter dealing exclusively with those countries. The relevant entries and references are thus

British Isles *see* Great Britain
England *see* Great Britain
Great Britain *see also* Ireland, Scotland, Wales
United Kingdom *see* Great Britain

There will inevitably be a long list of entries beginning with Great Britain. It is reasonable to shorten the list by omitting entries for subjects whose interest is not primarily national, such as the natural sciences and technologies, which may be expected to be sought under their own names, especially when the reader has in mind the birds, trees, railways, etc. of his own country. Under Great Britain will remain the subheadings for subjects which by their very nature are dependent on a particular country, such as Armed Forces, Criminal statistics, Foreign relations, Local government, Population. The reader scanning the Great Britain sequence must then be told that a residue of subjects will be found under their own names. There must also be a reminder that entries beginning with the word English will have relevance to Great Britain, since the terms English language, English literature, etc. will have been preferred to Great Britain – language, and Great Britain – literature, and English art is not the same as Art in Great Britain.

A reader's interest in a foreign country may well be diffuse, just as the library's collections may be less extensive regarding foreign countries. It is then a help to bring together under the name of the foreign country *all* subjects which relate to it, as

Spain – birds
    description and travel
    printing
    recreations – amusements
    textiles – manufactures

Similarly, interest in a purely local area, such as a town or county or other small, named region, like Wicken Fen, may be all-embracing, and should be served accordingly by the index:

Cambridgeshire – birds
Wicken Fen – Cambridgeshire – birds

Double entry in the catalogue or in the index?

A classification scheme which permits the complex subject of a book to be analysed into a succession of levels and of facets may give rise to index entries which *disperse* instead of bringing together related topics. For example, two books on Swedish architecture, one a general history, the other restricted to library buildings, will be classed at 720.9485 and 727.809485 respectively. The specific index entries will be

Sweden – architecture	720.9485
Sweden – libraries – architecture	727.809485

Intermediate entries may separate these two and mislead the searcher into thinking that he will find *all* material on Swedish architecture if he goes to the class number 720.9485. Two remedies offer themselves. One is to make an additional index entry, transposing the final link in order to bring together the 'distributed relatives', thus:

Sweden – architecture	720.9845
Sweden – architecture – libraries	727.809485
Sweden – libraries – architecture	727.809485

The other is to regard the second book as providing for two distinct subject interests: 1) architecture as it is practised in Sweden, and 2) library architecture, and to make two entries in the classified catalogue, one for each subject, instead of throwing the whole burden of collocation on the index and adding to the complexity of the reader's search.

The second remedy could automatically be adopted if a classification scheme with an articulated notation, such as the UDC, were in use.

727.8 : 72(485)
Library architecture : Architecture (Sweden)

72(485) : 727.8
Architecture (Sweden) : Library architecture

72(485)
Architecture (Sweden)

Transposed terms

In specialized subject libraries certain words of wide general application will have a narrowly focused meaning. In a library which supports the manufacture of some product, words like Testing, Maintenance, Coating, may all be entry words. In a general library it is assumed that the reader will first orient himself within his own subject before looking for aspects of it expressed in general terms, and I think one's own experience of reference work will support this assumption. It is the way one approaches any general list oneself: Catalogues – maintenance, Libraries – history, Computers – terminology. This is not because one is conditioned to this approach in the course of becoming a librarian, but because it is quickest to locate the *essential term* first, as other compilers of indexes and lexicographers have established.

Most of Dewey's 'standard subdivisions' fall into the category of 'non-entry words' or terms which will be unsought in the first instance. If they do not merit an entry when they form the final link in a chain, are they to be disregarded or should they be transposed? The *BNB* makes no index entries for history, theory, study and teaching, dictionaries, essays, periodicals, etc., restricted to a particular subject, leaving it to the reader to find his way from, say, 'Science . . . 500' in the index to the part of the classified sequence which shows the history or the study and teaching, etc., of science. But the *BNB* is published primarily for the use of librarians, booksellers and other bibliographers, who may be assumed to have some experience in these matters. The terms 'History of science', 'Study and teaching of science', 'Scientific periodicals' etc., are, however, in common use and it is possible that they will be sought in the index to a library catalogue. An interminable list under History, or Periodicals, of all the subjects which may have a history or may be written about in periodicals would defeat its own ends and, as we have presupposed, would not be much sought. A general reference to specific subjects might be a useful warning, as

History – general	900
History – specific subjects	
see the name of the subject required	
Periodicals – general	050
Periodicals – specific subjects	
see the name of the subject required	

At the entry for the subject, the links in the chain may be transposed, as

Science	500
Science – collections	508
Science – dictionaries	503
Science – history	509
Science – periodicals	505
Science – philosophy	501

Other very general terms, such as Equipment, Maintenance, Testing, which have little significance unless related to the process for which the equipment is designed, the machinery which is to be maintained or the product which is to be tested,

should also be transposed in a general index. Testing glass as a process in its manufacture would be classified in the Decimal classification as follows

660	Chemical technology
666	Ceramic and allied technologies
666.1	Glass
666.13	Tests, analyses, quality controls

The specific index entry would be

Glass – testing – chemical technology   666.13

Editing the chain index

The main function of notation in a classification scheme is to preserve the chosen order. It may be argued that its function is also to show gradations of division, but it is evident that Dewey – and Bliss and the Library of Congress – did not regard this as an essential function and often Dewey has preferred brevity to 'expressiveness' of notation, with the result that it is easy to overlook a class in the ordered descent if it has not been signalled with the expected notational symbol. The *BNB* shows the inclusive numbers covered by a 'centred heading', as in

Christianity	220/280
Manufactures – special materials	660/680
Geography, General – special localities	914/919
History, Modern – special localities	940/999
History, Modern – special localities – bibliographies	016.94/9

The inclusive numbering warns the user that the subject is not comprehended in a single class number. The warning needs to be supplemented by guidance in the classified sequence.

A neat device adopted by the *BNB* for use within an index entry is to combine an abstract or very vague term with the next term in the chain to make a qualifying phrase which begins with the more concrete term in adjectival form. Thus the crude entries

Concrete – materials – engineering	620.136
Iron – materials – engineering	620.17
Japan – policies – production – economics	338.952
Miracles – doctrine – theology – Christianity	231.73

199

become

Concrete – engineering materials	620.136
Iron – engineering materials	620.17
Japan – economic organization	338.952
Miracles – Christian doctrine	231.73

'Materials', 'Organization', 'Policies' are considered unsought headings and are therefore not used as entry words. Telescoping of terms within an entry not only shortens the entry, it can also lessen ambiguity, as

| Germany – British foreign policy | 327.42043 |

is preferable to

| Germany – Great Britain – foreign relations | 327.42043 |

Another device for shortening an entry, and at the same time making the meaning clearer, is to prefer the name of the inclusive class rather than a more specific term as the final qualifier. Thus the class mark 338.1771 analysed in full generates the following chain

| Milk – dairy products – special agricultural products – economic organization of special industries – economic organization – economics | 338.1771 |

but there is no ambiguity when this is reduced to

Milk – dairy industry – economics	338.1771
Milk products – economics	338.177
Agriculture – industries – economics	338.1
Industries – economics	338.1/4
Production – economics	338
Economics	330

There is a risk that such telescoping of terms may be practised inconsistently by different indexers and that more time and skill will be needed to assimilate editorial practices. Chain procedure was chosen initially by the editors of *BNB* because it could be applied with speed and economy.

Chain procedure set a pattern for subject indexing method which disposed of the need for individual determination of every vexatious question of component order and permutation. An important incidental advantage of chain procedure was that subordinate staff could be instructed very rapidly, and once familiar with the method, they had the satisfaction of working to a plan which they could understand rather than to the inscrutable edicts of someone in authority.[16]

These words on the application of chain procedure to the Decimal classification in preparing the continuous indexes to the *BNB* were written by E. J. Coates, who for ten years, almost from its inception, was in charge of subject cataloguing at the British National Bibliography. When he was writing, in 1960, the *BNB* was recording about 375 items a week. For the next ten years, while the number of imprints being recorded multiplied a hundredfold, chain indexing continued to provide an adequate means of access to them. It has also proved acceptable to the public in guides to the catalogues and shelves of a variety of libraries.

A sample index
In the list below the index entries proposed earlier in this chapter have been alphabetized and additional entries (marked with an asterisk) have been interpolated to show the general appearance of the index, the essential role played by the qualifying links, and the variety in the terminology, including synonyms and more inclusive terms, by means of which a reader may reach the specific classification number for a required subject.

*Animals – cruelty – ethics	179.3
Animals – ecology	591.5
*Animals – pests – agriculture	632.6
Animals – zoology	590
Anseriformes	598.41
Aquatic birds – geographic distribution	598.2924
Aquatic birds – taxonomic zoology	598.3
Aves	598
Behaviour – animals	591.51
Behaviour – birds	598.25
*Behaviour – ethics	170
Biology	570
Bird watching	598.07234
*Birds – bibliographies	016.598
*Birds – domestic animals	636.5

Birds – zoology	598
Cambridgeshire – birds	598.294265
*Cambridgeshire – history	942.65
Chordata	596/599
Dictionaries. *See the name of the subject required*	
Distribution – birds	598.29
*Distribution – newspapers	070.33
*Ducks – domestic animals	636.597
Ducks – zoology	598.41
East Anglia – birds	598.29426
*East Anglia – description	914.26
Ecology – birds	598.25
Ecology – zoology	591.5
England. *See Great Britain*	
*English literature	820
Europe – birds	598.294
*Europe – economic conditions	330.94
*Europe – minorities – politics	323.14
Fenland – Cambridgeshire – birds	598.2942653
*Geese – domestic animals	636.598
Geese – zoology	598.41
*Great Britain – cathedrals – architecture	726.0941
*Great Britain – emigrants	325.242
*Great Britain – foreign policy	327.42
*Great Britain – history	942
*Great Britain – maps and atlases	912.42
For other special topics treated in Great Britain see the name of the topic	
and also entries beginning with English	
Habitats – birds	598.252
Life – biology	570
Migration – birds	598.2525
Migration – ecology – zoology	591.525
*Migration – politics	325
Norfolk – birds	598.294261
*Norfolk – history – bibliographies	016.94261
Ornithology	598
*Periodicals – general	050
Periodicals – special subjects. *See the name of the subject*	
*Research – knowledge in general	001.4
Research – special subjects. *See the name of the subject*	
Swans – zoology	598.41
Taxonomy – birds	598.3
Taxonomy – zoology	592/599

Vertebrates	596/599
Water birds – distribution	598.2924
Water birds – zoology	598.3
*Waterfowl – hunting – sport	799.244
Waterfowl – zoology	599.41
Wicken Fen – Cambridgeshire – birds	598.2942653
Wildfowl – zoology	598.2924
Zoology	590
Zoology – dictionaries	591.03

It can be deduced from what has already been said that chain indexing may be used in conjunction with any logical classification scheme equipped with an acceptable notation. Step-by-step number-building is not a prerequisite. The Library of Congress has classified Gieure's book on Braque at ND553.B86G5.

The schedules give

N	Fine Arts
ND	Painting
ND 25-1257	General
ND 49-1113	History
ND 201-1113	Special countries, Table IV
ND 541-553	France

[Table IV gives: France 341-353. Applied to ND this becomes ND 541-553. Last number: special artists A-Z]

ND 553	Individuals
ND 553.B86	Braque
ND 553.B86G5	Gieure's book on Braque

(G5 is no longer part of the classification notation. It is the author notation, which distinguishes one book on Braque from another and when added to the class mark completes the call mark by which the book is identified.)

The index entries will be as follows:

Braque, Georges – French painters	ND 553.B86
French painters – biography and criticism	ND 553
French painting	ND 541-553
Painting – history and criticism	ND 49-1113
Painting	ND
Fine arts	N

Assessment of chain indexing

Chain procedure was included among the systems tested in the Aslib/Cranfield experiment, and in both specification and retrieval its performance, in conjunction with a faceted classification scheme, was found to be on a par with the three other methods of subject recording and retrieval which were tested, although, for the detailed analysis of reports and articles on aeronautics which the test required, it was found to be somewhat cumbersome.[17-20]

When highly complex subjects were allotted to a single place in the classification scheme and all the necessary facets were applied in the prescribed, fixed citation order, long chains of index entries necessarily resulted and they were apt to disperse related terms. When, however, the complex subjects were given double or triple entry in the classified sequence under the notation for their most important elements, qualified only by the aspects which related directly to those elements, the index entries became correspondingly shorter and simpler and hence less confusing to use. They led, however, to less specific placings in the classified arrangement. Clearly, for indexing in depth documents relating to a restricted subject, automatic recall and presentation of all aspects is necessary. This cannot be derived from a single reference to a chain index entry. However, the adequacy of chain indexing in a normal library situation was attested by librarians who saw no need to abandon it in favour of PRECIS (see p.213).

Ideally, precise indexing to a classified sequence on the shelves or in a catalogue demands precise specification by the classification scheme in use. (The formulation of chain indexing by Ranganathan referred to his fully faceted Colon classification.) Thinking back to the classified catalogue and index demonstrated at the beginning of this chapter it will be remembered that some of the numbers in the classified catalogue which have been supposedly located through the index will denote too broad a subject because the subject of enquiry has been sought under the name of the class to which it belongs rather than under its own name, as Zoology rather than Birds, or Birds rather than Ducks. Guides in the classified sequence will show how the class has been divided and will lead the reader to the specific subject, and, as I have already suggested, may disclose new openings on the way.

In certain other searches a class number may also prove to be that of an inclusive class rather than of a specific subject although the term for the specific subject was sought – and found – in the index. The specific subjects of Ducks and Swans, for example, have not been given class numbers of their own but have been thrown together with other components of their inclusive class – Anseriformes – so that though the index may distinguish them (as being the specific subjects of books classified) the classified catalogue cannot do so – at least not without departing from the standard classification schedule. The editors of Dewey have assumed that the number of books given the one class number will not be large, and that to scan the titles of a few books to find those that deal with any one component subject will cause but slight inconvenience. It might be suggested that it is improper to mislead a reader thus, and that only terms which have the same meaning as the class number to which they lead should appear in the index, but how can one deny the reader an entry under Ducks and expect him to think of Anseriformes?

Conversely, in making the vertical chain of index entries, it is possible to imply that material dealing with a class as a whole is available, whereas only books on parts of the class are in the library. To take an example from a different field, the horizontal chains

Pistols – small arms [– fire arms – arms and armour]   739.7443
Helmets – defensive arms [– arms and armour]   739.75

will give rise to the inclusive-class entry

Arms and armour   739.7

The reader interested in swords and daggers, or in body armour, may be misled into thinking that his subject is covered by a work in the library, whereas it is not: pistols and helmets do not add up to Arms and armour as a comprehensive class.

It was for this reason that the editors of *BNB* had introduced their extensions to Dewey numbers, together with their explanatory 'feature heading'. By means of those devices readers could trace a specific subject found in the index through the verbal extensions added to its Dewey number in the main sequence. They could also check whether a relatively general subject, referred in the index to a class number, was in fact covered by a correspondingly general book – in some cases an unrewarded search.

In the interests of international standardization the editors of the *BNB* decided that from January 1972 they would use the 18th edition of the Dewey classification as it stood, and abandon the use of the extensions and reorganizations which they had made (to the 14th and 16th editions) in order to obtain greater specificity and a closer semantic correspondence between the index entry and its class mark.

PRECIS

Objectives

By that time the yearly intake of the *BNB* was around 39,000 titles and automatic processing of the bibliography was inevitable. Preparation for computerization had provided the opportunity to refine the system of indexing so that subject specification did not depend only on the classification number, which in many cases would insufficiently distinguish items in such a vast bibliography. The decreased specificity of the classification notation was to be compensated for by the increased specificity of the index entry. The subject of each document was to be analysed and restated in a manner which should set out the specific subject, the way in which it had been treated, the form of presentation, and any other relevant aspect. In addition, the analytical subject statement was to be capable of rearrangement so that any term in it likely to be sought could become the 'lead' (i.e. leading) term of an index entry, and would itself be qualified by the other terms. No matter which term appeared in the leading position, the full statement of the subject would be presented and would refer to the complete class mark. Hence the name given to the new system – PRECIS – derived from its fuller designation – PREserved Context Index System. The system was designed to be wholly manipulable by automatic data processing. Its chief architect was Derek Austin, who has set out the history of its development,[21] and the details of its procedures, the latter in a manual[22] and also in a simplified form.[23] A primer is also available.[24]

An example will demonstrate the difference between chain indexing and PRECIS. Where chain indexing would generate the following entries:

Mathematical models – circuits – electrical equipment
                                    621.31920184
Circuits – electrical equipment   621.3192
Electrical equipment   621.319

PRECIS would generate:

Mathematical models. Circuits. Electrical equipment
                                    621.31920184
Circuits. Electrical equipment
    Mathematical models   621.31920184
Electrical equipment.
    Circuits. Mathematical models   621.31920184

The printed presentation of each entry has its own layout and terminology. The first term in the entry, the access word, is the 'lead', here shown in bold type. The term or succession of terms which sets the lead in its context follows the lead on the same line of type and is the 'qualifier'. The term or succession of terms which focuses on the most narrow division of the subject within the context of the lead takes a separate line and is the 'display'. In the first entry above, the whole entry is contained in the lead and its successively more comprehensive qualifying terms. In the second entry there is only one more comprehensive term to act as qualifier; the term which indicates the focus of the entry forms the display. In the third entry the lead is the most comprehensive term; its successive divisions are set out in the display.

Clearly the facility for producing such entries depends first upon rigid rules of subject analysis: the identification of the different elements of the whole, in conformity with a predetermined set of categories, and the recognition of the relationships of the elements with each other. It then requires a formal statement – a 'string' – of terms to express the individualized concepts together with their interrelationships. Into this string must also be encoded instructions to the computer for manipulation and printout. An index must always be a conventionalized presentation of words for the sake of brevity and consistency, but the terminology, the juxtaposition of terms, and the use of prepositions and other linking words in PRECIS have been kept as near to natural language as possible. Although its origins lie in chain indexing, PRECIS has a syntax, not a citation order. The computer has been programmed to manipulate the primary string so that significant elements from it become in turn the lead term, other elements are transposed, or 'shunted', to use Derek Austin's metaphor, prepositions are substituted according to the position of the phrase they are used in, and typographical variations are specified.

Concept analysis

Since a full exposition of PRECIS is available elsewhere, only a summary of the method of concept analysis and an indication of the devices used by the indexer to present computer-manipulable copy are given here, partly to complete the picture of a classified catalogue and its subject index, partly because a summary exposition is always useful as a preliminary to a study in depth.

Everything that exists or can be imagined is either an entity (a thing) or an activity (an action performed or suffered by an entity).

From the entities and activities which form the subject of a document, the indexer must pick out the 'key system' as his primary indexing term. This he does by stating the subject of the document in his own words and then looking first for the activity(ies) represented in his statement. An activity may be intransitive, having no object, as water flowing. It may be transitive, being an action performed by one entity upon another, as water eroding rocks, or by two entities reciprocally, as trading between two countries, implying mutual involvement. Secondly the indexer looks for the object(s) and the agent(s) of the activity(ies). The terms thus identified are then written down together with the 'role operators' assigned to them in Austin's table of role operators set out in Appendix 1 of his manual.

The key system, signified by the operator (1), is the object of a transitive action, or, in the absence of a transitive action, the agent of an intransitive action. The action itself is signified by the operator (2) and the agent of a transitive action by the operator (3). Thus, to take an example, the natural language statement 'Pollination of flowers by birds' is restated as (1) flowers (2) pollination (3) birds. To write a string which (when properly coded) instructs the computer to use each of the three terms as a lead, the indexer writes the terms in the order of their numerical operators and puts a tick above each term. He also ensures readability and clarity in the printout by instructing the computer to insert prepositions to read 'of flowers' and 'by birds'. This he does by using the connectives $v (downward reading component) and $w (upward reading component) before the relevant prepositions, so that when a higher term, that is, (1) or (2), takes the lead 'by' will be printed and when (3) takes the lead 'of' will be printed. The complete string is thus

(1) flŏwers
(2) pŏllination $v by $w of
(3) bĭrds

The resultant entries are

Flowers.
  Pollination by birds
Pollination. Flowers
  By birds
Birds.
  Pollination of flowers

The analysis and consequent string of terms required by the above example are very simple. More complex relationships of course exist between concepts in the mass of material to be indexed. Austin has set out those he considers essential in his Appendix 1. His text explains basic indexing decisions which lead the indexer through a series of questions and decisions to the identification of relationships and the correct coding of terms. A set of algorithms shows how to set out strings for computer manipulation.

The relationships other than those of key system, action and agent, may be summarized as follows. An entity, or system – the term is explained on page 144-5 – may be a whole or part of a whole. It may have specific attributes. Both parts and attributes are designated by the code letter (p), as Cars (p) bodywork, Cars (p) speed. Austin explains the impossibility of always maintaining a distinction between the two, and also the lack of necessity to do so. The truly generic relationship of an entity to its inclusive class is not specified in the analysis but is covered by a reference which will apply to all occurrences of the index term (see below). However, membership of a quasi-generic group, as (q) saloon cars, and of an aggregate, or assembly, as (r) second-hand cars, is noted.

Other contexts to be noted are geographical location, as Higher education (O) Great Britain, and what may at first sight appear to be a geographical location but is in fact the geographical limitation of a sample population or study region which might be considered typical of a larger survey, as in the Effect of environment on office workers (5) [studied in] Milton Keynes.

The viewpoint of the document's presenter may also be specified, as Marriage (4) Roman Catholic viewpoint, and also that of the target-user, as First aid (6) for motorists. Included with the latter are the form of presentation of the material in the document and of the document itself, since both also affect the choice or rejection of the document, as Road accidents (6) statistics, or (6) filmstrip.

Relationships that cannot with certainty be deduced from the juxtaposition of terms or by the use of simple prepositions, as in the example given of the pollination of flowers by birds, are explained using the operator(s) to denote the (unusual) role of some agent in an action, or an indirect agent, such as a tool, or an indirect action, such as the influence of one particular action upon another action.

An author's treatment of a subject may be influenced not by a point of view but by his use of comparison with another subject or by the use of a particular discipline to expound it, as the Teaching of reading (t) compared with the Teaching of mathematics or the Teaching of reading (t) psychological aspects.

A sete of 'differencing operators' is more directly concerned with the connections between terms and their placing among themselves in the index entries. Introduced by the dollar sign followed by a letter, they control the manipulation of compound terms, ensuring, for example, that the words of a

210

compound phrase always appear in their natural-language order, that only significant terms appear in the lead position and that a qualifying date appears in italics and immediately after the term to which it refers.

Finally, provision has been made for identifying co-ordinate concepts, using (g), as in two gardening examples:

(1) evergreens
(2) propagation $ &
(g) pruning

(1) ornamental trees $ &
(g) shrubs
(2) cultivation

Where co-ordinate concepts are related in a more complicated manner the operators (x), (y) and (z) are introduced to ensure that index entries are provided for each set of relationships.

References linking permanent relationships

There remain three sets of relationship which are permanent, whatever the context in which the relator occurs. They are covered by general references which are computer-generated whenever a term implying such a relationship appears as a lead.

The first relationship is between terms, not concepts. When terms, for the purpose of a particular index, are regarded as synonymous, one of them is chosen for use and the rejected terms appear only as references, as Corporations *see* Companies; Wages *see* Remuneration. Alternative spellings also are covered by this practice, Thibet *see* Tibet.

The second relationship is the hierarchic relationship which appears as a reference from the name of a more inclusive class to the name of a less inclusive class. This includes the truly generic to specific relationship, as Birds *see also* Gulls, Reefs *see also* Great Barrier Reef; the group-to-subgroup relationship as Clergy *see also* Bishops; and the whole-to-part relationship, as Buildings *see also* Doors, Windows; Sea bed *see also* Continental Shelf.

The third relationship comprises all the other linkings between terms that may exist in people's minds when consulting an index or which may, when expressed as references, direct users to a more appropriate term. These references are reciprocal. They include references between the name of a study and the name of the thing with which the study is concerned, as Numismatics *see also* Coins; and Coins *see also* Numismatics. They also link the name of an action with its agent, patient or product, as Education *see also* Teachers, Students; Cookery *see also* Food; Engineering *see also* Roads; Shipping *see also* Marine insurance. The names of mutually interactive systems such as Costs and Prices are also reciprocally linked. Terminological correspondences are similarly linked with *see also* references, as Oral *see also* Mouth; Mouth *see also* Oral.

All *see also* references precede entries beginning with the term from which they refer, so that the reader may check whether the most appropriate term has been found before proceeding to the classified sequence.

The categories of both conceptual and terminological relationships are set out in greater detail in the section on cross references in the dictionary catalogue in the next chapter.

Authority files

In compiling the *BNB*, when a term is first used as an index entry lead its relationships are sought and noted. The term is given a Reference Indicator Number (RIN), that is, an address within the computer, at which are stored codes to show whether a *see* or *see also* reference is required, together with the RINs of the terms from which references are to be made. Terms from which *see also* references are to be made will likewise be furnished with reference codes and addresses of *their* related terms, so that a whole hierarchy of references is automatically generated whenever a term requiring a reference is used.

A somewhat similar device used at the *BNB* is the Subject Indicator Number (SIN) at which are assembled all the data pertinent to the subject record of a document for which a unique subject analysis has been made. From such analyses authority files are generated and an indexer checking his subject analysis of any subsequent document against the authority file may find that it duplicates a subject record already held. If it does, instead of encoding the PRECIS

212

string, seeking the classification number, the LC subject heading and so on, the indexer merely inserts the SIN into the record and the computer generates the PRECIS index entry and the rest of the subject data.

Assessment of PRECIS

Although PRECIS is not widely applied in individual organizations, PRECIS indexes are widely *used* in searching bibliographical publications issued by BNB and UTLAS, and interest in the system is certainly widespread. That interest has been shown in a number of workshops held in North America, such as the one organized by the University of Maryland,[25] in the preparation of a bibliography (with plans for keeping it up to date) in Denmark,[26] in an experiment at the Deutsche Bibliotek,[27] in another at Woollongong University, designed to test the retrieval effectiveness of PRECIS in terms of recall and precision measures when used in an academic library catalogue,[28] and in the development of PRECIS as the framework of a translingual indexing system.[29]

The impact of PRECIS on library administrators and the cataloguers who apply it has been surveyed, perhaps prematurely since change takes time and few libraries at the time of the survey (1977) were using the new system.[30]

One of the reasons given for not using PRECIS was its complexity. Much study of classification, semantics and syntax, as well as of the potentialities of automatic data processing, preceded the formulation of PRECIS. It is not surprising that some study is necessary to understand and apply it. (Practical courses are arranged from time to time by the British Library.) Now that PRECIS entries are available online through BLAISE (with the rest of the catalogue entry), and that the PRECIS vocabulary and also a complete subject authority listing are available on microfiche from the British Library, there will be more confidence in its use. An open-ended vocabulary has advantages, but it can lead to chaos.

Another reason given for not using PRECIS was the adequacy of the library's existing indexing system, whether a chain index as used in the *BNB* until 1971 or a locally devised system. Chain indexing is certainly more economical in that its generation and manipulation do not require so much intellectual effort, and the entries, as one moves up the hierarchic chain are progressively shorter. The last consideration is important where repeated printing of the index is required, as, for example, in *LISA*, where economy of printing and paper must be considered.

Users' reactions to PRECIS indexes have also been surveyed.[31] Generally, users were favourably impressed with PRECIS indexes, especially by the precision of the entries, in contrast to the broad subject headings got from some existing authorities, although the lack of a thesaurus (at that time) was regretted. The Woollongong study also found that library users liked 'the semblance of an indicative abstract in the catalogue entry'.[32] A drawback commented upon was that although the PRECIS index entry is specific, the class number to which it leads may be less precise. Even in the *BNB* the verbal feature headings which add precision to the class number may not be set out in the same sequence of terms as the index entry and in catalogues which lack feature headings considerable search at the class number may be necessary.

Various other string index systems have been developed. They are akin to PRECIS in that, once generated, a string is computer-manipulable to produce entries under as many keywords as the subject requires, each displayed with its full context.[33]

The different indexing systems used in a number of libraries replying to a questionnaire in 1976/77 were tabulated by Hunter and Bakewell.[34] They show chain indexing to be predominant in both academic and public libraries (a total of 106 libraries), although in-house systems were reported by half that number of libraries, and PRECIS by 13. Special libraries generally used schemes of their own devising.

The author index

The classified catalogue is necessarily complemented by an author index, or more usefully, by a name catalogue (see Chapter 14).

References

1 Fumagalli, G., *Cataloghi di biblioteche e indici bibliografici*. Firenze: Sansoni, 1887, xiii.

2   Rostgaard, Frederik, *Project d'une nouvelle méthode pour dresser le catalogue d'une bibliothèque selon les matières, avec le plan*. 2.ed. Paris: 1698.

3   Garside, Kenneth, 'Subject cataloguing in German libraries', *Journal of documentation*, 6(4), 1950, 188-205.

4   British National Bibliography, *Supplementary classification schedules prepared to augment the Dewey Decimal Classification for use in the British National Bibliography and first introduced in January 1960*. London: BNB, 1963.

5   Coates, E. J., *Subject catalogues: headings and structure*. London: LA, 1960, 121-3.

6   Cutter, Charles A., *Explanation of the Cutter-Sanborn author-marks three-figure tables*, revised by Kate Emery Jones. Northampton: Mass.: Kingsbury Press, 1935. (Published together with the tables: *C. A. Cutter's alphabetic-order table...*; altered and fitted with three figures by Miss Kate E. Sanborn.)

7   Lehnus, Donald J., *Book numbers: history, principles, application*. Chicago: ALA, 1980.

8   Ranganathan, S. R., *Prolegomena to library classification*. London: LA, 1957, 371-8.

9   Jackson, Sidney L., 'Date treatment of broad subject headings in thirty major libraries: a report with comments', *Journal of cataloging and classification*, 9, 1953, 21-4.

10 Warner, Gilmore, 'Living, fresh and new', *Journal of cataloging and classification*, 10, 1954, 138-44.

11 See reference 2 above.

12 Lund, John J. and Taube, Mortimer, 'A nonexpansive classification system: an introduction to period classification', *Library quarterly*, 7, 1937, 373-94.

13 Ranganathan, S. R., *The Colon classification*. New Brunswick, N.J.: Graduate School of Library Services, Rutgers State University, 1965 (Rutgers series on systems for the intellectual organization of knowledge, vol. 4), 140-78.

14 Austin, Derek, *PRECIS: a manual of concept analysis and subject indexing*. 2nd ed. London: British Library BSD, 1984. (First ed. published 1974.)

15 Library of Congress. *Library of Congress subject headings*. 9th ed. Washington, D.C.: L.C. Subject Cataloging Division, 1980. (Updated and published in new edition quarterly on microfiche and microfilm.)

16 See reference 5 above, 119-20.

17 Cleverdon, C. W., *Report on the testing and analysis of an investigation into the comparative efficiency of indexing systems*. Cranfield:

Aslib Cranfield Research Project, 1962.

18 'The Aslib research project on the comparative efficiency of indexing systems', *Aslib proceedings*, 12(12), 1960, 421-9.

19 Cleverdon, C. W. and Mills, J., 'The testing of index language devices', *Aslib proceedings*, 15(4), April 1963, 106-30.

20 Swanson, Don R., 'The evidence underlying the Cranfield results', *Library quarterly*, 35(1), 1965, 1-20. (40 references in chronological order, up to April 1965.)

21 Austin, Derek, 'Progress in documentation: the development of PRECIS, a theoretical and technical history', *Journal of documentation*, 30(1), 1974, 47-102.

22 See reference 14 above.

23 Austin, Derek and Verdier, Veronica, *PRECIS: introduction and indexing*. London, Ont.: University of Western Ontario School of Library and Information Science, 1977. (String indexing)

24 Dykstra, Mary, *PRECIS: a primer*. London: British Library BSD, 1985.

25 *The PRECIS index system: principles, applications and prospects. Proceedings of the International PRECIS Workshop, sponsored by the College of Library and Information Services of the University of Maryland, 1976*; ed. by Hans H. Wellisch. New York: Wilson, 1977.

26 *A bibliography of PRECIS*. 2nd ed. compiled by Jutta Sørensen. Copenhagen: Royal School of Librarianship, 1979.

27 Maassen, Bernd, 'The PRECIS project of the Deutsche Bibliotek', *International cataloguing*, 13(2), 1984, 15-17.

28 Hunt, Roslyn, 'The subject catalogue in Australian academic libraries: PRECIS, LSCH and KWOC and the findings of the Woollongong University Subject Catalogue Study', *Australian academic and research libraries*, 9(2), June 1978, 61-70. 19 refs. (Full report on microfiche available from the (Australian) Education Research and Development Committee.)

29 Verdier, V., *Final report of the PRECIS translingual project*. London: British Library Research and Development Department, 1981.

30 Bakewell, K. G. B. and others, *A study of indexers' reactions to the PRECIS indexing system*. Liverpool: Liverpool Polytechnic Dept. of Library and Information Studies, 1978. (BLRDR 5433)

31 Peters, Helen Jane, *User reactions to PRECIS indexes*. Liverpool: Liverpool Polytechnic School of Librarianship and Information Studies, 1981. (BLRDR 5659)

32 See reference 28, p.68.

33 Craven, Timothy C., *String indexing*. Orlando, Fla.; London:

Academic Press, 1986.

34 Hunter, Eric and Bakewell, K. G. B., *Cataloguing.* 2nd ed. London: Bingley, 1983, 204-5.

12
The dictionary catalogue

Introduction
The term Dictionary Catalogue in English and American usage generally denotes a file of entries arranged in alphabetical order like an ordinary dictionary under the names of persons, corporate bodies, publications, classes of things, individual things and events, and forms of publication, as originally laid down by Cutter in the last century.[1] Under the name headings are subsumed descriptions of materials held in the library by or about the persons or entities or in the forms named. That will be the connotation assumed for this chapter. It will also be assumed that the reader has read Chapters 8 – 11 on the Subject catalogue, Terminology, and the Classified catalogue, and will not need repetition of details here.

Large dictionary catalogues are often divided into two sequences, one for authors and titles and for corporate bodies as producers of documents, the other for subjects and for forms of publication, that is, into an Author and a Subject catalogue. Alternatively, a dictionary catalogue may be divided into a Name catalogue and a Subject catalogue. (For what entries may be included in and excluded from a name catalogue see Chapter 14.)

The choice and form of names for persons and corporate bodies as originators of publications, and the form of titles of documents when they are required as filing entries, are not discussed here. They form part of the matter of the companion volume to this book (see Preface). When they are themselves the subject of publications, persons and corporate bodies appear under the same form of name as that established for them as authors, or originators, with, where necessary, some additional word or phrase to show the subject aspect. The rest of this chapter will therefore discuss chiefly the assignment of subject headings in a dictionary catalogue, or in the alphabetical subject catalogue. Particular reference will be made to the Library of Congress's list of subject headings (*LCSH*).[2] Emphasis has been placed on *LCSH* partly because it has given rise to the typical form of the dictionary catalogue, and partly because mastery of that list will make understanding and applying other systems relatively easy. Coates's *Subject catalogues* discusses most of the varieties of verbal subject-heading catalogues.[3] To them must be added the more recently devised PRECIS, which can function as effectively to generate an alphabetical subject catalogue as to produce the index to a classified catalogue.

Subject headings: specific and direct

The procedure for identifying the subject of a document is the same whether for a dictionary or for a classified catalogue (see Chapter 8).

Whereas the classified catalogue presents a subject in the context of its embracing discipline or system and often shows in its class notation the full hierarchy of division and sub-division from the main class to the specific topic, the dictionary catalogue presents a subject under the term that can name it most concisely. The naming is to be specific and direct. The two headings

ANIMALS – MAMMALS – BADGERS

and

BADGERS

are equally specific designations of the same subject, but while the former goes down in stages, indirectly, the latter names the subject directly in a single term. Using the classified catalogue, a reader not familiar with the classification scheme needs first to consult the alphabetical index to determine his point of entry into the main subject file. Using the dictionary catalogue, a reader goes straight to the word which he thinks denotes the subject of his search, and this simple, one-step access to the catalogue is claimed as its prime virtue, the coincidence of cataloguer's and reader's terminology and the simplicity of alphabetical arrangement being assumed.

Directness is shown also in the way in which a compound term is written, as Exterior lighting, rather than Lighting, exterior. The reversed order of words would, if applied also to other headings, such as Electric lighting, Interior lighting, Stage lighting, again introduce a classified sequence, which, in the alphabetical catalogue of a general collection presumed to hold a large number of documents on specific subjects, would, it is held, disappoint the cataloguer-user's expectation of finding subjects listed under the names by which they were commonly known. The alphabetico-classed catalogue is not without its uses, however. In a specialized environment, where readers' interests may be expected to be concentrated on recurrent aspects of a limited number of subjects, it may be most useful to display subjects in this way. For example, an agricultural library might use headings which followed a pattern similar to the (much simplified) one below.

```
CATTLE – Breeds – Ayrshire
              – Charolais
              – Galloway
              – Guernsey [etc.]
         Diseases – Anthrax
                  – Brucellosis
                  – Scabies
                  – Tuberculosis [etc.]
HORSES – Breeds – Clydesdale
                – Percheron [etc.]
         Diseases – Distemper
                  – Glanders
                  – Tapeworm [etc.]
SHEEP [etc. as above]
```

Just as librarians speak of 'the reader' (knowing quite well that there is no such composite figure but only a number of diverse individual readers) so readers form their own idea of 'the librarian', and in a general library may simplify a highly specific request by stating it in terminology which denotes a broader field more suited to the understanding of a non-specialist. Many librarians from Cutter onwards have reported their own experience of such requests. Sharp, for example, is inclined to favour a broader (class) heading, with a subheading denoting the (specific) subclass,[4] and Dunkin comments on proposals for double entry under both class and specific names.[5] On the other hand, in a library dedicated to serving a particular discipline or technology, the librarian is expected to be familiar at least with the terminology of the speciality, and it must be remembered that a national reference library will contain many specialist collections, each with its own librarian.

Words, as everyone knows, are slippery. 'Specific', to begin with, is an inexact word. How could it be possible to denote in a single term the whole content of a monograph? Even a comprehensive treatise is limited by the author's ignorance, in addition to any limitations of time, space or aspect which he himself voluntarily imposes on his subject matter. Degrees of specificity must be admitted. The degree of specificity required in any one catalogue depends on the number of publications recorded and the degree of interest in any one subject among the library's clientele. Any thesaurus compiled for a particular use distinguishes between 'core' subjects and 'fringe' subjects, the former being given more exact naming than the latter. The traditional dictionary catalogue assigns a heading which on its own designates the subject of a document as completely as the catalogue is thought to require, that is, by pre-coordinate indexing. One-word headings and one-term compound headings seldom suffice. The term denoting the key subject must often be qualified by a subheading denoting limitations in its treatment.

Library of Congress subject headings (LCSH)
The traditional dictionary catalogue has its most famous, and most voluminous, exemplar in the Library of Congress. The technique of making the catalogue was codified in 1951 by David Judson Haykin, then Chief of the Library's Subject Cataloging Division,[6] and from that time onwards the list of subject headings compiled in the Library of Congress *(LCSH)* has been based on Haykin's principles, although the compilation of other thesauri and the publication of relevant standards have not been ignored. Current practice within the Library has been described by Lois Mai Chan.[7] (Dunkin has provided a summary of American cataloguing practice leading

up to Haykin and also comments on Haykin's rulings.[8]

Many large libraries, particularly large academic libraries, use LC subject headings as the source of terminology and syndesis. Brunel University – though not large as academic libraries go – obtains 80% of all its cataloguing data directly from LC through MARCFICHE, and uses the headings as found.[9] Many other libraries use the simplified list of headings derived from the LC list known, after its first compiler, as *Sears list of subject headings*.[10] The introduction to *Sears* is such an excellent guide to the use of that list that here I merely refer the reader to it. The following pages will give some guidance on using the Library of Congress list of subject headings, at the same time setting out the general principles on which such lists are based and utilized. Some libraries have compiled their own authority list of subject headings, yet others use published thesauri.

Content and arrangement

LCSH lists in one alphabetical sequence terms which may be used as headings to denote subjects and forms of publications, and terms rejected as headings but required as 'see' references. The former are printed in bold type, the latter in light type. Where necessary, a scope note follows a heading to show the extent of the meaning attached to it within the list. Related terms, introduced by *sa*, are shown as a warning to the user of the list, that is the catalogue maker, to see also the terms which follow, usually terms narrower in meaning, and to consider whether one, or more, of them would more precisely express the subject of the document being analysed. Other related terms, introduced by *xx*, are suggested as references to be inserted into the catalogue for the catalogue-user's benefit. Their purpose and the categories they fall into are explained later.

Also listed are the subheadings which may be appended to individual entry terms. The subheadings follow, in their own alphabetical sequence, the terms they qualify. Complex subjects may need the addition of sub-subheadings. A lengthy example is the set of subheadings under UNITED STATES. ARMY.

Omitted from *LCSH* are most names of individual persons and corporate bodies (for which the correct form of entry can be established by applying the rules of *AACR2*), and a few other categories of heading, such as references from the name of a class to individually named members of that class, the need for which would depend entirely upon a particular library's holdings.

New concepts which have appeared in the literature to be catalogued, together with new terms which have become current, are discussed at weekly meetings of the library's subject cataloguers and classifiers, who decide on the establishment of new preferred terms, alternative terms to be noted and the references to and from existing terms which the incorporation of new terms into the list will necessitate. Most candidates for admission to the list name new developments in technology. Many such have been admitted during the last 20 years, including ABDOMINAL DECOMPRESSION, AERIAL PHOTOGRAPHY IN BOTANY, POSTAL SERVICE – Automation, SIMULATED WOOD. The social sciences also produce new terms, such as PREVENTIVE DENTISTRY, and MARCH ON WASHINGTON FOR JOBS AND FREEDOM, 1963. Among changed headings are DRILLING MUDS, which replaces OIL WELL DRILLING FLUIDS, and AERONAUTICS IN MISSIONARY WORK, which (regrettably) replaces FLYING MISSIONARIES. Suggestions for additional references submitted by other libraries have, from October 1982, been accepted for consideration.[11] Instructions for submitting proposals for a new term are given in the Library's *Subject cataloging manual.*[12] Updated editions of *LCSH* are available quarterly on microfiche or microfilm.

Because *LCSH* is vast, various and somewhat complicated, it is essential to read the introduction before making use of the list. It is also a great help to keep by one for reference at any time the supplementary guide prepared by LC's Subject Cataloging Division entitled *Library of Congress subject headings: a guide to subdivision practice.*[13]

Choice and form of headings

Subject headings in *LCSH* have been chosen because they are commonly used and seem likely to be permanent names for the things they designate. The variety of grammatical forms found in LC headings is hardly surprising. Language itself does not follow strict rules of development and a large catalogue which has been in the making for nearly a century is bound to contain inconsistencies. Inconsistencies may be accounted for in part by the fact that the literature and non-print materials which now come into a library for ordinary cataloguing (as opposed to specialist abstracting and indexing services) have tended to include more specialized subject matter than did monographs earlier in the century, and hence to require more detailed subject headings.

Introducing the sixth edition of *LCSH*, the then Chief of the Subject Cataloging Division, Richard Angell, said, 'The list is the product of evolutionary forces, among them the growth of the library's collections, semantic change, and varying theories of subject heading practice over the years. As a consequence the list is, at any point in time, an accurate reflection of practice but not a complete embodiment of theory.' The editor of the ninth edition qualifies that by saying that since computerization of the list 'it has become a less accurate reflection of practice, with some headings and subheadings remaining in the list in contradiction to current policies. It is far easier to announce a change in policy than to eradicate every example of an obsolescent practice in the list'.[14]

Thus we find headings consisting of a single noun, as AUTOMOBILES; a noun followed by a qualifier which prevents confusion with a homonym, as CONDENSERS (STEAM), HORN (MUSICAL INSTRUMENT); an adjective followed by a noun, or two nouns, the first of which is used adjectivally, as INDUSTRIAL STATISTICS, LOCAL GOVERNMENT, SCHOOL EMPLOYEES: such compound terms transposed, as FISHES, FOSSIL; and summary phrases, as DOMICILE IN TAXATION, GASTEROPODA AS CARRIERS OF DISEASE, MONTESSORI METHOD OF EDUCATION. 'Uninverted phrase headings are to be preferred', says Haykin, 'since they represent the normal order of words and it can be reasonably assumed that most readers would not look under the inverted form'.[15] The transposed form is still used, however, for phrase headings the second term of which appears as an independent heading, as does FISHES. We shall find also certain categories of terms, such as those denoting an activity and its agent, a thing and its opposite, used in combination because, although the terms may each be patient of separate definition, one member of the pair can hardly be discussed without reference to the other, giving such headings as BANKS AND BANKING, FOOD ADULTERATION AND INSPECTION. Literary warrant justifies the use of such combined headings as CHURCH AND STATE to denote the interaction of the two entities named. Finally, we may find parallel concepts expressed either as a direct heading or as a heading followed by a subheading as AGRICULTURAL EDUCATION and ART – Study and teaching. Examples to show the various forms used to achieve specificity in LC headings have been gathered by Hilda Steinweg.[16]

Using LCSH

Choice between topic and place
When a document to be catalogued treats one subject in relation to another subject the usual method of subject analysis will determine which is the real subject and which the subordinate subject, or aspect, or form, leading to the choice of main heading and subheading (called 'subdivision' in the Library of Congress). Thus, where a topic has been treated in relation to a place, the topic will take precedence, the locality will be named as subheading; where the place has been identified as the real subject, the place name will be the entry word, with a topical qualification forming the subheading. As a rule of thumb, subjects of scientific, artistic, technical, economic and educational interest are entered under the name of the subject, qualified where necessary by a place-name subheading; subjects of historical and descriptive interest, and also most subjects of administrative and social interest, are entered as subheadings to the name of a place

DIAMOND MINES AND MINING – India
                                   – South Africa
HEALTH EDUCATION – India
WINTER SPORTS FACILITIES – Scotland
INDIA – Description and travel
INDIA – Economic conditions

INDIA – Politics and government
INDIA – Social life and customs
GRENOBLE – Description – Guide books
GRENOBLE – History
GRENOBLE – Social life and customs

Where a town, or other small locality, is the focus of interest, the rule of thumb is frequently reversed, to bring the place name to the fore, as in the following examples.

GRENOBLE – Sports facilities
NEW YORK (CITY) – Buildings – Conservation and restoration
NEW YORK (CITY) – Stores, shopping centres, etc.

Geographical headings

The Library of Congress Descriptive Cataloging Division is responsible for establishing the form of geographical names which are potential author headings. Such names used as subject headings therefore take the same form as when they are used as author headings. However, a change of name does not imply multiple entries for places according to the date of the place's history to which publications refer. Where a place has had a continuous history, its latest name is to be used as entry word for all subject headings, with references from previous names. Thus, although (following *AACR2* rule 24.1B) government publications will be entered under CEYLON until 22 May 1972 and after that date under SRI LANKA, all subject entries will be entered under SRI LANKA.

Occasionally such headings are unexpected. For instance we find in *LCSH*:

ISTANBUL
  – Riot, 1955
  – – Pictorial works
  – Siege, 1203-1204
  – Siege, 1422
  – Siege, 1453
    xx Byzantine Empire – History
    Turkey – History – 1288-1453

Do we ever think of the Crusaders besieging 'Istanbul'? But imagine successive names being used for the history of our own country: ALBION for the Celtic period, BRITANNIA for the

226

Roman period, ENGLAND from the time of King Alfred, GREAT BRITAIN from the time of the Union! Ancient and modern Rome are, however, distinguished. The history of Ancient Rome up to A.D. 476 is entered at the heading ROME, while the modern city is designated ROME (ITALY).

Geographical features and regions which cannot be originators of documents are named by the Subject Cataloging Division. So far as possible, new headings are based on existing headings, with the United States Board on Geographic Names and national authorities available for reference. Territorial qualifiers, where needed, are added in parentheses, the name of a smaller region coming first. The examples which follow are taken from LC's own explanation of their current practice.[17]

EUPHRATES RIVER
PO VALLEY (Italy)
PELICAN LAKE (Otter Trail County, Minn.)
BEACON HILL (Boston, Mass.)

Geographical subheadings

Topical headings which may be subdivided by place names are indicated in *LCSH* by the word – in italics and parentheses – *(Indirect)*. 'Indirect' has the additional meaning that where a smaller locality than a country is concerned, the name of the country is interposed between the name of the subject and the name of the smaller locality, as

AGRICULTURE – France – Rhône Valley

Exceptions to the use of the country name as a gathering-up subheading are made for four countries – Great Britain, Canada, the United States and the Soviet Union. For the constituent countries, provinces, states and republics respectively of those four countries, the name of the constituent country, province, etc. immediately follows the topical entry term, as

AGRICULTURE – Scotland
AGRICULTURE – Ukraine

Perforce, regions not wholly contained within a country or within one of the excepted administrative regions mentioned

227

above, and islands far out in the ocean, must be named directly, as

SCULPTURE – Easter Island
TOURISM – Rocky Mountains

Exception is also made, for obvious reasons, for four cities – Berlin, New York, Washington, D.C., and Jerusalem, as

MUSIC – Instruction and study – Japan – Tokyo

but

MUSIC – Instruction and study – Jerusalem

The rather cryptic instruction (*Indirect*) was orignally used in contrast to (*Direct*). 'Direct' implied that a heading might be followed by the name of a locality within a country without the interposition of the country's name. It was applied to terms for subjects which might be affected by local, rather than national, circumstances. Thus BUILDING LAWS (*Direct*) resulted in such catalogue entries as

BUILDING LAWS – Aargau [a canton of Switzerland]
                – Buenos Aires [a city]
                – Bulgaria [a sovereign state]
                – California [a state of the USA]
                – Dade County – Fla. [an administrative
                  area of a state of the USA]
                – Hamburg [a city]

The practice was abandoned in the mid-1970s, and the computer printout of the 9th edition of *LCSH* responded to a program instruction which substituted (*Indirect*) for (*Direct*) after main headings, in order to collocate within the card catalogue all entries relating to a particular subject in a single country. (*Direct*) appears now only after subheadings, and has its original connotation, giving rise to such entries as

GREAT BRITAIN – Diplomatic and consular service – Oporto

Now that the online catalogue permits searching by qualifiers of either greater or lesser geographical extent, LC is considering reconversion to direct subdivision. If this proposal were adopted, place names would be used as geographical subdivisions in exactly the form in which they are established for use as headings, [as]

CANALS – Venice (Italy)

not

CANALS – Italy – Venice

[and]

SHEEP – Dorset

not

SHEEP – England – Dorset[18]

Care must be taken in applying geographical division to headings for which subdivision by topic is also used, because on some occasions the main heading is qualified by a geographical subheading and then by a topical sub-subheading, and on other occasions first by a topical subheading, and then by a geographical sub-subheading, as in the following entries, where the logic of the different sequences is evident:

EDUCATION – Wisconsin – Curricula

EDUCATION, BILINGUAL – Law and legislation – Belgium

Change of name and sovereignty

As I have noted elsewhere, there are many reasons why a country or a smaller locality may change its name. When a geographical name has been changed, LC requires the up-to-date name to be used for geographical subdivision of a topical heading, just as for an entry word where the place in question is the main subject. That ruling may give a sought heading for a subject of current or continuous interest, but may seem hardly appropriate to qualify a phenomenon peculiar to one time or context. LC's own example takes a book on the banks of Leopoldville in the Belgian Congo in 1910, which must appear in the catalogue under the heading

BANKS AND BANKING – Zaire – Kinshasa

just as the current name has been used as entry word in

ZAIRE – Description and Travel – to 1880

229

Hans Wellisch, in condemning the new practice as 'falsifying the representation of the subject matter of a book', adds that 'the belief that the present map of the world will remain static is unrealistic' and that costly changes in catalogues may need to be made. He also points out that 'direct' geographical subdivision would do away with the problem.[19] There are limits to the application of the rule.

Other categories of subheadings

Other aspects besides the geographical are common to many subjects and are expressed as formalized subheadings, such as Biography, History, Law and legislation, Terminology.

History may be further subdivided by period, as

INDIA – History – 1500-1765
INDIA – History – 18th century [1700-1799]
INDIA – History – British occupation, 1765-1947
INDIA – History – Rohilla war, 1774
INDIA – History – 19th century [1800-1899]

Certain other subjects whose name implies an historical approach may be divided directly by date, as

UNITED STATES – Foreign relations – 1789-1797
UNITED STATES – Foreign relations – Constitutional Period, 1789-1809

Well, not quite 'directly'. The two sets of examples immediately above have been taken from LC's own filing rules.[20] Why, since the arrangement is to be by date, the *name* of the period is interposed between the successive filing elements is hard to understand. If needed for reassurance that the wanted period had been found, the name surely could *follow* the date.

Some activities, component classes or parts, auxiliary devices, attendant evils, and so on are predictable of all individuals in certain categories, and can therefore be expressed in standard terms. (The terms are slightly modified when usage warrants, as can be seen in some of the examples below.) They form a subordinate element in the heading because their very generality or vagueness makes them unsuitable as entry words. Examples of headings and subheadings appropriate to different categories of entries are shown below.

Living things
BONES – Diseases
BONES – Diseases – Genetic aspects
CONIFERS – Diseases and pests
EAR – Diseases
EYE – Diseases and defects
HORSES – Diseases

Manufactured goods
FISHERY PRODUCTS – Preservation
FOOD – Analysis
FOOD – Preservation
FOOD – Storage
STEEL – Analysis
STEEL – Testing
SUGAR – Analysis and testing
SUGAR – Manufacture and refining
SUGAR – Manufacture and refining – By-products

Machines and machine systems
COAL MINES AND MINING – Equipment and supplies
COAL MINES AND MINING – Safety measures
RAILROADS – Equipment and supplies
RAILROADS – Safety measures
REFRIGERATION AND REFRIGERATING MACHINERY
– Maintenance and repair
REFRIGERATION AND REFRIGERATING MACHINERY
– Safety regulations
TELEVISION – Apparatus and supplies
TELEVISION – Repairing

Institutions and undertakings
DEPARTMENT STORES – Accounting
DEPARTMENT STORES – Buildings
DEPARTMENT STORES – Designs and plans
DEPARTMENT STORES – Management
DRESSMAKING – Accounting
SCHOOLS – Accounting
SCHOOLS – Buildings
SCHOOLS – Management

Disciplines and skills
BOTANY – Methodology
BUILDING – Study and teaching

231

CHEMISTRY – Study and teaching
SOCIOLOGY – Methodology

Subheadings are necessary also to separate different forms of presentation of subject matter and different media of publication, as

AGRICULTURE – United States – Directories
AUTOMOBILE RACING – Accidents – Statistics
DURHAM – Guide books
DURHAM – Road maps
FLYING SAUCERS – Bibliography
MAGNETIC AMPLIFIERS – Models
SIN – Sermons

It can be seen that more than one subheading may be necessary, particularly when attention needs to be drawn to geographical, chronological or formal aspects of a subject's treatment. Form subdivisions invariably come last.

The Library of Congress makes a further, arbitrary, division of material on a subject by dividing it by date, or period, of publication, so that early works, or works on a subject which preceded an important point in the subject's development, may be separated from more up-to-date material as

EDUCATION – Early works to 1800
ELECTRIC LIGHTING – Early works to 1870
PSYCHOLOGY – Early works to 1850

It seems to me a better idea to arrange subject entries for all works on the same subject in one chronological sequence as explained in reference to arrangement in the classified catalogue.

'Pattern' subheadings

Not all the subheadings which may be appended to a particular main heading are listed below the heading in *LCSH*. Certain headings have been chosen as 'pattern headings' and they show the subheadings likely to be useful in choosing appropriate entries for all members of the class of subjects to which they belong.

Thus the class of literary authors is represented by Shakespeare; (other persons – in a revised section of the guide – see p.238 below, have a more general list); Organs and regions of the body by Heart, and Foot; Livestock by Cattle – and so on, to a total of 35 categories of subheadings. The categories and their 'pattern headings' are listed on page 12 of the *Guide*.[21]

The *Guide* lists also a set of subdivisions to be used under place names, first for Countries, States, Regions, then Cities and towns, then Bodies of water, streams, etc.

A very useful section of the *Guide* lists the most commonly applied subdivisions (apart from those specific to certain of the pattern headings) that may be added to any heading that they may usefully qualify. The great value of this section lies in the notes which explain the scope and use of the subheadings and refer to possible alternatives.

Cross references

References are made in the catalogue to direct the reader from one entry term to another. References are of two kinds; 'see' references which the reader must follow if he is to use the catalogue successfully, and 'see also' references which he follows if they appear to lead to a more adequate expression of what he wants.

'See' references

When more than one term may be used to designate a single concept, one of the possible terms is chosen to represent the concept as often as it occurs, the other terms are always rejected. This is done in order to limit the number of entries in the catalogue and to use those entries consistently. The reader is directed by a 'see' reference from a rejected term to the term which has been used.

Such references are necessary between different verbal forms of what is essentially the same heading: different grammatical forms, different spellings, different forms of the singular and plural, translated terms, transposable words in a phrase, and terms which have been coupled with another term which has been preferred as the entry word, as in the following examples:

LAW OF NATIONS *See* INTERNATIONAL LAW
ESTHETICS *See* AESTHETICS

233

MOUSE *See* MICE
GREAT BEAR *See* URSA MAJOR
WEEDKILLERS *See* HERBICIDES
URSA SPELAEUS *See* CAVE BEARS
INDUSTRIAL ARBITRATION *See* ARBITRATION,
INDUSTRIAL
MATERIALS, STRENGTH OF *See* STRENGTH OF
MATERIALS
CARTOONS *See* CARICATURES AND CARTOONS

Just as some headings have been established in direct word order and others in transposed word order, so other headings can appear as direct headings or as main headings with subheadings. Because both patterns appear in the catalogue, the reader must be led from the unused form to the preferred form of any such individual headings, as

FLOWERS – Arrangement *See* FLOWER ARRANGEMENT
FOOD – Prices *See* FOOD PRICES
HORSES – Breeds *See* HORSE BREEDS
TOPOGRAPHICAL TERMS *See* GEOGRAPHY –
Terminology

(The unpredictability of the form taken by such headings led Marie Louise Prevost to propose a single, logical system of noun headings followed by a subheading, which might be an adjective or another noun.[22] Dunkin supports her.[23]

'See' references are also necessary between synonyms (and words used in the catalogue as synonyms) and between antonyms, where one cannot be discussed without reference to its opposite, as

ANIMAL KINGDOM *See* ZOOLOGY
CERAMICS (ART) *See* POTTERY

('Ceramics' alone has been used as the heading for the techniques of producing pottery.)

OBESITY – Control *See* REDUCING
INTOLERANCE *See* TOLERATION

From the last heading – Intolerance – the reader is also referred to Fanaticism; Liberty of conscience, Religious liberty.

Certain terms to which a reader may give a context in his

own mind when coming to the catalogue have been rejected as being too vague in the context of the catalogue to cover the literature usefully. Instead the reader is directed to the more precise terms under which he will find aspects of the subject, as

> STORAGE *See* COLD STORAGE; WAREHOUSES; and the subheading Storage under names of stored products, e.g. COAL – Storage; FARM PRODUCE – Storage

'See also' references

'See also' references, unlike 'see' references, do not imply equivalence or substitution. Both the term referred from and the term referred to are used in the catalogue. 'See also' references help a reader to find his way in the catalogue by showing how the constituent parts of a subject have been designated and also what cognate subjects might be of interest to him. For this reason 'see also' references precede all entries under a given heading, either giving reassurance to the reader that the most suitable heading has been found or offering a redirection before a search through specific entries begins.

Most categories of 'see also' references imply a generally recognized permanent relationship, such as that between 1) genus and species, as

> INSECTS *See also* BEETLES
> ENGRAVING *See also* STIPPLE ENGRAVING

2) a class and the commonly accepted groupings within it, as

> MATERIALS *See also* HAZARDOUS SUBSTANCES
> HAZARDOUS SUBSTANCES *See also* POISONS
> POISONS *See also* TOXINS
> TREES *See also* EVERGREENS

3) a discipline and its constituent studies, as

> SCIENCE *See also* GEOLOGY
> GEOLOGY *See also* PETROLOGY
> HOME ECONOMICS *See also* COOKERY

4) a class and its individual members, as

> BOTANISTS *See also* LINNAEUS
> INTERNATIONAL AGENCIES *See also* UNITED NATIONS

5) an entity and those of its parts which have been given entry under their own names, as

BUILDINGS *See also* FLOORS
GREAT BRITAIN – History – 1603-1625 (James I) *See also*
    GUNPOWDER PLOT, 1605
SCANDINAVIA *See also* DENMARK

Reference is conventionally made from a subject to the next lower subject in the hierarchy postulated for that subject, as in the references above from MATERIALS to HAZARDOUS SUBSTANCES, and from HAZARDOUS SUBSTANCES to POISONS, from SCIENCE to GEOLOGY and from GEOLOGY to PETROLOGY.

Because entry under the specific name of a subject is the general rule in a dictionary catalogue, it is not usual to make such references as the above reciprocal, that is, to refer also from the less comprehensive to the more comprehensive term. However, in a library where the stock is limited and the users unsophisticated, it may well help a reader looking, say, under the heading DENMARK to remind him that more material may be found under the heading SCANDINAVIA. In a very large library, where materials may be expected to be available on most subjects and where readers have some experience in using catalogues, a 'blanket reference' may replace a long list of specific terms, as

VERTEBRATES *See also* names of classes, orders, etc. and of specific animals

Where a special application of a subject has been expressed as a subheading to another term, the reader should be advised how to find the applied subject by such a directive as

POLITICAL SCIENCE *See also* subheading Politics and government, under the names of countries, cities, etc.

Connections must also be made between entries for certain other groups of permanently related subjects which are likely to be separated in the dictionary catalogue by the accidents of terminolgy and alphabetical arrangement but which may need to be considered together. The relationships here implied are those between 1) disciplines and the objects studied, as between ENTOMOLOGY and INSECTS, PNEUMATICS and

GASES; 2) theoretical studies and their application or technology, as ARCHITECTURE and BUILDING; HYDRAULICS and HYDRAULIC ENGINEERING, POLITICAL SCIENCE and POLITICS, PRACTICAL; 3) activities and their agents, as ASTERISM (CRYSTALLOGRAPHY) and CRYSTALS, BOTANY and BOTANISTS; 4) activities and the things acted upon, as SAFETY MEASURES and ACCIDENTS, SOIL MECHANICS and FOUNDATIONS; 5) activities and their products, as ACCIDENTS and DAMAGE, CIVIL ENGINEERING and BRIDGES.

Other closely allied subjects whose boundaries are not always mutually exclusive must be treated in the same manner, and 'see also' references made between BOATS and SHIPS, EDUCATIONAL PSYCHOLOGY and CHILD STUDY, GAMES and PUZZLES, and so on.

Finally there are the different verbal forms of headings derived from the same root or implying the same essential meaning of which readers must be reminded, so that, for example, looking under ELECTRICITY a reader is advised of additional headings beginning with ELECTRICAL AND ELECTRO-, or looking under WEATHER is advised to see also the sub-division CLIMATE under names of countries, cities, etc.

References which connect the above groups must be made in both directions. Some are shown below.

ARCHITECTURE *See also* BUILDING
BOATS *See also* SHIPS
BUILDING *See also* ARCHITECTURE
CHILD STUDY *See also* EDUCATIONAL PSYCHOLOGY
EDUCATIONAL PSYCHOLOGY *See also* CHILD STUDY
ELECTRICAL... *See also* headings beginning with
    ELECTRICITY and ELECTRO-
ELECTRICITY *See also* headings beginning with ELECTRICAL
    and ELECTRO-
ENTOMOLOGY *See also* INSECTS
INSECTS *See also* ENTOMOLOGY

All the references dependent on a single heading are combined into a single statement, together with any scope note which may be found necessary and any examples, or locational directives, which could be useful, as in the three examples which follow.

> ZOOLOGY
> See also ANATOMY, COMPARATIVE: EMBRYOLOGY:
> ENTOMOLOGY, ETC; DESERT FAUNA: MARINE FAUNA,
> ETC; FUR-BEARING ANIMALS: GAME AND GAME BIRDS:
> divisions, classes and orders of the animal kingdom, as
> INVERTEBRATES; BIRDS, INSECTS, MAMMALS; CETACEA,
> UNGULATA; and particular animals as ANTELOPES, BEAVERS

> DICTIONARIES
> Dictionaries of a particular language or subject are entered
> in the catalogue under the name of the language or subject,
> with the subheading Dictionaries.
> The Dictionaries for quick reference are shelved in the
> Reference Library at . . . They are arranged by subject. A
> complete list of them, under titles and subjects, is shown in the
> visible index at the end of the bookstack.

> TRAVEL
> Under this heading are entered publications about
> travelling, advice to travellers, etc. For general travels see
> VOYAGES AND TRAVELS. For travels in a particular
> country or region see the name of the place, followed by
> the subheading Description and travel.

The Library of Congress Subject Cataloging Division has cumulated and consolidated the subject cataloguing instructions which have appeared in *Cataloging service bulletin* into a desk manual to provide explanations of specific decisions and details of procedure.[24] It is in loose-leaf form to allow incorporation of new directives which continue to appear in *Cataloging service bulletin*.

The lattice structure of the dictionary catalogue
The separate 'see also' references used in my examples have shown a relationship within a single hierarchy, but the documentation of a subject may place the subject in many different hierarchies. Mice, for example, may be considered in the context of zoology as a species of rodent, in the context of

scientific research as laboratory animals, in the context of food storage as pests, in the context of family life as pets. The one term used in the catalogue must be connected with all its related terms in the different hierarchies so that the reader has before him a model of the catalogue's structure in so far as it covers his area of interest. The model may be more explicitly represented by a diagram showing the network of interrelations of which the subject is the centre. My illustration, shown on pages 240-1, has been derived from the LC list of headings and references and shows the connections discerned for Mineralogy. The whole system of references constitutes what used to be known as 'the hidden classification' which lies behind the dictionary catalogue. Modern thesauri usually display the classified arrangement, or the set of categories, from which the alphabetical list of terms has been compiled.

In the diagram overleaf, arrows show in which direction references are made, as

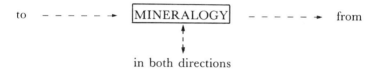

in both directions

Headings in capitals are headings used in the catalogue in relation to Mineralogy. Headings in lower case are put in to show hierarchies not explicitly shown in *LCSH*.

MINERALOGY and its related terms taken from the LC *List of subject headings* showing the 'hidden classification' within a syndetic alphabetical catalogue, or 'interconnected polyhierarchies forming a network or lattice'

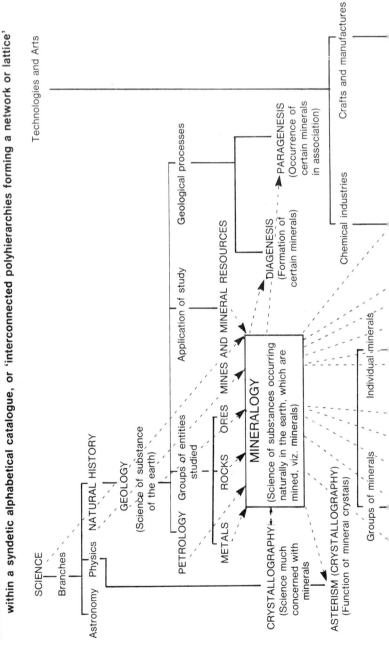

240

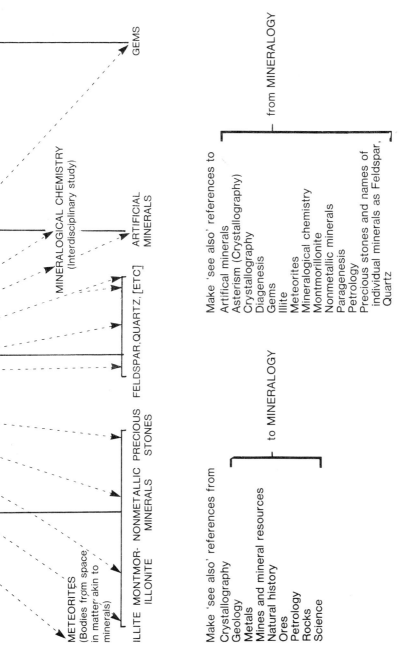

241

References

1 Cutter, Charles Ami, *Rules for a dictionary catalog*. 4th ed. Washington: Government Printing Office, 1904.
2 Library of Congress, *Library of Congress subject headings*, 9th ed. Washington, D.C., LC, 1980. (Supplements are published quarterly and cumulated annually. A completely new edition is available quarterly on microfiche and film.)
3 Coates, E. J., *Subject catalogues: headings and structure*. London: LA, 1960.
4 Sharp, H. A., 'Cataloguing: some new approaches', *Library world*, 57, 1955-6, 92-4.
5 Dunkin, Paul S., *Cataloging USA*. Chicago: ALA, 1969, chapter 5.
6 Haykin, David Judson, *Subject headings: a practical guide*. Washington: US Government Printing Office, 1951.
7 Chan, Lois Mai, *Library of Congress subject headings: principles and application*. Littleton, Colo: Libraries Unlimited, 1978. (Research studies in library science, no. 15.)
8 See reference 5 above.
9 Chapman, Liz, *How to catalogue: a practical handbook using AACR2 and Library of Congress*. London: Bingley, 1984.
10 *Sears list of subject headings*. 13th ed. by Carmen Rovira and Caroline Reyes. New York: Wilson, 1986.
11 Cochrane, Pauline A., *LCSH entry vocabulary project: final report*. Washington, D.C.: Council on Library Resources, 1983.
12 *Cataloging service bulletin*, 27, Winter 1985, 54-9.
13 Library of Congress. Subject Cataloging Division, *Library of Congress subject headings: a guide to subdivision practice*. Washington, D.C.: LC, 1981.
14 See reference 2 above, p.vii.
15 See reference 6 above, p.23.
16 Steinweg, Hilda, 'Specificity in subject headings', *Library resources and technical services*, 23(1), Winter 1979, 55-68.
17 'Qualification of geographic headings in current LC practice', *Cataloging service bulletin*, 11, Winter 1981, 87-94.
18 *Cataloging service bulletin*, 35, Winter 1987, 37-8.
19 Wellisch, Hans H., 'Poland is not yet defeated, or: Should cataloguers rewrite history? With a discourse on When is an island not an island?', *Library resources and technical services*, 22(2), Spring 1978, 158-67. (13 references)
20 Library of Congress. Processing Services. *Library of Congress filing rules*; prepared by John C. Rather and Susan C.

Biebel. Washington, D.C.: LC, 1980, 73.
21 See reference 13 above.
22 Prevost, Marie-Louise, 'An approach to theory and method in general subject heading', *Library quarterly*, 16(2), 1946, 140-51.
23 See reference 5 above.
24 Library of Congress. Subject Cataloging Division. *Subject cataloging manual: subject headings*. Rev. ed. Washington: LC, 1985.

13

Arrangement in catalogues and indexes

Following the ABC

By definition, the dictionary catalogue will be arranged according to the order of the English alphabet, that is, those Roman-alphabet letters that are used in writing English. Let us look at a list of entries arranged simply in accordance with the sequence of the letters they contain. (Not all the entries are necessarily to be found in the LC catalogue, but they all appear in a form that will be found therein, either as preferred entries or as references. Entries representing subject headings have been set in capitals; entries representing titles have been italicized.)

Entry	Arranged as	
A baker's life	ABAKE...	
Båken [The Scandinavian *aa* which has become å]	BAAK...	?
BAKE	BAKE ⎫	
B.A.K.E.	BAKE ⎬	?
B. A. K. E.	BAKE ⎭	
Bake and Take Café	BAKEANDTAKEC...?	
Bake & Take Restaurant [Ampersand spelled out]	BAKEANDTAKER...?	
Bake, John	BAKEJ...	?
... Bake me a cake	BAKEM...	?
BAKER, Adam	BAKERA... ⎫	?
Baker, Adam	BAKERA... ⎭	
BAKER (CALIF.)	BAKERC...	
Bake, R.E.	BAKERE...	
Baker, John Christopher	BAKERJOHNC...	
Baker, John, d.1558	BAKERJOHND...	
Baker, John, d.1716	BAKERJOHND...	
Baker-Jones, P.	BAKERJON...	

Baker Library	BAKERLI...
BAKERLOO	BAKERLO...
BAKER (OR.)	BAKERO...
Baker, Richard	BAKERR...
Bakers' Arms	BAKERSA...
Baker's dictionary	BAKERSDI...
Baker's dozen	BAKERSDO...
BAKER, Sir Richard	BAKERSI...
Baker-Smith, Richard	BAKERSM...
BAKER STREET IRREGULARS	BAKERST...
B.A.K.E.R.T.	BAKERT...
Baker, William	BAKERW...
BAKERY	BAKERY
Bakery Allied Traders Association	BAKERYA...
BAKERY – Bibliographies	BAKERYB...
BAKERY, POLISH	BAKERYP...
BAKERY – Study and teaching	BAKERYS...
BAKERY, VEGETARIAN	BAKERYV...
Baker, Zoe	BAKERZ...
Bake, Sam	BAKES...
Bake well at home	BAKEWELLA...
BAKEWELL (DERBYSHIRE)	BAKEWELLD...
Bakewell (Derbyshire), All Saints	BAKEWELLD...AL...
BAKEWELL (DERBYSHIRE) –	BAKEWELLD...AN...
Antiquities	
Bakewell (Derbyshire) St. John's	BAKEWELLD...ST...
Hospital	
Bakewell Historical Society	BAKEWELLH...
Bakewell, K. G. B.	BAKEWELLK...
BAKEWELL TART	BAKEWELLT...
B*K*R, Br**n	BKR...
5 bakers baking [Numeral spelled out]	FIVEB... ?
The baker's life	THEB...

Even such a short list has given rise to a number of questions to which knowing the sequence of the alphabet alone cannot provide answers. First, what is to be done with characters which are additional to the English alphabet? In the list above occur spaces, symbols (*, ...), a letter which is not found in the English alphabet (å), punctuation marks (comma, parentheses, full stop, apostrophe, hyphen, dash), numerals (5, 1558, 1716). Should capital letters be treated differently from lower case, and italic from roman type? Should *A baker's* *life* be separated from *The baker's life* by most of the alphabet? Should authors and titles and subjects be separated, or all mixed in together? These questions have been ignored, except where not knowing how to deal with them has led to their arbitrary placing in the list.

If a catalogue searcher had on his slip of paper for reference, or in his mind – the latter most unlikely – the exact sequence of letters used by the cataloguer in the above list, he might be able to go straight to the entry he sought. Most probably, however, the list would appear not straightforward but muddled, and the searcher would be unsure whether, having found an approximation to what he sought, he should continue the search forwards or backwards or conclude that his exact requirement could not be met.

It is clear that alphabetical arrangement is not as easy as ABC, and that a number of rules must be laid down if filing is to be helpful and consistent.

What is to be arranged?

To begin with, it would be useful to have in mind what will be in the file. What is to be arranged in a dictionary catalogue is the entire sequence of access points to descriptions of materials held in a library. The access points will be names of persons, corporate bodies, places, things, events, and publications. Each access point will be sought as a complete unit, which may contain more than one field, as an author's name may contain a surname and then a transposed forename, or a subject entry may contain a main heading and a subheading or a qualifier, or both. Some access points will be common to a number of entries and will therefore not suffice to arrange entries subsumed under them unless further filing units are taken into consideration.

Each entry has also a function as a member of the catalogue – as main entry, added entry, author reference, subject entry or subject reference – which may affect its form or placing.

The catalogue user may be seeking one specific entry, or may wish to browse among a number of related entries. For the benefit of the user, each entry should be headed by a recognizable filing unit within which each field has a predetermined place, both within the unit and in relation to other entries made

246

up of similar fields. A sought entry which is in the catalogue should always be findable; related entries should be intelligibly grouped.

Codes of filing rules

One might suppose that since the purpose, problems and possibilities of alphabetical arrangement have long since been familiar, a standard set of rules for arranging an alphabetical catalogue would by now be in general use. But this is not so. During the course of a single year, 1980, three new authoritative sets of rules for alphabetical arrangement were published, two by national libraries, the third by a national library association in the same country as one of the national libraries.[1-3] Since that date a revised British standard for alphabetical arrangement (BS 1749) has also been published.[4] These are in addition to systems established by individual libraries for their own use.

The new codes – from the Library of Congress (LC), the British Library (BL), the American Library Association (ALA), and the British Standards Institution (BS) – were thought necessary, and hence they differ, for a variety of reasons. The Library of Congress's new filing rules, to be applied to the new catalogue begun with the adoption of *AACR2* in 1981, were 'designed to enable the Library of Congress, with the least possible effort, to arrange large bibliographic files to satisfy a variety of needs.[5] The British Library stated similar objectives: '1) to draw up the code of filing rules for use by the British Library in its internal catalogues and external services, 2) to present the rules...as a contribution towards the formulation of a national filing standard.'[6] The name *BLAISE filing rules* denotes that the rules will form the basis of the computer sort programs used in the BLAISE/LOCAS service and other bibliographic listings issued by the library's Bibliographic Services Division.

The catalogues to which the two national libraries' rules were to be applied are, however, dissimilar. The Library of Congress catalogue is a full dictionary catalogue, listing books, serials, musical scores and sound recordings, and containing entries under names of authors, issuing bodies and all manner of subjects. *BLAISE filing rules*, in spite of its avowed intentions, gives the impression of having been designed primarily for the catalogue of the Department of Printed Books, which is a name catalogue listing persons, corporate bodies and titles of works only. That other libraries receiving BL cataloguing services will need directives for arranging subject entries is acknowledged by sections 4.2.3 and 4.2.4 of the rules, which briefly indicate how alphabetical and classified subject catalogues can arrange unit entries under a verbal subject heading or a class number either alphabetically by author's name or chronologically by date of publication.

The point of departure for the ALA Filing Rules Committee was the preliminary version of the LC rules, and contact between the compilers was maintained throughout the work on the two sets of rules. A very close correspondence exists between them, some of the wording and examples being identical. Nevertheless, in the pursuit of greater simplicity, the ALA Committee found sufficient grounds for disagreement to warrant the publication of a separate code. The major area of difference was in the arrangement of entries with identical access words.

As has been shown in Chapter 3, a published standard is frequently a compromise worked out to accommodate as many interests as possible. In BS 1749 not only librarians' needs were taken into account, but also those of book indexers, compilers of directories, providers of database services, and publishers. Both manual and automatic filing requirements influenced its decisions. The revision committee's point of departure was, necessarily, the existing standard that it had been asked to revise, with the three recently published codes at hand for reference. The word 'Recommendations' in the title of BS 1749 acknowledges that complete agreement on a single norm was impossible, and perhaps undesirable. A number of options have been included, partly to accommodate the requirements of on-going listings and partly to suit special needs.

The aim of all the codes was to make arrangement as simple as the mass of materials to be arranged would allow, and to avoid arranging what was written as if it were something else.

Basic filing order

Despite their care for differing needs, all four codes agree to a large extent. They are unanimous in the general directive which lists all the characters which are to be considered in arrangement, and establishes their sequence.

The basic filing order is to be

1 spaces, dashes, hyphens, diagonal slashes (all of which have equal value and any two of which occurring consecutively count as one; all are disregarded when they begin an entry)

2 ampersands

3 arabic numerals (The codes differ from each other in their somewhat complicated arrangement of numerals as entry words. When numerals occur as dates qualifying headings for authors or subjects, or as identifiers of sequential bearers of the same name, or of volumes, conferences, etc. in a series, all the codes assign to them their normal chronological or ordinal value)

4 Roman alphabet letters (Upper- and lower-case letters are interfiled; no distinction is made between letters in different founts or underlined)

5 letters from non-Roman alphabets (Since Library of Congress cataloguing practice romanizes all non-Roman scripts in filing units this item is omitted from LC)

Thus the fundamental decision whether to arrange letter by letter or word by word has been made in favour of word-by-word arrangement. That is to say, the filing units are compared, character by character, and because the character 'space' precedes the first letter of the alphabet, two words of different lengths which have identical letters up to the end of the shorter word will be arranged with the shorter word first, and all multi-word entries beginning with the same word will be arranged according to the characters of the second word and so on. The two methods of arrangement are contrasted in the following lists.

Word-by-word arrangement	*Letter-by-letter arrangement*
(nothing-before-something)	(all-through, or, solid)
hop	hop
Hopa	Hopa
hope	hope
Hope, Anthony	Hope, Anthony
Hope Point	Hopeh
Hope Town	Hope Point

Hopeh	Hopetoun
Hopetoun	Hope Town

BS 1749, having particularly in mind the arrangement of gazetteers and some encyclopaedias, allows letter-by-letter filing as an option.

Characters disregarded in filing

A number of characters and words are to be disregarded in filing.

1 Signs and symbols, having no generally accepted sequence and therefore little hope of being found, are ignored except for the ampersand – and that will not readily be found either! (Both ALA and BS optionally allow it to be arranged as if spelled out in the language of the phrase in which it occurs.) LC also creates a special sequence preceding the ampersand for 'names' consisting entirely of symbols, which must perforce be ordered according to some additional qualifier, forename, or title.

2 Punctuation is to be ignored except for those marks – dashes, hyphens and diagonal slashes – equated with spaces, and certain other marks when they perform a function in filing, as when a comma marks off a transposed forename from a surname, or a full stop divides a main heading from a subheading in a corporate name, or parentheses keep qualified terms together, or a colon implies a limit between fields.

3 Diacritical marks are ignored. Modified letters from other Roman alphabets are assimilated to their nearest equivalents in the English alphabet. *BLAISE filing rules* gives a list of such characters, mostly from phonetic script, particularly for use in written African languages, in its Appendix A.

4 The definite and indefinite articles are ignored when they occur in the nominative case as the initial word of a filing unit, except when a language convention requires retention of the definite article in a proper name.

5 There are certain other, minor, omissions, including the qualifier *ed.* which may be added to an author's name in a heading, *b.* or *d.* preceding the date by which a name is identified, and a title preceding a transposed forename. The last may be used to distinguish two names otherwise identical, as a final qualifier, as in

SMITH, Thomas, 1940-
SMITH, *Sir* Thomas, 1940-

Abbreviations

'Abbreviations are arranged exactly as written', says LC. Thus Mc and M' (abbreviations for Mac) are filed as MC and M respectively, St for Saint as ST, Dr for Doctor as DR, and so on. BL requires, and BS allows, abbreviations of Mac as a prefix to Scottish or Irish names to be arranged as if spelled out. Names from other languages, such as M'Boy, are to be arranged as spelled. Otherwise BL and BS agree with LC.

Initialisms and acronyms

Initialisms and acronyms are regarded as complete words, with varying exceptions. LC treats as separate words letters which are separated by marks of punctuation or spaces, BL and BS only letters which are separated by spaces. Rule 24.1 of *AACR2* warns cataloguers that, while their use of full stops or none should follow the predominant usage of corporate bodies when establishing names consisting of or containing initialisms, no spaces should be left between initial letters, whether written with full stops or not. References may be made from written forms which could be filed differently.

Same entry word or words

When entries beginning with the same word or words denote different classes of name – of person, place, corporate body, thing, and publication – they are grouped by LC, BL and BS in the following order, according to status, as

1 Personal name a) forename
                        b) surname
2 Place
3 Corporate body
4 Topical subject
5 Title of publication

Further grouping within those categories may be necessary, using dates, epithets, geographical qualifiers, and so on.

It is over the question whether to group entry words by status that ALA disagrees with LC. The disagreement was seen to be so fundamental as to require the publication of two codes. ALA simply arranges character by character, that is, the status of an entry word is not considered. Names are interfiled much as they are in the list on pp.244-5 (assuming the non-valid entries to be removed). Thus personal names will be intermingled with corporate, place, and subject names and with titles of publications. By this method the filing operation is simplified, and finding a precisely known entry becomes simpler, but the possibility of browsing among related entries is lost to the reader whose phraseology or spelling does not match that of the catalogue.

Sequence of entries by catalogue function
There is no disagreement between the four codes that the sub-arrangement of different entries with the same access point shall be according to the function of the entry. Entries are to be grouped as follows.

1 References under an author's name
2 Main and added author entries. This group includes entries for persons as main authors, joint authors, editors, compilers and other secondary authors, and for corporate bodies as issuing bodies, sponsors, etc. Any designation ('relator'), such as *ed.* or *defendant*, added to an author's name in the heading is disregarded in filing. If an added entry is formed by adding the secondary author's name as filing heading to a unit entry which already has a main author heading, that main author heading is usually disregarded.
3 References under a subject name
4 Subject entries

The American codes require sub-arrangement of subject entries by 1) author (or uniform title if that is the form taken by the main entry heading), 2) title, 3) date. *BLAISE filing rules* offers that arrangement as an option, the alternative arrangement being by date of publication.

All the codes offer schemes for arranging the works of 'complex' authors, that is, authors whose bibliography is complicated by the existence of numerous editions of their original works, adaptations and translations by other writers, and a body of criticism.

252

The following rearrangement of the list with which this chapter began exemplifies some of the rulings given in the codes discussed. It is evident from what has been said earlier that it is impossible here to present a single, much less 'the best', method of arrangement. The only course for the cataloguer to follow is to accept the set of rules chosen by his organization – or, in the event of setting up a new catalogue or preparing a bibliography, to choose a set of rules – master their complexities and use them consistently.

Entry	Comment	Filed as
5 bakers baking		[Numeral] 5 B...
B. A. K. E.	Initials with spaces	B A K E
B. A. K. E. R. T.	Initials with spaces	B A K E R T
BAKE	Initials without spaces	BAKE
B.A.K.E.	Initials without spaces. Full stops disregarded (but not in LC)	BAKE
BAKE, John	Personal surname, sub-arranged by forename, before other names	BAKE, J...
BAKE, Sam		BAKE, S...
Bake & Take Restaurant	Corporate names. '&' precedes word	BAKE & T...
Bake and Take Cafe		BAKE AND T...
...Bake me a cake	Symbols disregarded	BAKE M...
Bake well at home		BAKE W...
Båken	Diacritical disregarded	BAKEN
Baker, Adam *see also*	Author reference	BAKER, ADAM (1)
Baker, Adam	Author entry	BAKER, ADAM (2)
BAKER, ADAM	Same person as subject	BAKER, ADAM (3)
Baker, John, *d.*1558	Persons of the same name arranged by date. '*d.*' disregarded	BAKER, JOHN (1)
Baker, John, *d.*1716		BAKER, JOHN (2)
Baker, John Christopher		BAKER, JOHN C...
Baker-Smith, Richard	Compound surname	BAKER SMITH,

BAKER (CALIF.)	Place names, follow-	BAKER C...(1)
BAKER, (OR.)	ing personal names	BAKER O...(2)
Baker and bakery management	Title of serial	BAKER A...
Baker Library	Corporate name	BAKER L...
BAKER STREET IRREGULARS		BAKER S...
BAKERLOO LINE		BAKER.L...
Baker's dozen	Apostrophe dis-regarded	BAKERS D...
A baker's life ⎫ *The baker's life* ⎭	Initial article and apostrophe dis-regarded. Further filing element required	BAKERS LIFE BAKERS LIFE
BAKERY	Subject name	BAKERY (1)
BAKERY – Biblio-graphies ⎫ BAKERY – Study and teaching ⎭	Subject entry with subheading	BAKERY B...(2) BAKERY S...(3)
BAKERY, POLISH ⎫ BAKERY, VEGETARIAN ⎭	Subject entry-word qualified (Punctuation symbols serve as automatic devices for introducing a secondary alpha-betical sequence.)	BAKERY P...(1) BAKERY V...(2)
Bakery Allied Traders Association	Corporate name	BAKERY A...
BAKEWELL, K.G.B.	Personal name	BAKEWELL K...
BAKEWELL	Place name	BAKEWELL
BAKEWELL – Antiquities ⎫ BAKEWELL – Theatres ⎪ BAKEWELL – Views ⎭	Place name with subheadings arranged in a secondary alpha-betical sequence	BAKEWELL A... BAKEWELL T... BAKEWELL V...
Bakewell. All Saints Church ⎫ Bakewell. St. John's Hospital ⎭	Corporate names	BAKEWELL A... BAKEWELL S...

254

Bakewell Historical Society	Corporate name	BAKEWELL H...
BAKEWELL TART	Subject name	BAKEWELL T...
FIVE...*See also* the numeral 5 in the sequence which precedes the alphabetical sequence	Necessary reference. Precedes entries beginning with word 'Five'	FIVE...
Five dollars a day		FIVE D...

Grouped entries under a single personal name

1 BAKEWELL, K. G. B. *see also* ...

2a BAKEWELL, K. G. B. *jt. a.*
HUNTER, Eric J.
Cataloguing / Eric J. Hunter and K. G. B.
Bakewell. 2nd ed. London: Bingley, 1983.

2b BAKEWELL, K. G. B.
Classification and indexing practice /
K. G. B. Bakewell. London: Bingley, 1978.

2c BAKEWELL, K. G. B.
Classification and indexing practice
INCONNU, Q. d'
Comments on Bakewell's Classification
and indexing...

2d BAKEWELL, K. G. B. *ed.*
Management principles and practice: a
guide to information sources / ed. by
K. G. B. Bakewell ...

3 BAKEWELL, K. G B. – *Biography and criticism*
INCONNU, Q. d'
The works of K. G. B. Bakewell...

The entries above are

1 References to any other name(s) under which the author's works appear in the catalogue.

2 Main and added entries in a single alphabet:

a) Added entry for joint author – disregards *jt. a.* in the heading and also the main author heading;
   b) Main entry;
   c) Added (subject) entry – author/title heading to bring a critical work together with its subject;
   d) Added entry for editor – *ed.* disregarded;
3   Added (subject) entry under subject's name for critical works in general.

Helping the catalogue user

Because the arrangement of a large file is inevitably complex, as much as possible should be done to help the user in his search. Ideally, each entry in the catalogue should be set out exactly as it is to be filed, but we have not yet managed to conventionalize entries to that extent, and there remain sequences whose arrangement is not self-evident.

Also, in addition to the alternative procedures allowed by the current standards described earlier in this chapter, other deviations have sometimes been deemed appropriate to the nature and use of certain alphabetical listings. In the telephone directory, for example, account is taken of forename initials only, the remaining letters of a forename being printed out but disregarded in filing, the street name being taken as the next element to be considered. The Admiralty's *Sailing directions* and some atlases and gazetteers list all names beginning with Saint, San, Sankt, Santa, etc. under the simple initial S (what could be more reasonable?). Similarly, fine distinctions have been thought to be more of a hindrance than a help in some union catalogues. C. W. Berghoeffer, librarian of Frankfurt-am-Main, in 1891 introduced a system of interfiling entries cut out from different printed catalogues whereby entries under the same surname were interfiled, disregarding forenames and initials, and continuing to alphabetize by titles of the jumbled authors' works. The system was modified by the Swiss National Union Catalogue, in which names pronounced alike were also interfiled. The Berghoeffer system was adopted by the (British) National Central Library in 1962 for speedy integration of new entries into the union catalogue. Finding the location of requested publications was also easy, but search and correction were often necessary before a request could be

256

passed on to a lending library.[7] Now that co-operating libraries attempt to provide bibliographic as well as locational information, the Berghoeffer system is less suitable for interlibrary catalogues, although it is still used in some library systems as a locations catalogue.

Because so many varieties of alphabetical arrangement are in use, it is essential to explain the general principles of arrangement in any particular catalogue and to draw attention to the way in which problematic 'words', such as initialisms and abbreviations, have been treated. It is also necessary to draw attention to any non-alphabetical groupings, such as are made under topical headings in LC practice, where three sequences may occur under a single subject heading: 1) period subdivisions, 2) form and topical subdivisions, 3) geographical subdivisions. At points in the catalogue where arrangement is arbitrary, as at forename entries and at headings for 'complex' authors, a special explanation should be given showing how those entries have been arranged. In a printed catalogue or bibliography, as in the British Library's *General catalogue*, such explanations are plain to see and to follow. In a card catalogue they can unfortunately be easily overlooked. Direct 'see' and 'see also' references are a useful complement to them, as in the entry at the word 'Five' above.

The divided catalogue

Searching the dictionary catalogue becomes much easier if it is divided into two sequences, one an Author catalogue, offering access points under the names of persons, corporate bodies and individual publications, the other containing Subject entries only. Some libraries prefer three sequences, for Authors, Titles, and Subjects. Nearly all libraries have a separate sequence for serial publications, whether they appear also in other catalogues or not. The author catalogue is frequently expanded into a Name Catalogue, which is briefly described in the next chapter.

Summarizing the literature on the divided catalogue over the 35 years prior to 1976, Grady notes inconclusively that 'the divided catalog can be found in all sizes of library and in a number of forms . . . A divided catalog is neither a last resort nor the ultimate in catalogs, but it may be the one most suitable for some individual libraries'.[8] The Catalog Librarian of the University of Oregon, having described in detail the contents of the three catalogues – author, title, and subject – into which the library catalogue had recently been divided and also the process of the conversion, concludes: 'Patrons and staff find the divided catalog easier to use. Conversion to a divided catalog has reduced filing and revision time and has relieved the professional staff of filing revision. Congestion at the catalog has decreased'.[9] Both writers were concerned with the card catalogue. Now that the computer is taking over the task of filing for most of us, we can concentrate on the convenience of users, who must surely find it simpler to search in smaller, homogeneous sequences, whether turning over cards in drawers or manipulating fiches in a reading machine, provided that clear directions are given as to which sequence to use.

Towards an international standard for bibliographic filing
The International Organization for Standardization has published a generalized set of bibliographic filing principles for international use (ISO 7154:1983), but, after comparing usage in different countries, its Working Group on International Bibliographic Filing Rules found too much variation in detailed arrangements – some have been noted in this chapter – to warrant the promulgation of a standard at the present time. The filing rules which they devised to exemplify the principles remain, therefore, relatively simple, and have been published not as a standard but as a technical report (ISO/TR 8393:1985), in the hope that it will help to achieve more international uniformity in bibliographic filing and so lead to a true international standard.

References

1   Library of Congress. Processing Services, *Library of Congress filing rules*; prepared by John C. Rather and Susan C. Biebel. Washington, D.C.: LC, 1980.

2   American Library Association. Filing Committee, *ALA filing rules*. Chicago: ALA, 1980. (Carothers, Diane Foxhill, *A self-instruction manual for filing catalog cards*. Chicago: ALA, 1981, gives practice in applying the rules.)

3   British Library. Filing Rules Committee. *BLAISE filing rules.*
    London: BL, 1980.
4   British Standards Institution, *British Standard recommendations for
    alphabetical arrangement and the filing order of numbers and symbols.*
    London: BSI, 1985. (BS 1749)
5   See reference 1 above, p.1.
6   British Library. Filing Rules Committee. *Final report.* London:
    BL, [1979?], 3.
7   Garnett, Jane, 'The Berghoeffer filing system at the N.C.L.'
    and Simpson, Marjorie, 'Living with Berghoeffer: the user's
    point of view', *National Central Library. Occasional newsletter,* 11
    May 1971, 7-8 and 9.
8   Grady, Agnes M., 'Divided catalogs: a selected bibliography',
    Library resources and technical services, 20(2), Spring 1976, 131-42.
9   Kemp, Elaine A., 'Division of the University of Oregon
    catalog', *Library resources and technical services,* 20(2), Spring 1976,
    143-8.

14

The name catalogue

A typical name catalogue contains in one alphabetical sequence the following entries: 1) entries under names of persons and corporate bodies as directed by *AACR2* for main and added entries; 2) uniform titles and the titles of other anonymous works, collections, compilations, etc. assigned title main entry by *AACR2*, together with added title entries for works entered under an author's or corporate body's name (unless all titles are assigned to a separate title catalogue), and 3) certain subject entries. The subject entries are those which refer to persons, corporate bodies and publications already included in groups 1 and 2, or which might be so included. I do not know of a name catalogue which includes entries for places as subjects.

There is no standard definition of a name catalogue and no recent references appear in indexes to the professional literature. The content of name catalogues in use varies to suit the convenience of particular organizations and the arrangement of particular collections. The term 'name catalogue' may well supplant 'author catalogue', now that *AACR2* no longer recognizes corporate authorship.

The *General catalogue* of the British Library is a classic example of a name catalogue, carrying on an earlier tradition of assembling at one place in the catalogue entries for related publications, such as original works and commentaries on them and polemical works and answers to them. The subject entries in the *General catalogue* are restricted to those relating to personal authors and to individual publications.

Libraries which maintain a classified catalogue need to supplement it with an author and title (or name) catalogue, which may be combined with the subject index, although it is usually more convenient to display the subject index separately. Where, for example, the classified and name catalogues are on microfiche, the subject index may take the form of computer printout for easier scanning of consecutive entries.

Variations are found to suit particular needs. For example, the British Film Institute Library has an author/title catalogue, a classified catalogue with an alphabetical subject index, and a Personality index, which lists in one alphabetical sequence names of individual directors, actors, cameramen and other persons concerned in making the films in its collection. The library of the National Sound Archive likewise records all names of individual performers, conductors, choirs, orchestras, etc. It cannot be foreseen what historical materials may in future be sought in the Archive – a tape-recording of a speech to a local society made by someone later to become well known, the début of a famous actor, the contribution, otherwise undocumented, of certain individuals to oral history records – all may at some time need to be retrieved from the collection, hence the necessity of maintaining this detailed and accurate record.

The name catalogue offers the quickest approach to a work about a named individual or corporate body. It cannot, however, act as a substitute for that section of the classified or dictionary catalogue where subject entries for those individuals should be found. Entries for individual Italian painters, for example, while conveniently found if sought as individuals in the name catalogue, should not be omitted from the sequence of subject entries for Italian painting. A reference such as 'For works about individual painters see under their names in the Name Catalogue', together with a reference to shelf-location, might be permissible in a very large library, but would still leave the searcher in doubt as to which names to look for, and would abstract from the subject of Italian painting the bulk of its material. Double entry in name and subject catalogues seems essential.

Corporate bodies as subjects may present a problem. A professional or learned body or an academic institution will in most cases be the author of publications about itself: its annual report, yearbook, conference proceedings and so on. The rare historical monograph commissioned to mark an anniversary or other special event in the body's existence will give rise to a subject entry under the body's name which can be filed after the 'author' entries, which may themselves do double duty as author and subject access points. Generally the number of entries will not warrant further elaboration. Certain other bodies, however, of more general interest, will be the subject of written publications, films, illustrative matter, and so on, which will need arrangement among themselves in a manner for which provision is made in the subject catalogue, either by its class subdivisions or by the subheadings provided for ordering material on corporate bodies, as detailed in the LC *Guide* referred to in Chapter 12. It seems reasonable to file subject entries for such bodies as the United Nations and the Royal Navy in the subject catalogue, with a reference under the name of the body in the name catalogue, such as

GREAT BRITAIN. Royal Navy
    Here are entered only works put out by the Royal Navy and its subordinate bodies. Works about the Royal Navy are entered in the Classified Catalogue. The class numbers for different topics and periods will be found under the above heading in the Subject Index which is located . . .

The then Principal Cataloguer in the Manchester Public Libraries, N. K. Firby, whose description of the library's Name Catalogue had appeared in the libraries' own review,[1] answering a query from me about the extent to which subject entries for corporate bodies were included in the name catalogue, wrote:

Under the heading ROYAL NAVY in the name catalogue there are very few cards. Most official publications concerning the Navy are issued by the Admiralty or the Ministry of Defence, Navy Department. There are cross references between these headings . . . It would appear that the Navy has always been considered as too large and amorphous a body to be treated as an institution in the cataloguing sense. It would be difficult in fact to separate books on the naval history of Britain from books on the Royal Navy itself, and there would be so many entries it would be extravagant to enter them in both the subject and name catalogues. On the other hand books about special establishments within the

Navy, e.g. Royal Naval College, Dartmouth, are given name entries.[2]

Common sense appears to have solved the problem.

References

1 Firby, N. K., 'The Manchester Reference Library and its catalogues: some problems of growth', *Manchester review*, 10, Spring 1963, 1-18.
2 Private communication, quoted by permission.

Conclusion

In order that this volume should remain within the bounds of its allotted space, it has been necessary to separate into a companion volume[1] considerations (which logically follow) of the effect on individual cataloguing practice of the general situation here adumbrated. From this volume, however, it may be deduced that outside influences, such as linguistic evolution, the development of communications technology and of its agencies, and the standardization of practice, have an effect on the practical cataloguing of particular materials in particular situations that cannot be ignored.

Cataloguing may be a 'lost art', if we think of art as being a creative individual's response to the world around him, but it can never cease to be an intellectual pursuit, demanding an unceasing awareness of the changing scene and a greater sense than hitherto of responsibility towards others.

---

[1] Piggott, Mary, *The cataloguer's way: from document receipt to document retrieval*, London, Library Association, 1989.

Index

Where the context of cataloguing is understood, entries are specific. Authors cited are indexed (under name alone) only if their names appear in the text; other names appearing in the list of references appended to each chapter are not indexed. Abbreviations are used in subheadings for British Library (BL), *British national bibliography* (*BNB*), Library of Congress (LC) and *Library of Congress subject headings* (*LCSH*).

267

Bibliothèque nationale: host to
ISDS 52
bilingual countries: catalogues 105
Bishop, William Warner 9
BLAISE 23, 213
Blanck, Jacob 72
blanket references 236, 238
BLBSD *see* British Library.
Bibliographic Services Division
BLCMP Library Services Ltd 26-7
Bliss, H.E. 148
BNB see British national bibliography
Bochum University Library 57
Bodleian Library: catalogues 107
Bodmer, Frederick 97
Bokmål 84
book numbers 180
Booksellers' Association of Great
Britain and Ireland 71
Boole, George 166
Boolean formulae in retrieval
166-7
Boorstin, Daniel 32
botanical terminology 157-9
Bradford University 48
Brighton Public Libraries 22
BRIMARC project 22
Bristol University: host to
SWALCAP 27
British Film Institute Library:
catalogues 261
British Institute of Recorded
Sound *see* National Sound
Archive
British Library
ABACUS member 45
BLAISE filing rules 247-52
passim
CONSER Advisory Group
member 25
Cyrillic romanization tables
127, 129
General catalogue 106-7, 107-8,
129, 260

British Library. Bibliographic
Services Division 17-18
see also BLAISE; *British national
bibliography*
British Library. Department of
Oriental MSS and Printed
Books: catalogues 107
British Library. Document Supply
Centre 2, 3
British Library. Lending Division
see British Library. Document
Supply Centre
British Library. Research and
Development Department 50
British Library Automated Inform-
ation Service *see* BLAISE
British national bibliography 16-18
chain indexing 198, 199-201
extensions to DC numbers 179,
205-6
feature headings 182
PRECIS *see* PRECIS
British Standards Institution 39-41
endorses ISSN 49
glossaries 38, 111, 155
Glossary of documentation terms 38
*Guide to establishment and develop-
ment of monolingual thesauri* 164
machine-readable codes for
information exchange 57
*Recommendations for alphabetical
arrangement* 247-52
passim
*Recommendations for examining
documents, determining their
subjects and selecting indexing
terms* 145
romanization standards 121,
123-4, 125-6, 128
Root thesaurus 164-6
standards: revision policy 43-4;
serial numbers *see under* BS
broader terms in thesauri 163
Browning, Robert 139

Brunel University: use of MARC-FICHE 222
Brush strokes: Chinese characters 95-7
BS 589, 38; BS 881, 38; BS 1749, 247-52 *passim*; BS 2961, 111-12; BS 2979, 123-4; BS 4280, 121; BS 4730, 57; BS 4748, 57; BS 4812, 125-6; BS 5408, 159; BS 5723, 164; BS 6474, 57; BS 6529, 145; BS/PD 6483, 125; BS/RD 6505, 126
Burkett, Jack 28
Burmese script: book production in 104
Butcher, Judith, *Copy-editing* 158

CAG 29
call numbers 74, 180
Cambridge University Library: catalogues 107
Canada: languages 82, 105
Canada. General Directorate for Terminology and Documentation 155
Canadian Library Association agrees LC romanization tables 127
authenticates CONSER records 25
carrier format 61
Carrollton Press 30
Carter, J., *ABC for book collectors* 71
cartographic materials: cataloguing: ISBD(CM) 56
Case Western Reserve University 53
catalogues
administration *see* management considerations
definition and functions 1-5, 173-4

format 27, 30-1, 76-8 *see also names of different types of catalogue*
management *see* management considerations
research 26, 31 *see also* automated bibliographic systems; PRECIS
user friendliness 77-8, 256-8
Other aspects are entered under their own names
cataloguing
a necessary skill 7-9
state-of-the-art publications 9, 20, 30-1
Other aspects are entered under their own names
cataloguing-in-publication 18-19
cataloguing-in-source 18
Cataloguing practice notes for UK MARC records 28-9
centralized cataloguing *see also* automated bibliographic systems
early attempts 11-12
in UK 16
role of LC 14
centralized cataloguing department or subject specialization 151-2
Centre for Catalogue Research, Bath 31
chain indexing 183-206
assessment and use 204-6, 213-14
authority file 188-9
choice and form of terms 189-96
double entry 196-7
editing 199-200
methodology 183-9
sample index 201-3
transposed terms 198-9
Chan, Lois May 221
Chaplin, Hugh 53, 58

character sets for automated systems 52, 57
characters (written) *see also* languages and scripts: romanization; *and names of scripts*
disregarded in filing 250
order in filing 249-50
Cheshko, L.A., *Russian orthography* 85
Chinese-English dictionaries 96-7
Chinese languages and scripts
computer-aided typesetting 118
dictionaries: arrangement 95-7
literacy and book production in 104
romanization: Chinese systems 115-16, 117; Western systems and conversion tables 116, 125
typesetting 118
transcription 114-17
written characters 93-7
chronological arrangement in catalogues 176-7, 180-2
CIP 18-19
Clapp, Verner 18
classification notation: extensions 179-81
classified catalogue 173-206
advantages and use 173-9
arrangement 176-82
– by alphabetical extension 179
– by book numbers 180
– by date of publication 180-2
– example 176-7
guides 182-3
supplemented by index 182-3
see also chain indexing; PRECIS
supplemented by name catalogue 214
'closed' catalogue 30, 31
Coates, E.J. 145, 179, 219
in charge of subject cataloguing:

BNB 201
Coblans, Herbert 52
CODEN 48-9
coding for machine-readable files 56-8, 61
Cohen, Marcel, *La grande invention de l'écriture et son évolution* 132
collation 73
Collison, Robert 107
Colon classification: book number 109
colophon: definition 70
COM catalogues 22, 27, 31
common exchange format 46, 57, 60-2
for serials 52
UNIMARC 56-8
communications formats 20-1, 46, 52, 56, 57, 60-2
complex authors: filing 252, 255-6, 257
component parts: cataloguing: ISBD(CP) 56
compound terms 166
computer-assisted indexing *see* PRECIS; thesauri
computer files: cataloguing: ISBD(CF) 56
computerization *see* automation
concept analysis
use in determination of subject 144-5
PMEST 142-4
PRECIS 208-11
CONSER 25
CONSER/KWOC index 25
contents note 73
control numbers 46-9
Conversion of serials (CONSER) 25
Cooperative Automation Group (CAG) 29
Cooperation automation systems (UK) 26-30

Firby, N.K. 262
Flemish language: spelling changes
    86
forename entries: explanation of
    arrangement 257
form of document: important to
    note in catalogue entry 147-8
format: catalogues 27, 30-1,
    76-8 *see also names of different*
    types of catalogue
Foskett, A.C. 145
Foskett, D.J. 145
Foster, Gordon: development of
    SBN 47
France, Anatole 77
French language: use outside
    France 82, 83, 105
'frozen' catalogues 30, 31
Fumagalli, G. 173
function of entry: affects filing
    order 252

Garside, Kenneth 173
Geographical names: LC usage
    226-30
Georgian language and script
    91, 92
German language: use in Denmark
    83
German libraries: classification
    and cataloguing 173, 174
Gesellschaft für Information und
    Dokumentation 155
Giles, *Sir* Herbert, Chinese-
    English dictionary 96-7 *see*
    also Wade-Giles system of
    Chinese romanization
Giliarevskii, R.S. 124-5
Glaister, G.A., *Glaister's glossary of*
    the book 71
glossaries
    bibliographic terms 71
    importance of 155
    standard lists 158-9, 162-3

see also thesauri
Gorman, Michael 54
Gosudarstvennyi Komitet Standar-
    tov Soveta Ministrov, SSSR,
    Gost 16876 123-4
government concern with inform-
    ation 49-50, 51, 59
Grady, Agnes M. 257
Graphic Information Research
    Unit 77
'Great Britain' as entry word 195
Great Britain. Office for Scientific
    and Technical Information
    49-50
Greek language and script
    accents 55-6
    literacy and book production
        104
    transliteration 123 (reference
        40)
Grose, M.W. 2
Gruntvig, N.F.S. 81
guides to catalogues 77-8
Guo Moruo 118
Gwoyeu Romatzyh 115

Hamdy, M. Nabil 75
Handbook of oriental history 134
Hanyu pinyin 115-16, 117, 118
Harrod, L.M., *Librarians' glossary*
    159
Haugen, Einar 83, 84
Haykin, David Judson 221, 222,
    224
Heading: catalogue entry 74
    see also subject headings;
    terminology; thesauri
Hebrew language and script
    in Russia 92
    literacy and book production
        104
    romanization 113, 121
help for the catalogue user 77-8,
    256-8

International Centre for the
Registration of Serials 52
International Conference on Cata-
loguing Principles 54
International Congress of Orient-
alists 120
International Congress on National
Bibliographies 59
International Council of Scientific
Unions 50-1, 60-1
International Federation for
Information and Document-
ation *see* FID
International Federation of Library
Associations and Institutions
see IFLA
International Information Centre
for Terminology 53, 154-5
International Meeting of Cata-
loguing Experts 54-5
International Nuclear Information
System: cataloguing standards
42
International Organization for
Standardization 40
serial numbers *see under* ISO
standards for: bibliographic
interchange on magnetic tape
57, 60, 61; book numbers 47;
filing 258; romanization
121, 123, 124, 127
International Programme for UBC
58-9
International Serials Data System
48, 52-3
International Standard Book
Number 46-8, 74, 130
International standard numbers
46-9, 74, 130
International Standard Serial
Number 48-9, 130
international standardizing
agencies 49-62
see also names of agencies

international standards for
handling bibliographic information 46-67 *see also particular
topics*
International Standards Organization *see* International
Organization for Standardiz-
ation
inventorial method of cataloguing
173
Irish language: manual 85
ISBD(A) 56
ISBD(CF) 56, 69
ISBD(CM) 56
ISBD(CP) 56
ISBD(G) 56
ISBD(M) 55, 56
definition of monograph 143
required data for cataloguing
monographs 73-4
ISBD(NBM) 56
ISBD(PM) 56
ISBD(S) 56
ISBDs
incompatibility and harmon-
ization 42-3
origin and purpose 54-5
punctuation 55-6
revision 44
ISBN 46-8, 74, 130
ISDS 52-3
ISO *see* International Organization
for Standardization
ISO 9, 121, 123-4; ISO 233, 121;
ISO 259, 121; ISO 646, 57;
ISO 843, 121; ISO 2108, 47;
ISO 2709, 57, 60; ISO 3297
48; ISO 5426, 57; ISO 5427,
57; ISO 5428, 57; ISO 6438,
57; ISO 7154, 258; ISO/DP
2805, 125; ISO/TR 8393, 258
ISO/TC 46 Subcommittee 6: Bib-
liographic Data Elements in
Manual and Machine Applic-

276

277

MESH 162
microfiche catalogues 22, 26, 27, 31
Miller, R.A. 98
Mills, A.J. 145
Mineralogy: diagram of relationships 240-1
Minnesota Union List of Serials 25
modified letters *see* diacriticals
monographs: definitions 55, 143
multilingual, multiscript collections: catalogues 104-9, 178-9

name authority lists 18, 26
name catalogue 260-3
narrower terms in thesauri 163
National Agriculture Library 25
national bibliographies 59
  entries examined by Gorman 54
  need for standardization 54
  role in universal bibliographic control 11, 59
National Central Library: use of Berghoeffer system 256
National Federation of Abstracting and (Indexing) Information Services 49, 60-1
National Film Archive *see* British Film Institute
National Information Standards Organization (Z 39) 40
National Lending Library *see* British Library. Document Supply Centre
National Library of Australia
  ABACUS member 43
  CONSER Advisory Group member 25
  romanization 127
National Library of Canada
  ABACUS member 43
  CONSER project 25

romanization 127
National Library of Medicine
  Medical subject headings 162
  MEDLARS 13, 23
  serials records in CONSER project 25
National Library of Singapore: catalogues 108
National Program for Acquisitions and Cataloguing 15, 16
national script: symbolism
  Arabic 89, 90, 91
  Chinese 117
  Cyrillic 92
  Irish half-uncials 110
  Somali 100
National Serials Data Program 52
National Sound Archive: name catalogue 261
National union catalog 14
  pre-1956 imprints 5
near-synonyms 237
Nelson, A.N., Japanese-English dictionary 97
Netherlandic language: spelling changes 86
networks (UK) 26-30
  BLAISE/LOCAS 22, 27
  BLCMP 26-7
  JANET 7
  LASER 27-8
  SCOLCAP 27
  SWALCAP 27
new terms in thesauri 168-70, 223
New York Public Library: catalogues 107, 121
Newcastle University Library 26
NFAIS 49, 61
Nigeria: languages 99
non-book materials: cataloguing 4, 5, 56
non-entry words 198, 200
non-roman-alphabet letters: filing 249

279

Plaister, Jean   28
PMEST: formula for subject
    analysis   142-4
Polish alphabet   122
Portuguese language: spelling
    changes   85, 86
post-coordinate entry and retrieval
    165-8
    descriptors: definition and
        examples   165-6
    search in data bases   166-8
Potato Synonym Committee   158
pre-coordinate entry and retrieval
    165-6
pre-coordinate headings *see also*
    chain indexing; subject head-
    ings; thesauri
    definition and examples   165-6
    use in data bases   167
pre-natal cataloguing   19
PRECIS
    assessment   213-14
    authority files   212, 213
    bibliography   213
    compared with chain indexing
        207
    concept analysis   208-11
    objectives   206-7
    relationships and operators
        208-11
    singular or plural nouns   193
    terminology and layout   207-8
    translingual indexing system
        213
    use in alphabetic subject cata-
        loguing   219
    user surveys   213-14
preliminary pages: cataloguing
    data in   69-72
presentation of catalogues   30-1,
    76-8
presentation of material: affects
    reader's choice   147-8
Preserved Context Index System

see PRECIS
press mark   74
Prevost, Marie Louise   234
printed books: antiquarian:
    ISBD(A)   56
printed cards
    BLAISE/LOCAS   22, 27
    BNB   18
    LC   14-15
    OCLC   24
printed music: ISBD(PM)   56
Printing and the Mind of Man
    exhibition   86-7
processing: definition   13
processing centres   13
Program   20
proper names in subject catalogues
    218
property: concept in subject
    analysis   144-5
Publishers' Association   47, 71
publishing history of book on verso
    of title   71
punctuation marks: filing   249,
    250

qualifiers: LCSH   224 *see also*
    subheadings
Quebec: languages   82

Ranganathan, S.R.
    book numbers   109, 180
    chain indexing   183
    PMEST   142-4
    on cataloguing-in-source   18
    on vernacular bibliographies
        108
Readability of Print Unit   77
RECON   30
Reference Indicator Number:
    PRECIS   212
reference works: caution on
    linguistic changes   88

285

UNIBID 61
Unified Turkic Latin Alphabet
    91-2
UNIMARC 56-8
Union catalogue of Asian publications
    120-1
union catalogues 5
    as bibliographies 11 *see also*
        automated bibliographic
        systems
    for interlibrary loans 27
    Jewett's at Smithsonian 11
    LASER 27-8
Union of Soviet Socialist Republics
    see USSR
UNISIST
    *Guide to standards for information
        handling* 46
    INFOTERM 154
    International Centre for Biblio-
        graphic Descriptions 61
    programme 50-3
    Working Group on Bibliographic
        Descriptions 60
unit entries 76, 174
United Nations *see also* Unesco;
    UNISIST
    Bibliographic Information
        System 168
    controls own terminology 155
    thesaurus 164-6, 167-8
United Nations Educational,
    Scientific and Cultural
    Organization *see* Unesco
United States. Board on Geo-
    graphic Names
    authority for names in LC 227
    romanization systems 123, 124
United States. Higher Education
    Act 1965 15, 16
United States National Serials
    Data Program 52
universal alphabet 110
Universal Bibliographic Control

(UBC) 58-9 *see also* IFLA
universal bibliography 11-12, 58-9
Universal Copyright Convention
    71
Universal decimal classification 12
Universal Declaration of Human
    Rights 81
Universal Standard Book Code 48
University of Aston: founder-
    member of BLCMP 26
University of Bath. Centre for
    Catalogue Research 31
University of Birmingham:
    founder-member and host of
    BLCMP 26
University of Bradford: proposed
    Universal Standard Book
    Code 48
University of East Anglia: subject
    specialization 151
University of Exeter: Exeter tapes
    134
University of Leicester: centralized
    cataloguing 151
University of Maryland 213
University of Oregon: divided
    catalogue 258
University of Southampton 26
University of Toronto Library
    Automation System (UTLAS)
    26
    contribution to INFOTERM
    53
unsought terms 189, 198, 200
updating thesauri 168-70
US MARC 23
USBGN
    authority for geographic names
    227
    romanization systems 123, 124
USSR: languages and scripts 91-2
    catalogues 108
    literacy and book production
    104

USSR: languages and scripts
(cont.)
   romanization tables 123, 124-5
   Russian-English dictionary
     134
   spelling changes 85
   use outside Russia 82
UTLAS 26

vernacular scripts *see also* languages
   and scripts; *and names of*
   languages and scripts
   arguments for separate cata-
     logues 130-1
   emotive symbolism 90, 132
Verona, Eva 56
'version' and 'work' distinguished
   69
Vickery, B.C. 145
Vietnamese Roman alphabet 117
viewpoint of author 210
VINE 20
vocabularies 155, 158-9, 162-3
   see also thesauri
'voluminous' (complex) authors:
   filing 252, 255-6

Wade, *Sir* Thomas 115
Wade-Giles system: Chinese
   romanization 115
   conversion tables 116, 125
   use in LC 125
Walford, A.J., *Guide to foreign-*
   language courses and dictionaries
   134
Walford, A.J., *Guide to reference*

material 134
Walker, G., *Russian for librarians*
   133-4
Warner, Gilmore 181
Webster, Noah, *Dictionary* 87
Wehr, H. 90
Wellisch, Hans H. 104, 127,
   131, 230
   Conversion of scripts 134
Wells, A.J.: development of SBN
   47
Wersig, Gernot 38
Whitrow, Magda 129
Woodhead, P.A. 151
Woollongong University 213, 214
word-by-word filing 249-50
words not necessarily to be taken
   literally 145-6
world science information system
   see UNISIST
writing systems *see* languages
   and scripts; *and names of*
   languages and scripts
written characters *see also* languages
   and scripts
   basic filing order 248-50
   changes in 88-101
Wüster, Eugen 154, 162

Yale University. Institute of Far
   Eastern Studies 97

Zaunmüller, W., *Bibliographisches*
   Handbuch der Sprachwörterbücher
   134
Zulu language 82